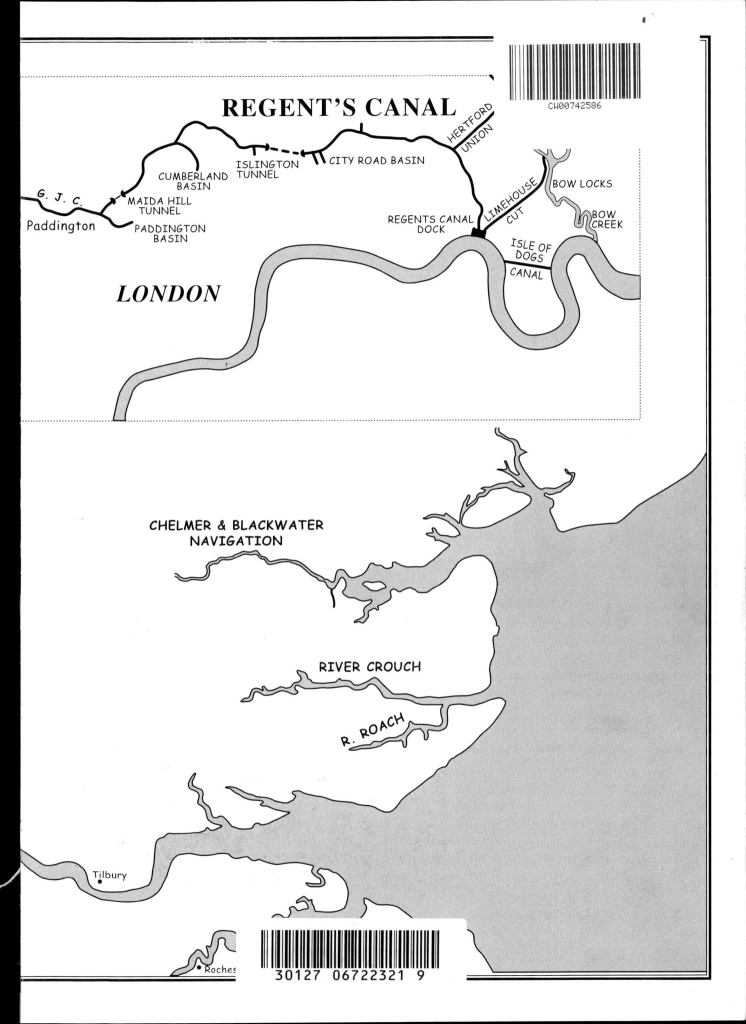

REGENT'S CANAL

G. J. C.
Paddington

CUMBERLAND BASIN

MAIDA HILL TUNNEL

PADDINGTON BASIN

ISLINGTON TUNNEL

CITY ROAD BASIN

HERTFORD UNION

LIMEHOUSE CUT

BOW LOCKS

BOW CREEK

REGENTS CANAL DOCK

ISLE OF DOGS CANAL

LONDON

CHELMER & BLACKWATER NAVIGATION

RIVER CROUCH

R. ROACH

Tilbury

Roches

The Regent's Canal
London's Hidden Waterway

The Regent's Canal
London's Hidden Waterway

Alan Faulkner

Waterways World Ltd

Burton-on-Trent, Staffordshire

First published 2005 by
Waterways World Ltd
151 Station Street
Burton-on-Trent
Staffordshire
DE14 1BG
Tel: 01283 742950

ISBN: 1 870002 59 8

A CIP catalogue record for this book is available from the British Library

Printed in Great Britain by Information Press, Oxford

Cover illustrations:

Top: **City Road Basin looking south towards the bridge carrying the City Road over the waterway. In the foreground a Pickfords' boat is being poled down the basin towards the firm's depot that was situated south of the bridge. This T. H. Shepherd drawing, dated 26 January 1828, is dedicated to Sir Culling Smith who served as a very active director of the company from January 1813 to June 1830.** Author's collection

Bottom: **A pair of Pickfords' boats shown passing through one of the City Road Locks on their way north with the 960-yard long Islington Tunnel in the background. This T. H. Shepherd print, dated 25 August 1827, was dedicated to Colonel John Drinkwater who was, in effect, the Regent's Canal Company's first Managing Director.** Author's collection

CONTENTS

LIST OF ILLUSTRATIONS

LIST of MAPS & PLANS

PREFACE

Although the Regent's Canal passes through a well-populated part of north London, it was largely unknown for many years as it pursued an almost secretive course in an enclosed world hiding behind wharves and waterside buildings and with little public access to the towpath. It was only in Regent's Park that the canal was more in the open, particularly for those visiting London's Zoo. Yet in its course of just over 8½ miles the Regent's Canal acted as a busy thoroughfare serving a wide range of businesses and a thriving dock at Limehouse, whilst it also had an inland port at the City Road Basin, a branch in Regent's Park and connected with numerous privately-owned basins.

In more recent times the opening up of the towpath by local authorities and the wholesale redevelopment of much of the waterside property has transformed the canal into a major amenity for the capital. And while commercial traffic has all but finished, the canal is increasingly popular with visiting pleasure craft and for permanent moorings.

My first encounter with the canal was in August 1951 when my parents took me on a trip on *Jason* from Paddington through Regent's Park to Camden. These trips had been started by John James as one of the many features of the Festival of Britain. At that time the canal was still busy with commercial craft and I remember that *Jason* had to push an unloaded barge through Maida Hill Tunnel to save delaying the trip as the boatman poled the barge slowly through, while the horse was walked over the top.

Over the years I used to visit parts of the canal, my interest being kindled by Herbert Spencer's *London's Canal* published by Putnam & Co Ltd in 1961. This book details the building of the canal and contains a fine set of photographs specially taken by Heinz Zinram at the time of publication.

Since then several other books have touched on various aspects of the waterway but the only other volume I know about devoted solely to the canal is Dr Michael Essex Lopresti's excellent guide *Exploring the Regent's Canal* published by Brewin Books in 1987. Michael's book and his series of conducted towpath tours have done so much to introduce thousands of people to London's canal.

I hope that this present book, written at a time of major change to the canal and to its surroundings, will build on the interest already created.

Alan Faulkner
March 2005

ACKNOWLEDGEMENTS

To produce this book about the history of the Regent's Canal I started serious research in January 1983 with the first of what eventually totalled over 60 visits to the Public Record Office at Kew. I am deeply grateful to the staff at Kew for the service I received, which was always efficient and helpful.

I visited many other locations of research material, some of them several times, and these include the London Metropolitan Archives; the Guildhall Library and its Manuscripts Section; the Bancroft Library covering Tower Hamlets; the Camden Local Studies Library; Hendon Library; Holborn Library and the London Gas Museum at Bromley-by-Bow. My thanks to all the staff involved.

I also have cause to be grateful to many individuals who have helped me over the years including David Allkins (Grand Junction Water Works Company); John Boyes (Limehouse Cut); Barry Fuller B.E.M (Welsh Harp Reservoir); Roy Jamieson of The Waterways Trust Archive at Gloucester; Nigel Perfect of the British Waterways Board; Tom Ridge (Regent's Canal Dock and the Commercial Gasworks); Martin Sach at the London Canal Museum; Tim Smith (Regent's Canal Dock) and Malcolm Tucker (Islington Tunnel and several other locations).

Particular thanks must go to Hugh Compton, a fellow member of the Railway & Canal Historical Society, for his great help and support throughout the project. Equally, I am profoundly grateful to Edward Paget-Tomlinson for producing his splendid series of maps and drawings. Sadly, Edward died on 12 November 2003. Thanks also to Euan Corrie for steering me efficiently through the publishing schedule.

Mention must be also made of the *Biographical Dictionary of Civil Engineers, Volume 1, 1500 to 1830*, published by the Institution of Civil Engineers in 2002, which was of especial value in giving information about many of those involved with the building of the canal.

For the illustrations I have drawn heavily on the collection housed in the British Waterways Archive at Gloucester, now controlled by The Waterways Trust, although many of them actually came from the Waterways Museum at Stoke Bruerne well before the Gloucester archive was established. And, although they have been published several times before, I have used the Thomas Shepherd series of historic prints again as they portray the canal in its earliest days and were the first pictures of the canal that I acquired over 40 years ago for my collection. In 1911 the Regent's Canal Company issued a well-illustrated publicity booklet and this has provided several illustrations. Several pictures were taken on some of my many visits to the canal and the others are acknowledged individually.

CHAPTER ONE

OBTAINING THE ACT

From the very earliest times the river Thames has been a major commercial thoroughfare catering for many of London's transport needs. Another early navigation was the river Lee, which joins the Thames from the north through Bow Creek at Canning Town.

Their success led to several plans to extend the benefits of water transport to other parts of London. The earliest scheme was in 1641 by Sir Edward Forde for a navigable river to bring water from the river Colne at Rickmansworth to St Giles-in-the-Fields.[1] In about 1766 a survey was made for a canal from the Colne at Uxbridge following the contour through Dawley, Northolt, Greenford and Alperton, crossing over the river Brent and passing near Acton, Kilburn and Paddington to terminate at Wellins Farm in Marylebone Park. Soon after, a slightly shorter route was proposed joining the Colne south of Uxbridge at Hobart's Mill, West Drayton.[2]

In 1773 Robert Whitworth, who was involved with the building of the Oxford Canal, was asked to survey a canal from the river Lee at Waltham Abbey to Moorfields in London and to look at continuing it across to Wellins Farm to link up with the proposed canal from the Colne.[3] He reported in October 1773, his line running 14 miles on the level from Waltham Abbey through Edmonton and Shoreditch to terminate in a large basin at Holywell Mount, near Moorfields. From there a canal nearly 4¾ miles long was to run to Marylebone with five locks rising up to Sadlers Wells, then with a level line to the north of St. Pancras and to the park. Whitworth's plans were enthusiastically approved but no action was taken.

In 1791 plans emerged to link the Thames in London with the Midlands canal system by a more direct route than through Oxford. There were two main schemes, the Braunston Canal from the Oxford Canal at Braunston, near Daventry in Northamptonshire, to the Thames at Brentford in Middlesex; or the London & Western Canal from the Oxford Canal near Aynho in Oxfordshire to Marylebone or to the Thames at Isleworth. The Braunston scheme, which became known as the Grand Junction Canal, attracted influential support and eventually triumphed over its rival, which had become known as the Hampton Gay Canal.

The Grand Junction's Act authorised a canal 90 miles in length.[4] In May 1794 William Jessop and James Barnes, the Grand Junction's engineers, surveyed a branch that was to run from the canal at Southall in Middlesex to a terminus at Paddington, then on the outskirts of London. Paddington enjoyed good access to the city as a new road had been built in the 1750s that ran almost due east across the north of London – today it is represented by the Marylebone, Euston and Pentonville roads. The Paddington Branch was authorised by the Grand Junction's fourth Act in 1796,[5] and while the starting point and terminus differed, its course was very similar to that proposed in 1766 with the contour being followed all the way and involving a substantial embankment across the Brent valley at Alperton.

Construction work on the Grand Junction's main line had started in May 1793 and the section from the Thames at Brentford through Southall to Uxbridge was opened in November 1794. The rest followed in stages until a through-route to Braunston was opened early in 1801, albeit using a temporary railway at Blisworth where the building of a long tunnel caused major problems and was not completed until March 1805.[6]

Construction of the Paddington Branch had started at the end of 1796 as it was realised this would be an important section of the canal. There were delays in purchasing the considerable area of land owned by the Church of England that was needed at Paddington, but the branch was opened with great celebrations on 10 July 1801.[7] The Grand Junction developed extensive wharves at Paddington and a substantial trade soon built up.

Early in 1802 a railway was proposed to run from Paddington to the London docks, but it was superseded in July by a plan to extend the Grand Junction on a similar course to that suggested by Whitworth in 1773. The line was to run some 7 miles from the east end of Paddington Basin to the New River Head at Islington and then across the City Road, skirting Shoreditch and Spitalfields, passing through the centre of Bethnal Green to Whitechapel, and then across the Commercial Road to link up with the West India Dock, which had its own connection with the Thames.[8]

At first, the Grand Junction was involved in the scheme, but later it withdrew as it still had many problems of its own to resolve, including that at Blisworth. It continued to support the scheme in principle but left matters with the sponsoring committee that had been set up led by Sir Christopher Baynes of Harefield. John Rennie,[9] a leading canal engineer, had made the survey but the moving spirit behind the proposal was Thomas Homer. He was connected with the Grand Junction and operated a fleet of boats on the canal bringing in coal and building materials to Paddington and taking away manure. Sir Christopher Baynes also operated boats on the canal; his craft being employed exclusively taking lime and bricks from Harefield to Paddington.[10]

Rennie's plan involved a wide canal, a towing path, and double locks and bridges able to accommodate barges. His estimate for the canal works was £187,712 but this was later increased to £196,712. Thomas Biggs, a surveyor, estimated the land and buildings needed would cost £107,600 but this, too, was soon increased to £140,000. After making an allowance for providing a supply of water the overall cost of what became known as the London Canal was £476,712.

Rennie foresaw water supplies as presenting the biggest difficulties for the new canal. He had looked at eight options:

1 A new canal from the Thames at Marlow feeding water into the Grand Junction near Cowley.
2 Taking water from the river Kennet at Reading, crossing the Thames by an aqueduct at Taplow, and feeding into the new canal to Cowley.
3 Pumping from a stream off the river Colne at Finches Allowance, Colnbrook, into the Grand Junction.
4 Using a proposed reservoir at Ruislip supplemented by floodwater from the rivers Bulbourne, Colne and Brent and back pumping at the Grand Junction's Norwood and Hanwell locks.
5 Drawing from ponds belonging to Hampstead Water Works.
6 Pumping from a canal to be constructed from the river Lee at Waltham Abbey to the Hackney Road, as surveyed by Whitworth in 1773.
7 Sinking a series of wells.
8 Pumping water from the Thames at London docks.

Rennie calculated the canal would carry 800,000 tons a year, equating to 54 barges a day six days a week for 50 weeks a year each carrying 50 tons. The locks were to be 88ft long, 15ft wide with an 8ft fall requiring 10,560 cubic feet of water. The 108 expected lock operations each day would require 1,140,480 cubic feet of water; approximately a ninety-fifth part of the average daily flow of the Thames. Rennie's report was dated 27 August 1802 and he favoured the option to link the Grand Junction with the Thames either at Marlow or Taplow.

A £400,000 subscription list was opened and this was soon filled. Sir Christopher Baynes then approached the Grand Junction about water supplies, but it refused to assist as it was poorly supplied at the time and was also getting involved in the public supply of water in the Paddington area. This rebuff and opposition from landowners, as the route crossed property scheduled for development, led to the scheme being shelved in 1803.

The plan was revived early in 1810 when Homer consulted John Holland, a surveyor who had been employed on several of the Grand Junction's works and had surveyed the proposed canal from the Thames at Marlow to Cowley in May 1801. Homer was encouraged by Holland's findings and commissioned James Tate to make a more detailed survey and to take levels. Once completed, Thomas Hogg was employed to obtain the names of the owners and occupiers of the land through which the canal was to pass and formal notice was given in the *London Gazette* of the intention to apply to Parliament for an Act. The canal was to run from the Grand Junction near the Harrow Road Bridge at Paddington but on a more northerly course than the London Canal to avoid the built-up area. It was to terminate at Limehouse where it joined the Limehouse Cut, part of the river Lee navigation.

At the end of 1810 Homer had a conference with the Grand Junction, but soon after he learned that the Duke of Portland's lease of Marylebone Park was due to expire on 25 March 1811. The freehold of the park belonged to the Crown and was managed by three commissioners of the Department of Woods & Forests & Land Revenues. Land bordering onto the park, such as the Portman estate to the west and the Southampton estate to the east, was already being developed and this had prompted the commissioners, led by John Fordyce, and their staff, to consider their own plans for the future of the park once the lease expired. Fordyce died in July 1809 but his plans for the park's development lived on. The commissioners' permanent staff included two surveyors, Thomas Leverton and Thomas Chawner, and two architects, John Nash[11] and his colleague James Morgan.[12] In October 1810 the four were entrusted with drawing up plans for the park; the general intention being for it to become, in part, a residential area, with a new barracks and a new church.[13]

Homer approached Nash who immediately realised the scenic and transport advantages that would accrue if the proposed canal was to pass through the park. Homer then arranged a survey for an amended route, which showed the canal passing through the middle of the park. His plan, dated 1 April 1811, envisaged a canal 8 miles 4 furlongs and 2 chains in length falling 86ft 5¼in to the Lee. Accompanying it was Tate's detailed estimate:

80 acres of land at £400 and 2 houses to be demolished	£34,000
2 miles deep cutting, 6 miles level cutting, bridges, approaches	£40,568
1,150 yards of tunnelling at £25 per yard	£28,750
12 locks	£12,975
29 bridges, forming roads over them and one culvert	£11,612
Gravelling towpath, posts, rails and quicking (hedges)	£2,592
Temporary damages and fences, Parliamentary expenses	£9,000
Contingencies, unforeseen expenses, salaries &c (33.33%)	£46,499
Total construction costs	£185,996
Average cost of three possible sources of water	£27,533
Compensation to Grand Junction Canal Co. and its tenants	£50,000
General contingency at 10% and amount to even up figures	£36,471
Grand Total	**£300,000**

The water supplies being considered, all of which involved pumping by steam engines, were from Finches Allowance with an initial outlay of £21,000 and annual costs of £1,800; from the Thames below London Bridge at £25,000 and £5,880 annually; and from the Thames at Pimlico via a heading to Paddington at £36,600 and £5,795 annually. The compensation to the Grand Junction covered the possible loss of income to that company and to the tenants of its wharves caused by reduced levels of trade at Paddington Basin.

Accompanying the estimate were projections of the operating revenues and expenses. Traffic was assessed at 150,000 tons of coal; 200,000 tons of bricks, lime and stone; 30,000 tons of timber and other building materials; 20,000 tons of iron, copper and other metals; 100,000 tons of manure and 200,000 tons of general goods – a total of 700,000 tons annually expected to yield £35,000 in tolls.

The outgoings were the cost of water £5,000; salaries and management expenses £3,700; wages for toll clerks and lock keepers £1,500; general repairs £1,700 and sundry items £600, a total of £12,500. This would have produced a surplus of £22,500 and a 7½% return on the £300,000 estimate.

Nash and Morgan's plans were effectively in competition with Leverton and Chawner's for acceptance by the commissioners but Nash was very confident about his chances. Although the plans did not have to be submitted until July 1811, in March Nash outlined his proposals, which included the canal, to banker Sir Thomas Bernard who then became a prominent supporter of the canal.[14] Nash's confidence may have stemmed from the patronage he enjoyed from the Prince of Wales, who became the Prince Regent in 1811, and it was his plans that were accepted by the commissioners.

On Friday 31 May 1811 a meeting of those interested in the proposed new canal was held at the Percy Street Coffee House.[15] Thomas King took the chair and both Nash and Homer were present. The meeting resolved that a canal from Paddington to the Thames below London Bridge would be of great public utility by giving the advantage of water carriage to the whole of the north of the metropolis, by cutting the costs of carriage by land, and by reducing congestion caused by carts and wagons in the capital's narrow streets. The meeting agreed that the line suggested in 1802 was now impracticable owing to the large amount of building work since carried out, but Homer's amended route seemed to be convenient and practical. Nash was asked to arrange for it to be re-surveyed to see if it could be improved still further.

Nash and Morgan then went over the whole line again with Homer and Tate and most of Homer's route was approved, except for a small deviation at Paddington. At the eastern end, however, it was felt the canal should join up with the Thames and not with the Lee. The route agreed was from the Broadwater on the Grand Junction by the Harrow Road bridge at Paddington, under the Edgware Road opposite Maida Hill in a 165 yard tunnel, through Marylebone Park between Wellins Farm and the northern perimeter, and passing north-west of Camden Town to reach Islington where an 880 yard tunnel would be needed through the narrowest part of Islington Hill and under the New River.

The line then passed Hoxton, Kingsland Road, Agostone, Cambridge Heath and Bethnal Green to Mile End. From here the suggested deviation started, for instead of passing to the Lee near some rope walks, the line was now to pass through the north end of Stepney, to cross the Commercial Road, Queen Street and Narrow Street in Limehouse and to enter the Thames at Harrity's Deal Yard. An extra ¼ mile was involved, making the total length 8¾ miles.

The canal was to be level from Paddington to Camden Town, where the first of four locks dropped the line down to Islington, with another eight locks from the eastern end of the tunnel to the junction with the Thames where a 1½-acre barge dock was proposed. Whilst this dock could be made larger, the intention was for canal craft to go out onto the river to load or unload alongside shipping. A revised estimate, dated 19 June 1811, of £280,000 was presented by Nash; this allowed for an increase to 87 acres for the land, which included two meadows belonging to the City of London between the Commercial Road and Queen Street at Limehouse needed for the dock. The cost of the land was now estimated at £39,000, the heading from Pimlico £38,000 and the Grand Junction's compensation £40,000. Total revenue was assessed at £43,100 and expenses at £12,000.

The second meeting was held on 19 June at the City of London Tavern when Nash's report was approved and he was asked to prepare a prospectus. A week later a committee, with Sir Thomas Bernard in charge, was appointed to examine the proposals, Tate being asked for fuller details of his estimates while Homer was asked to verify the tonnage figures. On 16 July, Tate and Holland's revised estimate of £256,155.14.2d (£256,155.71) was approved but this figure excluded any compensation to the Grand Junction and, to be prudent, a £400,000 subscription list was recommended in shares of £100 each.

On Wednesday 17 July 1811 there was a general meeting at the London Tavern when the subscription list was opened. The minimum holding was set at five shares; the maximum at 50 and a 2% deposit was to be paid. Early in August it was decided to restrict the subscription to £260,000 of which £80,000 was to be reserved for the landowners along the line, and £80,000 for the subscribers to the original 1802 scheme.

On 7 August another general meeting was held, this time at the Freemason's Tavern at St Giles-in-the-Fields when Nash made the important announcement that the Prince Regent had not only approved the plans for the canal but also had agreed that it could be called the Regent's Canal.

By the middle of August £100,000 had been promised and £1,630 paid in deposits and the subscription had risen to £135,300 by the end of the month. Meanwhile, the first suggestions were being made for a branch canal towards the Grays Inn Lane to bring the canal nearer to the City. On 14 September Tate reported on the idea, which became known as the Aske Terrace Branch, and it was adopted just in time to be included in the Parliamentary notices. Shortly after, the plans were deposited with the Clerk of the Peace.

On 12 November, Homer reported that as only a few of the 1802 subscribers had exercised their share options the balance of the £80,000 had been opened to general subscription and £52,000 had already been raised. At the same meeting John Edwards and James Lyon were appointed solicitors to the undertaking, whilst Morgan was appointed engineer. Early in January the final preparations were being made for conducting the Bill through Parliament and on 1 February Lord Yarmouth (Francis Charles Seymour), Lord Robert Seymour, Sir Thomas Bernard, John Nash, Joseph Delafield and Charles Monro were appointed as a sub-committee to oversee the Bill's passage.

Their services were soon needed as introducing the Bill into Parliament unleashed a storm of protest. Vested interests saw the proposal as a major threat and quickly made their fears known, one group even having a handbill printed which set out 18 points of concern. Some were rather fanciful, such as the damage that could be caused if the banks failed as the water was 86ft above the level of the Thames, which conveniently overlooked the fact that none of the summit-level was to be on an embankment but was to be excavated into the surrounding land. The threat to health of 300 acres of standing water was condemned, but this overstated the water-area and ignored the natural movement of the water with the passage of craft and the use of the locks. Concern was also expressed about the interruption of natural springs and of drainage channels. Some fears were more realistic, such as the stability of the two tunnels proposed, particularly that through Islington Hill, which was partly covered by houses. The adequacy of the estimate was also questioned. Against these accusations the steering committee issued its own handbill answering each of the 18 points in turn.

Opposition from some quarters had been expected. Landowners were concerned about the effect of the canal on their properties and how it would impede their immediate and future building development plans. Some were totally obdurate, but others were willing to negotiate. Edward Berkley Portman, who controlled an extensive estate at the west of Marylebone Park, refused to countenance the canal passing through his property under any circumstances. He ensured a special clause was written into the Bill to cover this, forcing the promoters to move the proposed line northwards

To prevent any similar problems on the neighbouring estate of Henry Samuel Eyre the committee agreed to several concessions to assist with the development of the land. They included the provision of two bridges, the building of a new sewer to drain from St Johns Wood into the public sewer in Baker Street North, and an agreement to take out a building lease for the land on either side of the canal. The lease involved 26 acres at £1,035 per annum, but 7 acres were to be used for the canal and another five for the slopes of the cutting. In return Walpole Eyre, who managed his brother's affairs, agreed to allow the canal to be cut in the open and not in a tunnel.

In the event, the company found it was not empowered to enter into a lease of this nature and the actual agreement with Eyre was made on 29 July 1813 between Nash, Delafield and Monro as trustees. It provided for the first five houses to be built within five years of the agreement and the new sewer to be completed within two years. Rather than develop the land itself, at the end of 1817 the company arranged for a speculative builder, James Burton, to construct the houses with it paying him £6,000 to assist.

On Lord Southampton's estate, which lay at Chalk Farm between Marylebone Park and the Hampstead Road, precise conditions were laid down to minimise any damage, as the canal was to be in a cutting; even the type of fencing was specified. His Lordship was under age but his guardians also extracted an agreement for three bridges to be built on the estate should they be requested. Lord Camden obtained similar promises for bridges to be built on his land near Kentish Town as did George Thornhill near the west end of the proposed Islington Tunnel, Samuel Rhodes and Samuel Pullin near the east end of the tunnel, and Nathaniel Lee Acton near Shoreditch. Several landowners obtained promises that steam engines would not be erected on their lands, including the Bishop of London at Paddington, the parish of St Marylebone, and the governors of Harrow School at Maida Hill.

Predictably, the Grand Junction was concerned to protect its position and, more particularly, its water supplies. A stop-lock at the junction was a necessary prerequisite with precise conditions as to its operation. The Grand Junction was also concerned to safeguard the revenues from its Paddington wharves, which, prior to the proposals, attracted a considerable demand. This had led to increased rents being charged which the Grand Junction wanted protected as the provision of wharves on the new canal much nearer to the City could hardly fail to attract traders away from Paddington, thus devaluing the wharves there. An agreement was reached whereby if on the expiry of the existing leases the wharves could not be re-let at the premium rental the new company had to make good the difference.

The original seal of the Regent's Canal Company, which was used from 13 July 1812 until the company was dissolved from 31 March 1883. The seal incorporates the Prince of Wales feathers reflecting the patronage given by the Prince Regent who became George IV in 1820.

The Waterways Archive, British Waterways Archive, Gloucester

The wharfingers at Paddington and also those at Bulls Bridge at the junction of the Grand Junction's Paddington Branch with its main line were similarly concerned about their position. They petitioned Parliament against the Bill, seeking protection from any devaluation of their leases. They too were then protected by an agreement that obliged the new company to purchase their interests in their wharves and buildings at such prices that would have been obtained if the new canal had not been built.

Several water companies were unhappy about the new canal. The Grand Junction Water Works Company, which was based at Paddington and drew water from the canal, was concerned to ensure its supplies were protected. The East London Water Works Company was also involved, both in the sale of land needed for the canal and by possible interference to its pipes by the excavation works. One of its mains ran across the site of the proposed entrance channel at Limehouse and provision had to be made for this to be carried under the waterway in a siphon.

The interests of the Commissioners of the Department of Woods & Forests also had to be safeguarded. It soon became clear that Nash's original plan to pass through the centre of Marylebone Park would not be approved, but the commissioners were prepared to allow the park to be used provided the line was diverted to the northern perimeter. The difficulty was that instead of a fairly shallow cutting being involved, substantial earthworks would now be needed.

Another problem arose early in February 1812 when it became clear that the commissioners would only give their consent to this new alignment provided a branch canal was constructed to a basin proposed on the east side of the park.[16] The proposal was considered by the Parliamentary agents acting for the promoters, but it was felt that it would be impossible to include such a major work at this late stage without endangering the whole Bill. Instead, the promoters agreed that they would apply for an enabling Act to construct the branch canal and basin in the next session of Parliament.

Other interests also made sure their rights were safeguarded, including Charles Hampden Turner, who had a wharf on the east side of the proposed canal entrance from the Thames at Limehouse, and John Boulcott, whose timber yard adjoined the entrance lock. Stringent conditions were also imposed on the promoters to provide proper bridges to carry the various turnpike roads across the proposed canal.

By meeting the objections where possible and by negotiating to remove fears and demands, both real and imaginary, the Bill progressed through its committee stages and was reported to the House of Commons at the end of April. Early in May the Earl of Bridgewater was asked to take the Bill under his protection during its passage through the Lords. With his and with other influential support the Regent's Canal Act received the Royal Assent on 13 July 1812.[17]

The Act named 168 individuals who were incorporated as 'The Company of Proprietors of the Regent's Canal'. They included the Earl of Yarmouth, Lord Robert Spencer, Lord Robert Seymour, Lady St John and Lord Glenbervie and collectively they were empowered to construct a canal from the Grand Junction Canal at Paddington through the parishes of Saint Mary la bonne (Marylebone), Saint Pancras, Kentish Town, Camden Town, Pentonville, Saint James Clerkenwell, Islington, Newington Green, Kingsland Green, Saint Leonard Shoreditch, Hoxton, Hackney, Cambridge Heath, Saint Matthew Bethnal Green, Mile End Old Town, Saint Dunstan Stebon Heath (Stepney), Saint George's Ratcliff Highway to join the river Thames at Saint Anne's Limehouse. This was a course of some 8¾ miles falling 86ft through 12 locks and with an entrance lock at Limehouse. They were also empowered to make a 726-yard branch canal in Shoreditch to Aske Terrace, together with a heading from the Thames at Chelsea to Paddington and a feeder from Friern Barnet to Marylebone to supply the canal with water.

To finance the work £300,000 divided into £100 shares could be raised with a further £100,000 if required. The additional funds could either be in shares or could be borrowed on mortgage or promissory notes. There was no restriction on the number of shares that could be held, and each share carried a vote, but no shareholder could have more than ten votes.

The Act laid down the tonnage rates applicable to the new canal. Every ton of goods coming in at Limehouse or Paddington was charged a special entrance toll of 6d but thereafter charges were on a distance-related scale. Building materials, which included lime, chalk, bricks, tiles, slate, metals, stone and timber, from Limehouse to any destination up to the Mile End Road had to pay 8d per ton over and above the entry toll; another 6d up to Cambridge Heath; 4d to Kingsland Road; 4d to the Aske Terrace Branch; 9d through the tunnel at Islington to Maiden Lane; 4d to Kentish Town; 4d to the entrance to

Drawn by Thos H.Shepherd.

Engraved by S.Lacey.

JUNCTION OF THE REGENT'S CANAL, AT PADDINGTON.

Published May 24, 1828, by Jones & Cº. 3, Acton Place, Kingsland Road, London.

The Broadwater on the Grand Junction Canal at Paddington was the starting point of the Regent's Canal. This view by Thomas Hosmer Shepherd published on 24 May 1828 shows the towpath bridge and the Grand Junction's Toll Office on the left with the canal to Paddington Basin in the right foreground and the entrance to the Regent's Canal middle right. Later, this area became known as Browning's Pool or more usually as Little Venice.

Author's collection

MACCLESFIELD BRIDGE, REGENT'S PARK.

TO JAMES MORGAN ESQ: ARCHITECT, THIS PLATE IS MOST RESPECTFULLY DEDICATED BY.
T. H. SHEPHERD.

Published June 16, 1827. by Jones & Cº 3. Acton Place, Kingsland Road, London.

Above: *A view of Macclesfield Bridge in Regent's Park by T. H. Shepherd, dated 16 June 1827. The bridge was named after the Earl of Macclesfield, the company's chairman, but the drawing is dedicated to James Morgan, the company's engineer.*

Below: *A Thomas Shepherd print of a barge on the Regent's Park branch heading past Park Village East and away from the terminal basin that, from 1830, also served the New Cumberland Hay Market.* both Author's collection

PARK VILLAGE EAST, REGENT'S PARK.

GAS WORKS, NEAR THE REGENT'S CANAL.

The gas works at Maiden Lane, St. Pancras built by the Imperial Gas Light & Coke Company and opened in August 1824 are shown in this T. H. Shepherd print. A short basin led off the main canal into the works.

CITY BASIN, REGENT'S CANAL,
TO SIR CULLING SMITH, BART. THIS PLATE IS RESPECTFULLY INSCRIBED.

Published Jan.y 26, 1828, by Jones & C.o 3.Acton Place.Kingsland Road.London.

Above: *City Road Basin looking south towards the bridge carrying the City Road over the waterway. In the foreground a Pickfords' boat is being poled down the basin towards the firm's depot beyond the bridge. Dated 26 January 1828, this T. H. Shepherd drawing is dedicated to Sir Culling Smith, a very active director of the company from January 1813 to June 1830.*

Below: *A pair of Pickfords' boats shown passing through one of the City Road Locks on their way north. The 960-yard Islington Tunnel is in the background. This T. H. Shepherd print, dated 25 August 1827, is dedicated to Colonel John Drinkwater who was, in effect, the company's first Managing Director.*

both Author's collection

THE DOUBLE LOCK, & EAST ENTRANCE
TO THE ISLINGTON TUNNEL, REGENT'S CANAL.
TO COLONEL DRINKWATER THIS PLATE IS MOST RESPECTFULLY INSCRIBED.

Published Aug.t 25. 1827. by Jones & C.o 3. Acton Place. Kingsland Road. London.

Drawn by Thos. H. Shepherd. Engraved by F. J. Havell.

ENTRANCE TO THE REGENT'S CANAL, LIMEHOUSE,

TO THE REGENTS CANAL COMPANY, THIS PLATE IS DEDICATED.

Published Jany. 26. 1828. by Jones & Co. 3. Acton Place. Kingsland Road. London.

The entrance from the river Thames to the Regent's Canal's Limehouse Dock with a barge being poled out as depicted by T. H. Shepherd. The bridge, which in reality was a swing bridge, carried Narrow Street across the entrance channel.

THE LIMEHOUSE DOCK, REGENT'S CANAL.

TO THE EARL OF MACCLESFIELD, THIS PLATE IS RESPECTFULLY INSCRIBED.

Published Augᵗ 25. 1827. by Jones & Cº 3 Acton Place. Kingsland Road. London.

Above: *Limehouse Dock showing canal barges and sea-going sailing ships. The entrance lock to the canal itself is in the middle distance and to the left of this the land is shown sloping into the canal. Initially, all the land around the dock sloped in this way and jetties had to be built for ships to moor and unload to land-based vehicles. This T. H. Shepherd print, dated 25 August 1827, is dedicated to the Earl of Macclesfield, the company's chairman.* Author's collection

Below: *The mouth of Islington Tunnel in August 1819 prior to the portal being completed and the water being admitted. Whilst the main construction work had been finished in September 1818 difficulties acquiring land at the tunnel's eastern end had prevented it being fully opened.* Gentlemen's Magazine – Author's collection

Gent. Mag. Aug. 1819. Pl.I. p. 105.

T. Bonner del. et sculp. 1819.

Mouth of the TUNNEL, on the REGENT'S CANAL, Islington.

SKATING IN THE REGENT'S CANAL TUNNEL.

Above: *In February 1855 the weather was so cold that the water inside the tunnel froze, enabling people to skate all the way through until policemen were stationed at either end to stop this dangerous practice.* Illustrated London News, 3 March 1855

THE CANAL FROM VICTORIA PARK.

Right: *A horse drawn barge heads up the canal above Old Ford Locks and alongside Victoria Park.*

From a postcard in the Ian Wilson collection

A narrowboat is about to leave Commercial Road Lock and head up the canal on 5 June 2001. The remains of the hydraulic capstan system survive on the lockside and the Commercial Road Bridge spans the head of the twin lock chambers.

Author

Above: *Today the main user of the City Road Basin is the Islington Boat Club, some of whose craft were afloat on 19 April 1999. The former wharves around the basin are gradually being replaced, mostly by housing and the development on the left has been named Pickfords Wharf. More land around the basin is likely to be similarly redeveloped for housing.*

Author

Left: *The preserved hydraulic pumping station alongside the railway viaduct at Limehouse on 27 June 2002. The building was refurbished jointly by the London Docklands Development Corporation and the British Waterways Board in 1995 and is open to the public on certain days.*

Author

Marylebone Park; and 9d through the park and the tunnel under the Edgware Road to the Grand Junction. There was a concession if the goods went the entire length of the canal, limiting the maximum toll to 3/-, which included the entrance toll, whilst the toll on goods from the Grand Junction to Cambridge Heath was limited to 2/4d per ton.

All other goods, except for coals, coke, minerals and manure, had to pay an additional 50% on the building materials toll, but for manure the basic toll was halved. The same proportionate increase or reduction applied for travelling the whole length of the canal – 4/6d general goods, 1/6d manure – and from the Grand Junction to Cambridge Heath – 3/6d general, 1/2d manure.

A special scale applied for coal, coke and minerals – between the Thames and Cambridge Heath 1/- per ton; to Kentish Town another 6d and to the Grand Junction another 1/-. A flat toll of 2d per ton was to be charged on all goods on the Aske Terrace Branch. There was an overall minimum of 30 tons per boat, unless the water level was such as to prevent this tonnage actually being carried, when only the true tonnage could be charged.

In all the Act ran to 217 clauses, many of which covered what the company could, or could not, do. Others set out procedures for dealing with disputes for such matters as land purchases. These procedures were to be well tested.

CHAPTER TWO

THE FIRST PHASE OF CONSTRUCTION

With the Act obtained, the shareholders assembled at the Freemason's Tavern, St Giles-in-the-Fields, on Monday 10 August 1812 for their first general meeting, Sir Thomas Bernard taking the chair. Proprietors with 705 shares attended, while a further 165 shares were represented by proxy. Twenty-six proprietors were then nominated to serve as directors on the general committee and given full powers to purchase land and build the canal. James Morgan was appointed engineer, architect and land surveyor; George Ward, a

partner in bankers Martin Stone & Company of Lombard Street, was appointed treasurer; solicitors John Edwards and James Lyon became joint clerks; and Thomas Homer was to be employed in such appropriate role as the directors saw fit.

The meeting urged the directors to ensure that the two proposed tunnels were built sufficiently strongly to allay continuing doubts being expressed about them. This was due to general disquiet in London at the time about tunnelling following the collapse of a road tunnel through Highgate Hill in April 1812. The

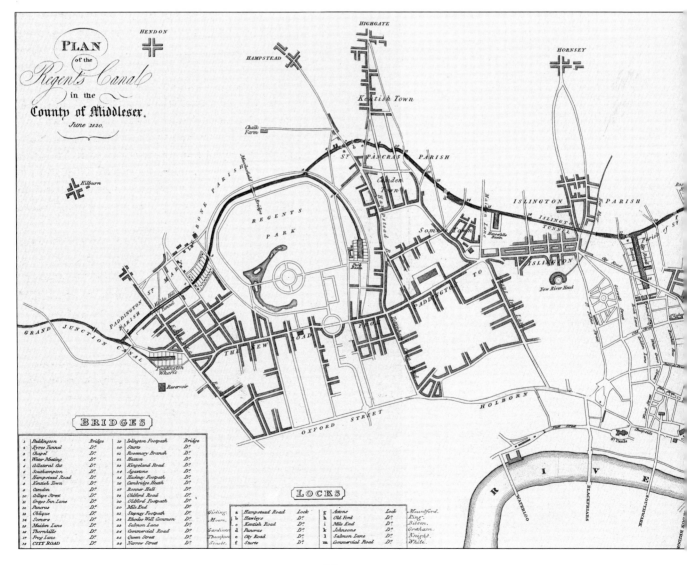

shareholders also urged the directors to adopt duplicate locks for the new canal. In conclusion, the Earl of Bridgewater and Earl Stanhope were thanked for their assistance in helping steer the Bill through Parliament, as was John Nash for his major contribution to the project.

The committee met immediately afterwards with Charles Monro in the chair and instructed Morgan to begin staking out the line of the canal from Paddington and to advertise for proposals for excavating the various stretches. It also asked Nash to offer a 50 guinea (£52.50) reward for the best design of a tunnel, and a similar sum for the best design of a lock. At the same time the clerks were instructed to open negotiations for the land needed, initially concentrating solely on the stretch from Paddington to the Hampstead Road. A fortnight later Morgan reported that the canal had been staked out from the Broadwater on the Grand Junction Canal to Marylebone Park.

On 28 August, Homer was appointed superintendent of the canal on a salary of £400; he was to devote himself entirely to the overall management and the concerns of the company. On the same day Edmund Snee was appointed minutes clerk at £200. It was not until December that the committee specified Morgan's duties; he was to have complete control of the making and perfecting of the canal and other works, provide all drawings, specifications and plans, help to make agreements, regulate all contracts and certify all bills and accounts. His only assistance was a resident clerk of works to supervise the day-to-day affairs. For all this he was to receive a salary of £1,000, payable in quarterly instalments backdated to 10 August.

To honour its agreement with the Commissioners of Woods & Forests, on 31 August the company instructed its solicitors to apply for an Act for the branch to the proposed basin in Marylebone Park, while Morgan was instructed to prepare a detailed plan to accompany the application. The company presented its petition to the House of Commons for the Bill on 26 November and the measure had an easy passage through Parliament, the Act receiving the Royal Assent on 15 April 1813.[1] It contained only nine clauses and authorised the construction of the branch to the southeast corner of the park. The work was to be completed within a year of the passing of the Act and no extra funds were authorised but an additional toll of 3d (1p) per ton was granted on all goods passing along the branch.

By the end of August eight tenders to excavate the main canal had been received and were considered by Morgan and a group of seven directors who made up a committee of works. On 12 September it was decided to employ Samuel Jones,[2] who had been involved assisting Morgan and Tate with some of the

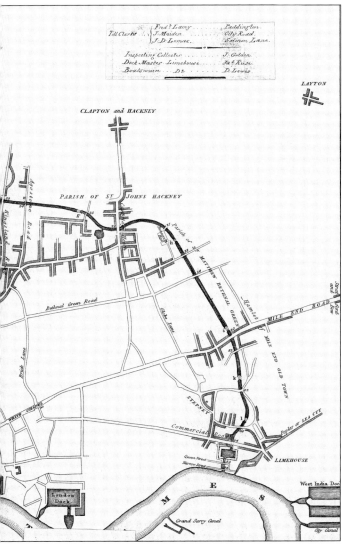

A plan of the Regent's Canal issued by the company in June 1820, shortly before the canal opened throughout, showing the 12 locks and the original 36 bridges. Regent's Park Basin is shown as originally built, before it was extended northwards; there are two small basins above Hampstead Road Locks, both of which were built when the canal was opened to this point from Paddington in August 1816; Horsfall's Basin was not finished at this time and the City Road Basin has just one side dock. Author's collection preliminary surveys, and Hugh McIntosh of Poplar.[3] On Wednesday 7 October work started with Sir Thomas Bernard putting in the first spade and Colonel John Drinkwater the second, in Marylebone Park near Primrose Hill.[4] Drinkwater had been involved with the canal since November 1811, was one of the first directors and was soon to take an increasingly active role in the company's affairs.

The request for designs for tunnels and locks attracted several entries and a panel of three engineers, led by Josias Jessop,[5] was asked to judge them. While they made an award,[6] none of the designs was deemed original and instead Morgan was asked to draw up plans.

In December 1812 the company started work on Maida Hill Tunnel under the Edgware Road, which was originally to have been 165 yards long and estimated to cost £30 per yard. It had been intended to put the work out to tender; instead it was decided to undertake it on a day-work basis under Morgan's direct supervision. The tunnel proved more expensive than expected mainly owing to a spring of water and some quicksand being encountered in the excavation, which delayed progress for a while and

The eastern end of the 272-yard long Maida Hill Tunnel that takes the canal under the Edgware Road (A5). The conduit on the right contains six high voltage electricity cables that were installed by the Central Electricity Generating Board and run under the towpath down to the Hertford Union Canal, canal water being used to keep them cool. The CEGB also installed concrete slabs on the towpath giving it a good surface for walkers and cyclists.

Author – 19 May 1984

caused several casualties among the workmen. Extra labour was brought in to overcome the problem and materials, especially timber, had to be left in the earth to increase its stability.

Meanwhile the alterations at the eastern end, where the canal had to take its more northerly course, led to the length of the tunnel being increased to 272 yards. This realignment also meant that a small second tunnel was needed under the avenue – now Lisson Grove – on the Eyre estate. This became known as Eyre's Tunnel, was 53 yards long and cost £3,061 up to the end of September 1814, although it still needed further minor works.

By June 1814 excavation of the canal from Paddington to the Hampstead Road was progressing well with only a few yards of Maida Hill Tunnel and a short stretch at the east end of the tunnel to be undertaken. The tunnel was completed in August at a cost of £14,730 with miners' wages comprising £3,809, bricklayers' and labourers' wages £1,468 and bricks £4,853. The cost had come out at £54 per yard and this was after allowing £1,254 for timber, ironwork and other equipment subsequently transferred to Islington. The wing walls at both ends cost a further £2,361.

Hugh McIntosh carried out the bulk of the excavation to the Hampstead Road. Samuel Jones did work in Marylebone Park valued at £9,956 but McIntosh's account totalled £58,460, which included £2,202 west of the tunnel, £1,092 on the tunnel itself, £14,298 from the tunnel to the park, £23,363 in the park itself, and £12,378 for work on the branch canal. These costs were far in excess of the estimate, most being caused by having to reroute the canal away from the centre of the park to the northern boundary because of the Commissioners' revised plans and the opposition from Portman. As a result, the depth of the cutting through the Eyre estate and through the park was increased considerably. By the end of September 1814 £49,084 had been spent on the section to the Hampstead Road against the estimate of £18,516. A further £4,000 was paid to Thomas Lord to give up his cricket ground so as to avoid still deeper cutting. Lord had moved to North Bank, St Johns Wood, in 1809 from his original site in Dorset Square and now moved again to the present location on St Johns Wood Road.

By the beginning of 1815 the canal was virtually complete to the Hampstead Road, as was the branch canal. Six bridges had been finished, five on the main canal and one on the branch, while the foundations for two others had been constructed, one being to carry a new road into Marylebone Park from Primrose Hill and the other was to take Warwick Avenue across the entrance to the canal at Paddington. A small aqueduct had also been completed carrying the river Tyburn, which drained part of St Johns Wood, into the park. Certain minor works remained to be carried out but these were being deferred until the water could be let in; they included re-grading the banks between Maida Hill and Eyre's tunnels and gravelling the towpath, both of which could be performed more efficiently and cheaply by using boats. The physical connection to the Grand Junction, which involved the construction of a stop-lock, also had to be provided.

Once work on Maida Hill was completed, Morgan made a start, in September 1814, on the much bigger task at Islington Tunnel. In the original plans this was to have been 880 yards long and, as at Maida Hill, was estimated to cost £30 per yard. This was now revised upwards to £40 per yard but it was hoped that the experience gained at Maida Hill would help contain the costs and cut down on the time taken. Much of the equipment that had been used at Maida Hill had been moved to Islington and a construction depot was set up on rented land at Pentonville. On 20 October 1814 the company contracted with Thomas and William Rhodes to supply the large number of bricks that were needed.

The main work was again undertaken by direct labour and at first good progress was made. By the beginning of 1815 four shafts had been sunk to their working depth, 140 yards of tunnel had been completed and 368 yards of the pilot heading had been driven. Two months later the company reported 250 yards complete, 500 yards of heading driven creating a connection between the four shafts, and two more shafts were about to be sunk. So far, the

A busy scene at Walker's Purfleet Wharf at Camden Town in 1911. This wharf, served by a short basin was situated just above Hampstead Road Locks and was one of first to be built on the canal, being opened in 1816. It is now known as Dingwall's Dock.

Regent's Canal & Dock Co booklet in the author's collection

ground had proved ideal for excavation, no water had been encountered and the tunnel, which was being driven eastwards, had been carried under one of the main streets in Pentonville without apparent difficulty. A series of railways was installed both in the tunnel and on the surface to handle the excavated spoil and construction materials. At the beginning of August 661 yards had been completed and the heading to the two new shafts was nearly finished, but delays had been caused in both shafts as water was encountered. More seriously, an acute shortage of money was now facing the company, forcing it to consider suspending all the work.

At the time of the first General Assembly 2,225 shares had been issued but this had risen to 2,541 by the end of 1812 when the directors decided to close the list. The first call of 2% had been made as early as 17 July 1811 to meet the preliminary expenses and as these built up another 2% was called prior to the Act. At its meeting on 24 August 1812 the committee was presented with bills for £12,411, which included £9,729 to Edwards & Lyon for Parliamentary and legal expenses with payments to Tate, Morgan and Jones for the engineering surveys, to Thomas Hogg for the land surveys and to George Woodfall for printing.

To meet these costs another 4% was called and further calls then followed at regular intervals:

Called	Amount
Prior to the Act	4%
28 August 1812	4% immediately
30 October 1812	10% by 1 December 1812
18 February 1813	7% by 25 March 1813
15 June 1813	10% by 17 July 1813
27 August 1813	10% by 29 September 1813
9 December 1813	10% by 22 January 1814
7 April 1814	10% by 16 May 1814
20 July 1814	10% by 1 September 1814
6 December 1814	10% by 16 January 1815
11 July 1815	10% by 1 August 1815
11 September 1815	5% by 13 October 1815

These calls should have raised £254,100 but there was a shortfall due to a defalcation by Homer, the company's superintendent. In March 1815 Monro, the chairman, received a letter from an aggrieved shareholder about drafts accepted for timber being many days overdue for payment. As Homer was in charge of the accounts Monro and Delafield met him on 30 March to inspect the books. Homer produced some of the records but claimed that in view of the short notice he had been unable to find them all. A further meeting was arranged for the following day, but Homer failed to attend. Instead he wrote in saying he was still attempting to trace the missing items and until he had found them he could not bear the idea of a meeting. Monro then learned that Homer had not been home for several days and a further letter was then received from him saying he could not remain in the country and that certain apparent defaults by some shareholders were not correct. He also revealed that he had previously been declared bankrupt, but had withheld this information from the committee when he was appointed.

Following this unwelcome news the committee offered a 100-guinea (£105) reward for Homer's arrest and his sureties, who were liable for £1,000, were told he had absconded with a large sum. Subsequently the sureties were found to be insolvent. On 17 April the committee learned Homer had been to Ostend but had since returned to London and then boarded a ship bound for Scotland. Thomas Foy, an officer from the Public Office in Marlborough Street, was dispatched by mail coach in hot pursuit. By the end of the month Foy had apprehended Homer and brought him back to London where he was examined and imprisoned at Tothill Fields, Bridewell. John Edwards was instructed to prosecute him, while Edmund Snee, the minutes clerk, was appointed to take temporary charge of the office and, as he would now be handling petty cash, was asked to provide sureties for £1,000.

Homer was tried on 15 May on the company's charge of embezzlement. He pleaded guilty and was sentenced to seven years transportation. Meanwhile Foy claimed the reward, which was paid together with his travelling expenses of £54. Investigations revealed that several shareholders had paid calls to Homer for onward transmission to the treasurer. While Homer was very much involved with the company's finances, the instructions to shareholders were to pay calls direct to George Ward, the treasurer, at his banking house. Counsel's opinion was sought, which suggested the company had a valid case against the defaulting shareholders. Ninety-two shares were involved, including 17 owned by Stamp Brooksbank, brother of Henry who was a committee member, on which £340 was outstanding, and 20 owned by Lord Dundas on which £1,200 was owing.

As there was doubt about the position, the

company instituted a test case against Stamp Brooksbank to try and resolve the matter. The results were inconclusive, as the company could not prove the appropriate notice had actually been given to the shareholders, as Homer would have done this. In 1828 there was still some £2,640 outstanding from seven shareholders, but by then the company was resigned to the fact that it could only compel payment by withholding registering the transfer in the case of a sale. By this means most of the arrears were eventually recovered but it took many years.

Up to the end of 1814 £170,453 had been spent on the canal works, mainly between Paddington and the Hampstead Road but with small amounts at Islington, Limehouse and elsewhere, but the expenses were already £72,725 over the estimate for that part carried out. The main reasons were the additional excavation through Eyre's estate and Marylebone Park totalling £30,567; the extra costs of Maida Hill Tunnel £11,375; buying Thomas Lord's cricket ground, including expenses £4,057; Eyre's Tunnel £3,061; the increased cost of the Act £8,483; extra fencing £1,551; and the cost of the collateral cut and basin in Marylebone Park £13,648, which had not been in the original plan.

These details emerged from a report by a special committee appointed on 19 August 1814 to investigate the company's finances and which estimated a further £253,421 would be needed to complete the canal, including £10,290 to finish the work to the Hampstead Road.

It was now obvious that additional moneys were going to be needed, but the report was not presented until the end of January 1815, it being held up by Nash being called away on other business. By then only two more calls remained on the original subscription and consideration had to be given to how to raise the extra funds. One option was borrowing, but an approach to the Solicitor General for guidance produced the unwelcome news that the company could not borrow the additional £100,000 on mortgage as authorised by the Act until the original subscription of £300,000 was complete.

At its meeting on 10 February the committee decided to recommend to the next General Assembly that if the shareholders would subscribe the required £45,900 to make up the £300,000, interest would be allowed at 5% on moneys already paid up to 5 April. Each shareholder was asked to contribute an additional 20% by 1 May and the payment could be reduced by the interest to be received. From 5 April interest on the old and the new capital would be allowed at 5%, payable in half-yearly instalments. The proposal was adopted on 23 February and by 5 April £36,100 had been promised.

The plan to pay interest, however, did not meet with universal approval and Charles Taylor filed a suit in the Court of Chancery in July to restrain the company from applying any part of the money received from shareholders to paying interest. The company then abandoned the plan and asked the shareholders if they would simply provide the extra 20% required. There was a mixed response; 18 proprietors with 248 shares agreed; 24 with 328 shares agreed but subject to various conditions; 15 with 273 shares declined; but the vast majority – 148 with 1,692 shares – failed to respond. As the company was having problems acquiring land and as the additional money sought was only part of what would be needed, the whole question of fund raising was deferred.

With the prospect of the money about to run out, the ends of the Islington Tunnel workings were faced up and secured early in August so that if the work had to stop it would not deteriorate. Morgan estimated that it would cost only £60 per week for another seven weeks to complete the heading between the fifth and sixth shafts, which was important as it would determine the nature of the soil in that part of the tunnel still to be driven. His suggestion was taken up, but once finished at the end of September all work on the tunnel came to a halt.

Up to the suspension £33,179 had been spent at Islington; wages for the miners and bricklayers in sinking the shafts, driving the heading, and excavating the tunnel totalled £9,849; bricks had cost £8,103 and timber £6,987. Completing the remaining 218 yards was estimated to cost £10,200, which included £2,400 for removing the spoil and for the rental of the land on which it had been temporarily deposited. This was equivalent to a figure of £35.15/- per yard – comprising £11.2/- for 4,200 bricks at £2.13/- per thousand; £12.12/- for labour and mining; £9.10/- for timber, cement and stone; and £2.11/- for equipment and incidentals.

The suspension led to a claim for compensation from the Rhodes over their brick-making contract. The settlement of this claim dragged on for many months but in August 1818 they were awarded £519, following arbitration by James Burton.

Hardly any work had been carried out between

WEST ENTRANCE TO THE TUNNELL, REGENT'S CANAL, ISLINGTON.

The western end of Islington Tunnel as depicted by T. H. Shepherd. There appears to be some artistic licence here as there is no bend in the canal on the approach to the tunnel. The small hut to the right of the portal was used by one of the two tunnel keepers who regulated the passage of barges so as to ensure they did not meet in the tunnel, as it was not wide enough for them to pass.

Author's collection

Hampstead Road and Islington owing to major problems in obtaining the land, although a contract to excavate this section had been awarded to Hugh McIntosh in January 1813. East of Islington several land purchases had been made or agreed but no work had been started.

At Limehouse the original Act had authorised the construction of a small basin for barges to be connected to the Thames through a tide lock. The cost of the 2 acre basin was estimated at £19,590 and the entrance lock at £7,200. At only its second meeting, on 24 August 1812, the committee had received a suggestion from George Brown of Ratcliffe Cross for a much larger dock. With the decision to start work at the western end of the canal no action was taken, but at the end of October the

company's solicitors opened negotiations for the land required with the principal landowners involved. The main freeholders were the Corporation of the City of London, while Charles Hampden Turner owned a wharf just off the Thames where the canal was intended to join the river; John Boulcott ran a timber yard between Narrow Street and Queen Street and the Commercial Road Company was responsible for the main roads in the area. By the end of 1813 the company had acquired just over 7½ acres of land for £5,485, but no work was carried out except to fence the site to make it secure.

In December 1813 the proposal for a dock at Limehouse was re-examined, the idea being to enlarge the basin and entrance lock sufficiently to accommodate sea-going colliers and other shipping and enable them to discharge in still water and greater security than would have been possible on the open river. An estimate for a 5¼-acre basin was £76,600, of which the excavation was £25,000 and the brickwork £21,800. The solicitors were asked to determine just what powers the company had under its Act and Morgan was asked to prepare a full report. Brown attended the next meeting to champion his idea but the committee felt the scheme was too ambitious, although a more modest plan might be feasible. Morgan then prepared a series of estimates covering the various options available to the company. While considerable extra revenue would be attracted from ship dues it was not felt this would be sufficient for the much heavier outlay involved. The idea was rejected again and instead detailed plans for the barge basin and tide lock were prepared. In September 1814 a revised estimate of £23,535 was produced but with the cessation of work no action was taken.

At Paddington, Morgan outlined the steps needed to form the link with the Grand Junction and was told to carry them out in July 1815, the main item being the stop-lock estimated at £578. In August Charles Harvey, the Grand Junction's superintendent, refused to allow the removal of the earth dam until the lock and the lock keeper's house were finished.

Looking back to the entrance to the Regent's Canal on 19 May 1984 and showing the former toll keepers' houses by the Warwick Avenue Bridge. Originally there was a stop lock at this point to ensure that the Regent's Canal did not take any water from the Grand Junction Canal to which it was not entitled.

Author

Agreement was reached in October when it was hoped the canal could be opened to Hampstead Road by 4 December. The stop-lock was completed on time and several boats passed through to carry out the gravelling of the towpath.

Despite this, the formal opening was deferred, probably owing to the Grand Junction's continuing fears about its water supplies. Eventually the two mile stretch of the main canal, together with the 1,230-yard branch in the park, was opened for traffic on Monday 12 August 1816.[7] The date was singularly appropriate – it was the Prince Regent's birthday.

The company's main problems in acquiring land between the Hampstead Road and Islington stemmed back to 31 March 1810 when William Agar, a barrister at law of Lincoln's Inn, purchased 72 acres of land, comprising the Manor of St Pancras, at auction for £8,000.[8] When the plans were being drawn up for the canal it was found there was little alternative but to cross Agar's estate and the original idea was to carry the line to the southwest of his house where the ground was reasonably level.

As early as August 1811, however, Agar sought a route that would be less damaging to his property. Tate examined the plans to see if the request could be met and went over the ground with Morgan. They reported that Agar's alternative plan was practicable but it would be costly as more earthworks would be required. Agar raised other objections and four clauses in the company's Act related solely to him; the main one being that the canal was only to be made on the northeast side of his estate unless he agreed otherwise. This involved a considerable increase in distance and expense as a deep cutting needed another 3½ acres of land.

In addition, the company was not to erect any steam engines on the estate without permission, Agar could make a wharf for his own use if he so wished, and the company was not to leave any excavated materials on the banks or allow them to be used for brick making. Instead, the spoil had to be deposited where Agar directed, provided it did not have to be moved more than 100yards, unless it was taken entirely out of his grounds.

On 9 April 1813 Morgan, having first written to Agar and called at his house, set out the line through the estate to determine the general direction of the canal and the actual amount of ground needed. He did as little damage as possible, following the line specified in the Act and the deposited plans. The action produced a strong protest from Agar about people trespassing on his estate, digging up his lawn and driving stakes into his garden, all without his permission.

Agar followed up his complaint by obtaining an injunction in the Court of Chancery restraining the company from carrying the canal through his estate at all, alleging that the Act gave no powers to do so. The company appealed and the Lord Chancellor subsequently dissolved the injunction. At the beginning of June 1814 the company, hoping the matter had been resolved, took steps to have the required land valued. Agar, however, instituted further legal proceedings with another hearing before the Lord Chancellor on 25 November 1814, but the results were inconclusive.

Matters rested until March 1815 when Morgan, having agreed with the contractor, Hugh McIntosh, on the work needed through Agar's land, asked the solicitors to deposit the money for the purchase and give formal notice that work would begin on Monday 13 March. On that day Agar set his gardeners and servants to guard the entrance that had been created for the company's workforce to gain access to the estate. Agar's clerk demanded to know on whose authority entrance was now being attempted and was told his employer had been served with the usual notice. McIntosh's men then started taking in their barrows and planks and Agar's men attempted to stop them but gave way as the workmen pushed forward with their planks between them. Having gained access the workmen started to strip the soil off the line of the canal for the rest of the day.

There was some opposition on the following day, but at 9am an officer from Bow Street appeared and arrested Francis Lewis, Morgan's assistant, and Henderson, McIntosh's foreman. Both were taken before the magistrates and charged with making a forcible entry onto the estate and assaulting one of Agar's employees in a riotous way. The magistrates, on being told that the company had bought and paid for the land, dismissed the complaint. Agar then issued a writ in the Court of Exchequer against Morgan, Lewis, Monro and Lyon. The company's solicitors were told to defend the charges and to consider a counter-action against Agar for trespass on the company's land. On 27 May Agar filed a new writ against several other committee members and against McIntosh. The actions were heard before a special jury, starting on 26 June and lasting three days. Monro was acquitted but verdicts of guilty were brought in

against the other defendants and Agar was awarded £500 damages. The court's decision was influenced by doubts about the scale being used on the plans, the company having assumed that the conventional 1in to 1-mile was that intended by the legislators. As a precaution, work on Agar's land had been suspended on 24 June, and after the adverse verdict the materials were removed.

Following this setback the company suggested the appointment of a panel of five engineers – two for the company, two for Agar and one neutral – to resolve the line of the canal. Agar rejected the idea and the Earl of Stanhope now took on the unenviable role of mediator. Stanhope was not a director but took a major interest in the company's affairs.

In September 1815 Morgan reported that after a series of meetings to try and resolve the position he had investigated a new line to the northeast of Agar's house, but further away than originally proposed. It posed major difficulties in crossing Kentish Town Road, while an embankment would be needed that would cause problems on adjoining land owned by the Marquis of Camden which had been laid out for building. He had also investigated a line to the southwest of the estate, which used less of Agar's land for the canal and spoil banks but required an embankment to which Agar objected. This line also passed too near a workhouse and a burial ground.[9] Stanhope then suggested a compromise line crossing the estate as directly as possible, but providing Agar with three bridges, instead of the two originally proposed. This line seemed much better than any of the others suggested so far.

Early in October Agar started a new action against Monro, Morgan, Lewis and Lyon for alleged trespass on and after 28 April, although Agar's solicitor said they would be willing to settle out of court. In November Agar sued Cockram, the gardener employed by the company to value the crops on the land, for trespass on 13 May 1815 and on subsequent occasions, for breaking into the garden and fields, and for causing £200 damage to the grass, vegetables and plants but the company quickly offered to cover any unintentional damage caused. Meanwhile the action against the officers went ahead with the solicitors recommending that as the first action had been lost, the company should simply suffer judgement by default and leave it to the jury to assess damages. In June 1816 the court assessed further damages of £1,000.

With these problems the company was

considering returning to Parliament to clarify the question of the line to be taken by the canal. In November, Morgan was asked to produce estimates for three alternatives – the line directed by Parliament, the new direct line discussed between Agar and Stanhope, and a line avoiding the estate altogether. A new factor had arisen; the company had now acquired an option on the freehold reversion of Agar's land from the Prebendary of St. Pancras. Agar wanted to take this over, but at no cost to himself.

By the middle of January 1816 Stanhope was losing patience due to the series of petty difficulties constantly being put up by Agar. Almost in desperation, Stanhope had investigated ways to minimise the impact of the canal on the estate, which included making the canal narrower to reduce the excavation but Morgan was opposed to such measures, feeling they would only cause problems later.

In the middle of February, after seven months of fruitless negotiations, the committee decided it had had enough and broke off the talks. This action seemed to bring a sense of realism to Agar for before the end of the month he had sent in a draft agreement, which met with Stanhope's complete approval. It involved an additional payment of £700 to Agar, making £5,200 in all, and it was speedily agreed.

The company still felt it essential to include the route in an Act and a finalised agreement was crucial to meet Parliamentary deadlines. Agar continued to be devious and unhelpful but on 23 March the agreement was finally signed by him and sealed by the company. Even then there were problems as Lord Shaftesbury objected to the way the clause was presented in the Bill and to the amount of the payment proposed to be made to Agar. Matters were smoothed over and the Act received the Royal Assent on 2 July 1816.[10] Its nineteenth clause referred to the doubts over the true line of the canal through Agar's estate that had arisen from the original Act; then specified that the line indicated by the first Act, on the northeast of the estate, was to be the true line. Two other clauses covered the period for payment and the valuation procedure.

Almost immediately after, and seemingly in complete disregard of the new Act, Agar applied to the Court of Chancery to commit Monro and officers of the company to the Fleet Prison for a breach of the injunction granted by the Lord Chancellor restraining the company deviating from the line of the canal marked on the plan deposited with the Clerk of the Peace. Perhaps not surprisingly the application was rejected, but these continuing problems with Agar were a major contributory cause of cessation of work on the canal.

CHAPTER THREE

THE SECOND PHASE OF CONSTRUCTION

With work on the canal suspended, efforts were concentrated on the all-important matter of trying to raise more money. By early 1816 it was obvious further Parliamentary powers would have to be sought and the company's third Act authorised raising an additional £200,000, either from the existing proprietors, from new subscribers, or by borrowing on mortgages or annuities and, if necessary, half shares of £50 could be created.[1]

In March 1816 revised estimates were presented showing that of the £253,421 specified in September 1814 as the amount needed to complete the canal, £66,105 had been spent – mainly on Islington Tunnel and on land purchases – leaving some £187,316. The new estimate was £220,673 to complete the canal, an increase of £33,357, and this assumed lifts were to be used instead of locks. A long struggle then followed to try and raise these additional monies.

The first proposal, in July 1816, involved a complicated plan: £40,000 in £100 shares; £40,000 in options of £70 each bearing interest at 5% and subsequently convertible into £100 shares; £40,000 in redeemable annuities on lives over fifty years at 12%, and £40,000 by a tontine commencing at 7%.[2] There was a poor response; 31 shareholders offered £25,700 (£8,000 of which was conditional on at least £130,000, the amount calculated to open the canal to Aske Terrace and to cover the interest payments, being raised); 49 declined and the remaining 125 failed to reply. Some of these were thought to be either dead or bankrupt. A deadline of 1 September had been set to raise at least £80,000 but this was not achieved. The opening of the first stretch of the canal to Hampstead Road was only made possible by members of the committee providing a loan.

A debate followed as to whether the company should persevere with its plan to open the canal to Aske Terrace at a cost of £110,000; should build the canal from the Hampstead Road to the Thames, omitting the basins at Aske Terrace and Limehouse until later, at a cost of £200,000; or should build from the Thames to Islington, or as far as the money would go, again omitting the basins. None of the options provided an easy solution and no decision was taken.

On 4 October 1816 an important meeting took place between Drinkwater and Nicholas Vansittart, the Chancellor of the Exchequer, to discuss the company's finances and Drinkwater was given a letter of introduction to the Governor of the Bank of England. The idea was for a £150,000 loan to enable the company to construct the canal from the Thames to Islington and, hence, enable it to start earning considerable revenue. Nash and Brooksbank accompanied Drinkwater to the Bank where the Governor asked for a formal statement of the company's finances for his Court of Directors. The Bank subsequently turned down the request, influenced by the unwillingness of the company's directors to provide personal security, although a mortgage of the canal was offered.

Soon after, the company began receiving delegations from parishes through which the canal was to run to see if unemployed people could be used on the works. There were considerable advantages; the company would have access to a cheap, albeit unskilled, labour force; the parishes would be saved some of their costs in providing for the poor; and the people would be doing meaningful work. The first approach came from Limehouse, but Stepney, Spitalfields, St Pancras, Bloomsbury and Marylebone were also interested. Spitalfields offered a subsidy of 5/- (25p) per man per week and wanted to employ 2,000 people, whilst Marylebone offered 6/- (30p) per week and St Pancras 1/- (5p) per day.

Morgan, on whom the burden of organising this labour would fall, was far from enthusiastic, as insufficient land had been purchased to enable worthwhile lengths of canal to be dug. He was also dubious about the benefits of employing the poor in this way unless the parishes could guarantee to perform the work for a specific price and to complete what they had started. In any case, everything now depended on some form of government help and a deputation comprising Sir Culling Smith, Brooksbank and Monro went to the Treasury on 8 January 1817 to renew the appeal for a loan, but again they were unsuccessful.

Meanwhile, on 4 December 1816, the General Assembly decided to try to raise £150,000 and authorised additional shares of a nominal £100 being issued at £25 each. These were to be offered first to existing shareholders, and then to the general public. By the end of February 1817 £42,725 had been offered, but as the negotiations for a government loan had made no progress no action was taken and the talks with the parishes were suspended. In March another elaborate scheme for raising £300,000 by a tontine was agreed, but it attracted only a minute response and was withdrawn.

The various approaches to the government had not been totally in vain as they had prompted a measure to be introduced into Parliament for commissioners to be appointed to lend money for the completion of major public works suspended for the lack of funds.[3] In May, Snee was instructed to prepare a case for submission to the Exchequer Bill Loan Commissioners, whilst on 3 June Josias Jessop made an independent report on the costs of completing the canal. His figure was £144,899 excluding the water supply arrangements, but an additional £4,500 would be needed if the upper line through Agar's estate was adopted, and a further £3,500 if the locks were equipped with side ponds. Morgan also made an estimate and this formed part of the submission to the Commissioners on 24 June.

The Commissioners response was to appoint Thomas Telford,[4] to inspect the canal, their secretary, William Holden, arranging a preliminary meeting at the Salopian Coffee House on Thursday 17 July. Telford's report was favourable and the Commissioners decided at their meeting on 27 July that the work would be of great public benefit and useful in providing work for the poor. A £200,000 loan was approved on various conditions; all the existing debts had to be paid off; the company was to raise another £100,000 with the Commissioners making their advances in £50,000 instalments as each £25,000 of this new capital was received and as the work itself progressed. The company also had to undertake to complete the canal at its own expense if the costs exceeded the estimate, and a mortgage of all the company's lands and properties was required as security.

On 4 June, and with government help in prospect, the shareholders were asked to subscribe for two new shares at £25 each for every share already held. With forfeiture the number of shares in issue had reduced

to 2,501 but the total was later restored to 2,541. By the beginning of July £93,250 had been offered and the list was closed. Once the Commissioners had made their offer, another £15,000 was needed to meet the company's debts – standing at £7,927 – and to bring the balance of the new subscription up to £100,000. Further shares were offered at the General Assembly on 6 August and subscribed immediately. The calls on the new subscription were:

6 August 1817	20% by 12 September 1817
6 August 1817	20% by 12 November 1817
12 November 1817	20% by 15 January 1818
27 May 1818	20% by 11 July 1818
20 January 1819	20% by 23 February 1819

The additional £15,000 was called in one amount on 21 May 1819, payable by 21 June.

Lyon visited the Commissioners' office in Great George Street on 12 August 1817 to learn that a case had been submitted to the Attorney General to find out if the need for personal security could be dispensed with. This was finally agreed, but the company had to enter into a bond undertaking to complete the canal.

With construction work suspended a settlement with Agar had been less important. Desultory negotiations had continued through much of 1817 but with the financial position looking more encouraging the company gave formal notice to determine the line through his estate, as required by the Act. The company was still looking at possible alternatives and talks were started with Lord Camden and with the Governors of St Bartholomew's Hospital for a major deviation of the line to overcome Agar's continuing intransigence. In January 1818 the General Court of the hospital was agreeable, but early in May it became apparent that Lord Camden's terms would be unacceptable.

In August 1817 Thomas King, one of the canal company's directors, was approached by people in the sugar trade about the enlargement of the proposed Limehouse Basin to accommodate shipping. Morgan produced a new plan and estimate early in September together with details of those traders likely to support the venture and the solicitors were asked to clarify the legal position. Early in October there was a meeting at Limehouse with John Craven, the traders' representative, to discuss the proposal. There seemed little doubt that the basin would be well used by colliers unloading their cargoes for the sugar refiners and other consumers in Ratcliffe and its immediate district, but not much coal would proceed up the canal. On the legal side the Act seemed to give the necessary powers but it was felt that the City of London would be entitled to a duty on the coal so discharged. Craven was asked for his suggestions as to how the enlarged basin should be laid out, and also what funds would be forthcoming towards the additional costs.

Meanwhile, with its financial problems apparently settled, the company could at last consider resuming construction work that had been halted for nearly two years. The first monies were due to be received early in September 1817 and at its meeting on 6 August the committee instructed Morgan to resume work on Islington Tunnel on Tuesday 12 August and to advertise for contractors to undertake other works. This prompted a note from Hugh McIntosh, writing from Bloomsbury, pointing out that he had been awarded the contract to excavate the canal from Hampstead Road to Islington Tunnel in 1813. With the passage of time the committee seem to have overlooked this and Lyon was asked to report on the validity of McIntosh's claim.

At the beginning of October, Francis Read was awarded the contract to erect the new bridge in Marylebone Park to carry the road from Primrose Hill. Two weeks later Thomas Douglas was appointed to oversee this work and to be responsible for the delivery of materials, while James Maiden was appointed to do the same at Islington Tunnel. Good progress was made on the tunnel and by early December nearly a quarter of the remaining length had been completed.

Early in January 1818 George Roe's tender to excavate the canal between Commercial Road and Mile End was accepted on Morgan's recommendation, while in May contracts were awarded for other works on this section – Francis Read was to build Stepney Common Bridge and the nearby Rhodeswell sewer while McIntosh was to erect the bridges at Salmon Lane and Commercial Road. In the same month Roe contracted to excavate the canal from Mile End to Cambridge Heath, McIntosh to erect two bridges at Old Ford while Richardson & Want started on Mile End Road Bridge.

By January it was apparent that the attempt to raise any significant sum of money from the traders to enlarge Limehouse Basin had failed, the company having hoped for £20,000. Despite this Craven and King remained keen about the larger basin and in February the committee decided on a compromise – to build the lock and entrance channel to the basin large enough to accommodate ships, but to leave the size of the basin itself unaltered. Morgan was asked to obtain tenders for carrying out the work on this basis with a view to getting it started as quickly as possible. With the restricted nature of the site, excavation would be a major undertaking as the spoil could only be removed by barges at high tide. The estimate for the ship lock, ship channel and barge basin was now £27,265 but if it was subsequently decided to enlarge the basin the contractor was to be expected to do the work at equivalent rates.

On 11 March McIntosh's tender of £24,640 was accepted, this being easily the lowest. Two weeks later he was instructed to start the work, which was to be completed in ten months so as to recoup some of the time lost in the ship basin negotiations. The company still hoped that Craven and his associates would come up with some of the money for a ship basin and suggested that he should raise one-third of the cost, and the rest might then be borrowed from the government. There was a setback early in May, however, when the Attorney General decided that the company did not have the power to construct a ship basin.

McIntosh started on his contract and the first stage payment was made to him on 24 June. Almost immediately a problem arose as Morgan became apprehensive that the works would seriously injure premises adjoining those acquired by the company from Boulcott. The owner was offered £1,100 as the building could ultimately be used by the company as an office, and the acquisition enabled the lock to be moved slightly westwards to avoid another property.

At their meeting in June 1818 the shareholders learned that only 40 yards of Islington Tunnel remained to be completed; Telford having inspected it and reported very favourably on the materials used and the quality of the workmanship. During the course of the work a large spoil bank had built up at the western end and the company was keen to have this moved. Initially it was hoped to use this spoil to build up land to form a basin near White Conduit House, but following an approach by William Horsfall early in 1815 it had been agreed to use the material at Maiden Lane, some 400 yards away, to build up the land and create a large basin there.

After the approaches from the various parishes, the company had taken on some of the unemployed people from Marylebone in January 1818 to start moving this spoil from the tunnel. Early in February Morgan reported that 317 men were at work on various parts of the canal, including about 150 from Marylebone, part of their wages being born by the parish. Their progress was slow and in May Morgan tried to chivvy the parish trustees into getting the work speeded up. A few weeks later, however, the trustees decided that as the people should be able to find other work during the summer they were to be withdrawn from the middle of June, but they asked for the remainder of the work to be held over until next winter. This was unacceptable to the company as after all the delays caused by Agar it was anxious to get the excavation between the tunnel and Hampstead Road started.

In May 1818 Bernard suggested that it might still be possible to get Agar to agree to the southwest line as originally intended in 1811 and as later discussed with Stanhope. Bernard and Harvey Combe, another of the directors, were given full powers to negotiate with Agar. A week later they produced an agreement for the southwest line with the route precisely specified on a map signed by them all and the line had been staked out on the estate and marked on the ground with a spade. The price for the land for the canal, towpath, cuttings, embankments, fencing, crops and all compensations was to be no less than £15,750. It was a large amount to pay for the 5 acres but, after all the aggravation, perhaps cheap at the price. The company sealed the agreement with Agar on 27 May and on the following day the treasurer agreed a short-term overdraft to enable the purchase to take place.

All that remained was to acquire the option to purchase the Prebendary of St Pancras' freehold interest, which was agreed for the relatively modest sum of £735.

Once a settlement had been reached with Agar it was crucial to resolve McIntosh's claim to do the excavation work. He had already offered a reduction on the prices previously agreed, but the company considered these inadequate. As a result the work was re-advertised and three other tenders came in. McIntosh and his solicitor made it quite clear that they would resort to legal action if necessary, so Morgan was asked to reach an agreement with them. At the same time Nash and Lyon took counsel's opinion on the original contract, but this revealed the company's position was weak and that it would be best to try and obtain a settlement. On 16 July agreement was reached whereby McIntosh was to complete the work by the end of 1818. His contract also included the completion of the work started by the Marylebone Trustees in moving the spoil to Horsfall's Basin.

McIntosh made an immediate start and Richardson & Want began on three bridges that the company had agreed to build as part of the settlement with Agar. One was Oblique Bridge, which carried the private drive to Elm Lodge, Agar's house; it was a handsome affair with decorative ironwork and was plastered with cement. Some problems remained as the negotiations with Lord Camden for the land needed for part of this stretch were still not finalised and it was not until the end of March 1819 that the company took formal possession. Even then there were problems over a sewer to carry the Fleet Ditch. Eventually these were resolved enabling McIntosh to get on with this part of his contract. Richardson & Want contracted for the sewer and they also built the Maiden Lane and Caledonian Road bridges, both of which were finished early in 1819.

The original plans had included the ½ mile branch to Aske Terrace in Shoreditch, leaving the main canal near Canonbury Road Bridge and running southeast, passing under the New North Road just south of its junction with Bridport Place, which was an extension of the Southgate Road. The branch was to terminate in a basin about 300 yards north of Old Road and close to the present-day Aske Street, which would have provided convenient access to the City. Some 3½ acres of land were needed for the branch and 8 acres for the basin and surrounding wharves. The £14,104 estimate included £7,350 for the land, £3,388 for the excavation, £1,780 for walling the basin and £468 for the road bridge.

On 26 August 1818 Nash reported that he had met the landowners concerned but their terms were so excessive there was no hope of any agreement being reached. Instead he had looked elsewhere and particularly at a site on the north side of City Road near the east end of Islington Tunnel. This was better situated than Aske Terrace, was likely to cost less, had better access to the City while the Paddington wharfingers, most of whom wanted to move as near to the City as possible, were keen on the alternative now offered. The problem was that an Act would be needed, as part of the branch would pass through church land. An approach had been made to Doctor Samuel Parr, the tenant, and while he had no objection in principle he pointed out that the Bishop of London, as freeholder, and his own sub-tenants would need to be satisfied. Nash's suggestion was adopted and a draft notice of an intended application to Parliament for a new Act was approved.

It was decided to include in this Act powers to enlarge Limehouse Basin, the cost being estimated at an additional £24,000, and to admit and charge shipping. A formal proposal to enlarge the basin was passed on 18 December when it was decided that at least £24,000 must be raised from the shareholders. On 23 December, Craven met the committee again to discuss the enlargement plans and following this James Walker, an experienced dock engineer, was appointed to advise the company.

Walker reported early in January 1819 supporting the enlargement plan as the company already owned most of the land, the dock would be closer to the City than other docks except London Dock, while the Commercial Road provided good access and the canal was an added advantage. Walker had been asked considered two plans. The first was for a 2¼ acre ship basin on the west side separated from a 1¾ acre barge basin by a new road the Commercial Road Trustees were planning to build from the Commercial Road southwards to a long-established ferry across the Thames. A ship lock and ship channel would give access to the ship basin and a brick bridge would carry the road over the link to the barge basin, which would be connected to the canal.

The second plan was for a single 4⅛ acre basin, 600ft long, 300ft wide with 1,680ft of wharves enabling it to accommodate 13 ships of between 200 and 300 tons while others could lie in the basin to tranship to barges. Walker recommended the single basin although it would cost £16,335 against £12,810 for the twin-basin scheme.

Morgan supported Walker's recommendation and it was decided to go ahead, negotiations being started with the Mercers Company for some extra land needed at the northwest of the site, with timber merchants Richardson & Son for an access road through their land, and with the Commercial Road Trustees as a re-alignment of the new road would now be needed. As Walker already acted for both Richardson and the Trustees it was hoped there would be few problems, but plans were made for a more modest scheme if difficulties should arise.

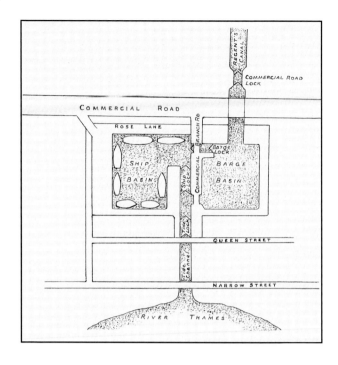

A plan showing James Morgan's proposed scheme for a ship basin at Limehouse completely separate from a barge basin and from a passage for barges from the Thames to the canal. This plan was sketched out to accompany a letter sent by Morgan to the company's chairman in 1819.

Edward Paget-Tomlinson

To finance the new basin a subscription list was opened offering one new £25 share for every five old shares held and by 27 January 1819 £30,550 had been raised and the list was closed, but one further share was issued on 10 February to a subscriber who had been abroad and only just returned. On 11 August 1819 the company called these funds, the shareholders having to make payment by 20 September.

Meanwhile the application to Parliament for powers to operate a ship dock and admit ships was going ahead. Walker had also recommended that the canal locks should be built wider to allow 15ft-wide sailing barges to work up at least as far as the proposed City Road Basin. While Salmon Lane Lock had already been started, alterations could still have been made to allow for the increased width. Morgan, however, felt that most of the sailing barges were unsuitable to be towed up the canal and there would also be a large increase in the demand for water. As a result Walker's suggestion was not taken up.

While all this was being decided Lyon had opened negotiations for the land for the City Road Basin. A meeting of those interested in Doctor Parr's prebendal land had been held and it soon became clear the company would have to purchase the whole estate, and not just the land needed for the canal. It was decided to seek Parliamentary authority on this basis and to include powers to let land around the basin to the Paddington wharfingers and to sell off the surplus land in due course.

In Parliament the company's Bill was read in the Commons for the first time in the middle of March and was expected to receive its second reading on 22 March. This was thwarted by the government, which was concerned about how its mortgage over the company's lands would be affected. A deputation comprising Drinkwater, Monro, Lyon, Morgan and Snee met the Exchequer Bill Loan Commissioners on 25 March when a settlement was reached. The Bill was read a second time on the same day and was then referred to a Commons committee. Craven gave evidence in support of the company, as did several of the Paddington wharfingers such as Pickfords, James Holt and John Rutty.

There were several objectors. The Commercial Dock Company wanted to stop timber and deals coming into the new dock for storage under bond and the City of London was concerned about dolphin piles being placed in the river at Limehouse to assist ships entering and leaving the new dock. Then Lord Shaftesbury insisted the company surrender its powers for the Aske Terrace Branch, while Boulcott and the East London Water Works Company wanted clauses to protect their interests. The government stepped in again with a clause to prevent West Indian and Colonial produce from being handled in the dock but a meeting was held with Vansittart which led to timber, corn and grain being excluded from this ban.

By mid-May the Bill had completed its passage through the Commons and had been read twice in the Lords. It was referred to a Lords committee on 13 May, some delay having been caused by the need to exclude the City Road land to be leased to the wharfingers, together with the surplus land to be re-sold, from the terms of the government's mortgage. By the end of the month the Bill had completed its passage through the Lords and only awaited the Royal Assent, which was given on 14 June 1819.[5]

In anticipation of this, at the beginning of June, Morgan had been instructed to proceed with the single large basin at Limehouse and to invite tenders for excavating City Road Basin. Soon after, McIntosh agreed to complete the additional work at Limehouse in three months. On 9 June tenders were considered from the Coalbrookdale Company, the Butterley Company, and Richard Salisbury & Company for two iron swing bridges to take Queen Street and Narrow Street across the entrance lock and channel. Salisburys' bid was accepted along with their tender for the lock gates.

On the same day Morgan's plans for the City Road Basin were approved, and it was agreed the basin would extend southwards of the City Road, which would be bridged. The company sealed the agreement with the Bishop of London and Doctor Parr for the land on 14 June and paid over the £28,200 purchase price soon after.

This left the tenants to be settled with, the main ones being two farmers, Samuel Fuller and Stephen Pepper. Pepper's interest was valued at £1,350 with a further £1,340 for stock, crops and compensation while Fuller's interest was valued at £1,040 with £4,710 for fixtures, stock, crops and compensation; he retained some of his holding and a new lease was agreed for him. With small payments to others this brought the cost of the City Road land to £36,745, against which the sale of the crops produced just over £1,000 for the company. In October just over 9 acres of the surplus land was sold to Nash for £7,360.

On 16 July five tenders for excavating the City Road Basin had been received. The lowest was from Samuel Jones but he lacked the resources to complete the work in the very short time scale now required by the company. Morgan favoured McIntosh who was also being considered for the adjoining stretch of the main canal and in September he was awarded the basin contract. On 31 August vandals tore down and stole part of the fence enclosing the company's property round the proposed basin and there were similar problems on 29 September when a number of people gathered outside Fuller's old house and pulled down part of the railings. The matter was reported to the Worship Street magistrates and two policemen were stationed on the site to prevent further trouble.

In December 1818 six tenders were received for excavating the canal from Cambridge Heath to the Rosemary Branch and on 13 January Morgan recommended that George Roe and his son John's offer of £4,996 should be accepted, although it was not the cheapest. The work was to be completed in four months. In May, Robert Streather contracted to build Cambridge Heath Bridge and in the following month he also started on a bridge carrying a footpath to Hackney. Cambridge Heath Bridge was completed in August when Streather contracted for Agostone Lane Bridge and in October he undertook to build the two other bridges on this section carrying Kingsland Road and a private road at Hoxton.

Once the decision had been taken to adopt conventional locks for the canal (see chapter 5) tenders could be invited for their construction and four offers had been received by the end of July 1818. The company then had second thoughts and decided that rather than have the contractor build the entire structure, it would be better to employ two gangs of experienced carpenters to construct the lock gates and other fittings using timber supplied by Sargent & Rutty, merchants at Paddington Basin. This would leave the contractors responsible solely for the excavation and masonry work. Despite this little seems to have been done until December when excavations for Salmon Lane and Johnson's locks started. In January 1819 Richardson & Want began building these locks, together with St Pancras Lock.

The company was still undecided whether to have duplicate locks and no other sites were started but once the decision was made special arrangements were concluded with Richardson & Want to try and speed up the completion of the remaining contracts. These contractors, who were becoming increasingly involved with the canal works and enjoyed Nash's patronage, made a start on Kentish Town Lock in June. At the same time Francis Read started on Hawley's Lock where additional land had to be acquired from Sir Henry Hawley to accommodate the second lock chamber, and Streather started on Acton's Lock, as he was already working on the bridges on this stretch. Considerable progress had been made on all three locks by the end of the year while Salmon Lane and Johnson's locks were nearly ready for the fitting of the gates. At both these sites and at St Pancras Morgan had set out the site of the duplicate lock and brickwork was about to begin.

Work on Islington Tunnel was completed in September 1818 except for some brickwork at the two portals; it had been a major undertaking and involved the laying of over 4,000,000 bricks. It was 960 yards long against the original 880-yard estimate, the extension being at the eastern end to facilitate passing under the New River, which had had to be

diverted for part of June while the tunnel was being driven. The extension increased the cost by £2,568 to over £43,000.

The tunnelling had caused Morgan several problems. In a detailed report explaining why it had exceeded the estimate he pointed out that much heavier timbers had to be used to support the whole face of the earth while the arch was being formed underneath. This was due to the nature of the soil and the presence of water making the workings prone to collapse. In his estimate he had expected the earth would be self-supporting until the masonry was complete. Then cement, rather than mortar, had been used to give extra strength to the arch together with a much better quality brick since the ordinary stock brick was unlikely to have supported the weight. These factors had meant that the centres had to be kept in place for far longer than envisaged to allow for the gradual settlement of the work. In turn this meant more centres were needed and they required almost constant repairs due to the pressure of the

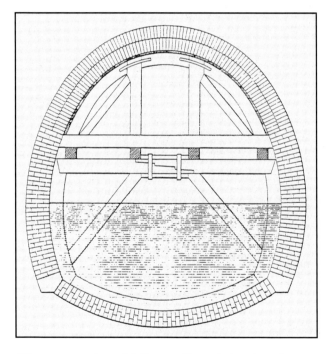

The cross section of Islington Tunnel showing the timber centering in position. This drawing appeared in the third part of **Voyages dans la Grande Bretagne** *by Charles Dupin, published in Paris about 1824. The tunnel's dimensions were 17ft wide at the water line and 18ft 6in high from the invert to the crown of the arch.*

A drawing of work underway inside Islington Tunnel. Railways were laid down both in the tunnel and on the surface to speed up the disposal of the spoil and bringing in the large quantity of bricks and other materials necessary. Six shafts which were sunk down from the surface, also speeded up the construction work.
Greater London Council

earth. All this led to extra labour and extra expense in materials and cartage to and from the construction depot at Pentonville. The provision of railways in the tunnel to transport the spoil to the shafts had also added to the costs. At the head of the shafts gins were set up to hoist the spoil to the surface where further railways transported it to the dumps, while the construction materials went in the reverse direction. Morgan had had further difficulties when a spring was encountered during sinking the last two of the six shafts.

Despite all his endeavours some damage was caused to properties above the tunnel. In July 1815 a claim was received for damage to 42 Chapel Street, Pentonville; a month later another came in for number 36 and others followed including property in nearby White Conduit Street. A valuer was appointed to assess the claims and the first payments were made in January 1816. By March of the following year £1,759 had been paid out, but several claims were still outstanding and these all added to the ultimate cost of the tunnel.

While the works were making good progress at the western end of the tunnel there was no possibility of opening it as no work had started at the eastern end due to major problems in obtaining the land. Matters had been delayed by the decision to abandon the Aske Terrace Branch and substitute the City Road Basin, but the main difficulties were over land owned by Samuel Pullin and Samuel Rhodes. In January 1819 an arbitrator awarded Rhodes £4,834

for his land and compensation, which was accepted with some reluctance. Rhodes also had an interest in some of Pullin's land as tenant. In February Pullin was awarded £1,800 and the company offered to pay this money into court to enable work to start. Pullin rejected the award outright and a jury had to be summoned to reach a settlement. In July the jury awarded £2,626 for the 4 acres involved, but Pullin was still dissatisfied and consulted William Agar to decide on further action. On learning of this unwelcome development Lyon hastily paid the money awarded into court and took possession of the land on behalf of the company.

Before any work could start an injunction was served on the company on the grounds that Pullin's trustees were acting for minors, whose interests had not been properly considered. A new jury was summoned and on 30 September it awarded an additional £74 over and above the £2,626. This, the company considered somewhat cynically, was merely to saddle it with the costs of the trial. Even this was not the end of the matter as in December further proceedings were instituted in the Court of Chancery to try and have the jury's verdict set aside. The Lord Chancellor refused to suspend the works and merely directed that the money paid into court by the company should remain there until the question of how it was to be divided between the freeholder and the tenant had been settled. The crucial plot of land lay diagonally across the eastern end of Islington Tunnel and extended down to Frog Lane.

In the hope that a settlement was about to be reached the company had re- examined the tenders for excavating the canal from the tunnel to the Rosemary Branch in June 1819, four offers having come in following an advertisement as far back as September 1817. It was decided to re-advertise, but before doing so Nash asked McIntosh to tender at the same time as he tendered for the City Road Basin. Five offers were received including from McIntosh and from the Roes. Morgan clearly favoured McIntosh for while his was not the lowest

offer he was able to guarantee completion of the work in the two months required once the company finally obtained possession of the land, no other contractor possessing the large numbers of horses and carts that would be required. Only relatively light works were required on the stretch involved and once the legal problems were sorted out McIntosh made an immediate start and by the end of October had performed work to the value of £3,000, which was nearly half the total of the contract.

Early in October 1819 John Atherly and Thomas Sowter contracted to purchase the soil that was suitable for brick making from the excavations near the east end of the tunnel. They also undertook the brickwork of Frog Lane Bridge, the lock on Rhodes and Pullin's land near the City Road Basin, a culvert nearby and a bridge carrying a footpath from City Road to Islington. A month later Richardson & Want contracted to build the bridge carrying City Road across the new basin together with the bridge on the main canal near Sturt's Lock. The contract for the lock itself went to Streather as well as for the Rosemary Branch Bridge carrying the Southgate Road while Richardson & Want were awarded the contract for Mile End and Old Ford locks and Bonner Hall

A towpath tractor and a horse above Sturt's Lock in the early 1950s waiting to tow their respective barges further up the canal.
The Waterways Archive, British Waterways Archive, Gloucester

Hampstead Road Locks in 1938 with the large Gilbeys warehouse on the left hand side occupying the site of several earlier wharves and basins. The diagonal bridge was erected in 1845 to carry the towpath.

Bridge. Meanwhile, Read had started on the reconstruction of the Hampstead Road Lock now that the caissons and other machinery had been removed (see chapter 5). The work included an additional arch to Hampstead Road Bridge to provide access to the new duplicate lock

It would have been too much to hope for an end to Agar's harassment. All went well until it was decided to construct the duplicate lock at St Pancras, which necessitated a small amount of additional land. Agar

Bonner Hall Bridge now gives access to Victoria Park, an attractive feature, which runs alongside the canal down to the Old Ford Road. Author – 30 May 1984

contended the company had no right to construct double locks on his estate as the agreement covered a single lock only. Lyon and Combe saw him early in November 1819 but he persisted in his objection. In the short term there was no alternative but to agree to operate the lock at St Pancras as a single lock with the duplicate, on which work was well advanced, being used as a side pond. Matters were further complicated as Agar had constructed a wharf on part of the land now needed by the company.

In March 1820 Agar's solicitor claimed for the costs of the actions in the Court of Chancery and offered to settle for £1,500, but Lyon contended Agar had no further claim on the company. This matter, and the question of the double lock, was then referred to counsel. In the meantime the company decided on more resolute action and Morgan was ordered to fence off the land for the double lock and to complete the work on the lock itself. This was too much for Agar who prevented the company's men from carrying out the work and insisted that the entrance to the duplicate lock should be sealed off.

Counsel's opinion was received early in May stating that Agar had no grounds to recover any costs from the company, and it would be best to ignore the matter at this stage, leaving Agar to take whatever steps he wanted. As the company's case would be weakened if it seemed to be conceding Agar's claim by not using the duplicate lock, counsel recommended making a strong protest insisting on the right to use both locks as and when necessary. Lyon was instructed to make such a protest but Agar was unmoved and in July matters were no further forward. Lyon then suggested that an impartial barrister should be brought in to settle the dispute but Agar rejected the idea leaving matters still in an unsatisfactory state.

Meanwhile the loan moneys from the Commissioners had been drawn in four equal instalments, in May and December 1818 and July and September 1819. After the final instalment the Commissioners called for an estimate of the costs of completing the canal, which revealed that £151,709 was still needed. After allowing for funds in hand and to come in, and for payments to be made including interest and capital repayments to the Commissioners, there was a shortfall of £95,000. An application was made for a further £90,000 loan with the company undertaking to raise another £15,000.

Drinkwater called on the Commissioners on 11 November to discuss this request but they refused to see him and subsequently he learned that it was being viewed unfavourably. An emergency committee meeting was held on Saturday 13 November and Snee was despatched to Shirburn Castle in Oxfordshire, home of the Earl of Macclesfield the company's chairman, to enlist his aid. On Sunday Drinkwater met one of the Commissioners at Ewell in Surrey and then went on to see their chairman, who lived at Dartford in Kent, but he was unable to have a proper discussion.

Another emergency committee meeting was held on the Monday with the Earl of Macclesfield in the chair and a deputation was appointed to attend the next meeting of the Commissioners, while the Earl was to write to their chairman. Despite these efforts the Commissioners, acting on the advice of the Attorney General, declined to help. Instead they indicated that they were considering legal action to compel the company to complete the canal in accordance with the original agreement.

On 24 November the committee, and 22 invited shareholders, met to discuss the situation. They decided to recommend to the General Assembly to be held a week later that £105,000 be raised by issuing further shares at £25 each. Any shortfall could be borrowed on the security of the City Road Basin land, which was not involved in the mortgage to the Commissioners. This suggestion was adopted, the committee having already contributed £29,475 themselves.

The new shares were first offered to the existing shareholders on the basis of three for every five old shares held. The list was filled comfortably before the deadline of 6 January and another £44,000 had also been offered. The new subscription was called in three equal instalments – on 28 December 1819 payable by 12 January 1820, on 8 March 1820 payable by 14 April, and on 14 June payable by 15 July. This brought the capital up to £497,725.

By the December shareholders' meeting all the contracts had at last been let. At one time the company had hoped to have the canal completed by this time but the delays in acquiring the land had made this impossible. Considerable efforts had been made to make up for lost time and the excavation of the upper part of the canal from Hampstead Road to City Road Basin was expected to be finished by mid-January. On the lower part of the canal most of the excavation and most of the bridges were finished, several locks were completed and the rest were almost ready. Even then there were setbacks as poor weather delayed progress considerably while frosts damaged the new brickwork, resulting in parts having to be taken down and rebuilt.

At City Road, McIntosh had made good progress but he had problems at Limehouse where the restricted access to the Thames caused long delays in barging away the spoil. To speed up the work some of the spoil was dumped temporarily on land to the north of the basin. At the end of December 1819 Salisburys delivered the two sets of iron lock gates and by this time most of the excavation work had been finished and efforts were being concentrated on the brickwork in the entrance lock and entrance channel.

By April 1820, Salisburys had completed Narrow Street Bridge and expected to have the Queen Street Bridge finished early in May, a temporary bridge having been provided while it was under construction. At the beginning of June the basin, now upgraded to the status of a dock, and the entrance lock were virtually complete except for a few small items which prevented the removal of the coffer dam, one being the erection of jetties at the entrance to the canal as the Thames Navigation Committee had raised objections. A compromise was reached whereby

dolphin piles that were to have been driven into the bed of the river, were replaced with buoys that would cause less interference to traffic in that crowded part of the river. David McIntosh attended the committee on 21 June on behalf of his father and agreed to erect the jetties in only 17 days instead of the expected month, for an extra £40 on the contract price.

At the beginning of June 1820 the canal was basically complete except for the final works at Limehouse. On 21 June Richardson & Want navigated a laden barge from Paddington to City Road Basin carrying construction materials for the brickwork they were carrying out around the basin. The company had decided to postpone the formal opening until some of the wharfingers had had time to establish themselves at the new basin.

Leases had already arranged with several of the leading carriers. For instance Pickfords took the large Nos 1 and 2 wharves at the south end of the basin, James Holt took Nos 3, 4 and 5, Richard Snell Nos 6, 7 and 8 and John Rutty Nos 11 and 12. The carriers were to erect their own buildings on the land with a view to moving from Paddington as soon as the canal was open and their buildings were complete.

CHAPTER FOUR

THE CANAL IS OPENED

With the works at last within sight of completion the company could start planning how to operate the canal and in March 1820 the committee decided on the numbers of toll clerks, lock keepers, dock staff and other officers needed and their salaries and wages. The first appointment was John Golden as Toll Clerk at City Road from 6 April on an £80 salary with an extra allowance until a house could be provided for him; he had to put up a £100 security and provide two guarantors for £100 each. A week later John Lomax was appointed to Salmon Lane and soon after Frederick Lacey to the third toll station at Paddington. In July, Golden became Inspecting Collector and James Maiden took his place at City Road. At the same time a table of tonnage rates was advertised widely in the national press.[1]

At the beginning of April 1820 work at the dock at Limehouse was sufficiently advanced for the company to appoint James Ruse as Overseer at £150 and the use of a company house; his title was changed to Dock Master a month later. On 19 July draft regulations were published for the use of the dock, the rates were set out and David Lewis was appointed Boatswain at £70. John Knight's tender to repair a house in Queen Street for Ruse and construct an extension was accepted on 1 July on condition the work was carried out very speedily.

David Lewis had been the first lock keeper appointed early in May at 21/- (£1.05) per week but soon after he was transferred to assist Ruse at Limehouse with another John Knight taking his place. A further ten lock keeper appointments followed as candidates came forward and were adjudged suitable, although most did not take up their duties until mid-July.

In the middle of April, Morgan submitted plans for houses for the toll collectors and the lock keepers, but it was not until 14 June that

To ensure the speedy passage of traffic and the correct operation of the locks each one had its own keeper and most had houses for those keepers. The Regent's Canal Company issued workers at its Limehouse Dock with a uniform and the Grand Union Canal Company extended this to the lockkeepers. This picture was taken at Camden shortly after nationalisation in 1948 as the keeper has a Docks & Inland Waterways Executive badge on his cap but his serge coat has GUCCo on its lapels. The Waterways Archive, British Waterways Archive, Gloucester

The lock keeper's cottage stands on the right at Old Ford Lock (30 May 1994) but the buildings also included a former pumping station and stables to house horses used for towing on the canal. The duplicate 'offside' lock chamber has been stanked off.   Author

the first contracts were awarded for their construction – Thomas Sowter for the lock keeper's and toll clerk's houses at City Road for £314; Francis Read the lock keeper's houses at Kentish Town and St Pancras for £204 each; and John Knight for four lock houses from Commercial Road to Mile End for £101 each. Soon after, Robert Streather contracted for the lock houses at Old Ford, Acton's and Sturt's for £102 each, and Knight for the toll clerk's house at Paddington for £180, one at Salmon Lane for £100, and, in August, the lock house at Paddington for £105.

Meanwhile with the prospect of much more work having to be handled in the office, the company decided it would need larger premises having occupied a house owned by Thomas Jackson at 28

Grafton Street, Fitzroy Square, since the autumn of 1812. It now agreed to rent 108 Great Russell Street, owned by the Duke of Bedford, for £156 per annum, including a coach house and stables. The staff moved in early in July 1820.

A significant event took place on 12 May when the committee decided to honour its Chairman, the Earl of Macclesfield.

As a memorial of the high sense the General Committee entertain of his Lordship's obliging acceptance of the Chair, and constant attention to the

One of the canal company's tugs towing four loaded barges near Hanover Lodge at the western entrance to Regent's Park.

The Waterways Archive,
British Waterways Archive, Gloucester

Interests of the Regent's Canal, the Iron Column or Ornamental Bridge in the Regent's Park be styled The Macclesfield Bridge and that his Lordship's Family Arms cast in iron, agreeably to the design now submitted for approval, be placed in the centre compartment of the Railing over the centre arch of the same, on each side, and that the same be executed with the least possible delay.[2]

At the same time the committee decided to name the various other bridges; those carrying public roads were generally named after those roads and several of the rest after the landowners on whose property they had been constructed. The same principle was adopted for the locks, but it was hardly surprising that William Agar's name was not chosen for any of the bridges or the lock on his land at St Pancras.[3]

On 14 June, Drinkwater and Culling Smith were asked to oversee the final works on the canal, start preparations for the official opening and to expedite negotiations with the Paddington wharfingers. On 12 July, Morgan was asked what would be the earliest date the canal could be opened and he promised that everything would be ready by the beginning of August.

As the Grand Junction had now agreed to provide a temporary supply of ten locks of water a day for six weeks the committee meeting on 17 July opted to open the canal on Tuesday 1 August 1820 and the arrangements were put in hand.

The Earl of Macclesfield passed the news to King George IV; the Prince Regent having ascended to the throne on 29 January 1820 on the death of his father. In his reply the king expressed his pleasure at the completion of the works and hoped the undertaking would fulfil its purpose in providing commercial benefits to the metropolis and the empire as a whole.

The opening ceremony was rightly celebrated as a great event.[4] The committee, with many of the shareholders and their friends, assembled at Horsfall's Basin near Maiden Lane, where they embarked at 11am on the City State Barge and other barges provided for them. The craft were decorated with flags and streamers and had two military bands on board. They then passed in procession through Islington Tunnel and through City Road Lock to enter City Road Basin where they were greeted by a gun salute and great cheers from the crowds gathered round the basin. The official procession was followed by several craft loaded with manufactured goods, coals and building materials; one having arrived, fortuitously, all

The east end of the 53-yard long Eyre's Tunnel taking the canal under Lisson Grove. It is so named after Henry Eyre, the landowner. Author – 19 May 1984

the way from Manchester that same morning. Once in the basin there was considerable competition as to which one would unload the first cargo, the honours going to *The William*.

The official party continued down the ⌐˘ ¹ to Limehouse and as the tide was right ˙ ˙ ᵤ₁ₑ to navigate out on to the Thames at 6pm to land at the Custom House Stairs. From there they proceeded to the City of London Tavern where nearly 100 sat down to dinner at 7.30pm with the Earl of Macclesfield in the chair. After all the difficulties over the previous eight years the canal was finally open.

Thomas Homer was obviously not at the opening ceremony and in view of his conduct it is not surprising his name is little remembered today. He was, however, very actively involved in the 1802 project and responsible for reviving the plan in 1810 and promoting it until others could take over. Prior to this he had been employed by the Grand Junction as the clerk of the works at Blisworth Tunnel during the first unsuccessful construction attempt between 1793 and 1796. Later he was involved with the railroad over Blisworth Hill and drew up the regulations for its operation. From 25 March 1802 he was appointed as the Grand Junction's Inspector General & Superintendent of Trade, Packet Boats & Navigation on a £300 salary.[5] On the same day John Holland, who later assisted Homer with the early surveys of the

Regent's Canal, was appointed the Grand Junction's Assistant Engineer.

Homer seems to have been responsible for setting up the Grand Junction's service of packet boats between Paddington and Uxbridge. In 1804 he took over the boats on a three-year lease and this was renewed in 1807 for another five years.[6] He was also involved with the arrangements to begin supplying water to parts of Paddington. In 1802 he owned at least four barges, two of which had just been built for him at Reading, and six canal narrow boats, all of which were newly built for him at Banbury.[7] By 1806 his fleet had increased significantly, but it seems he over-reached himself and perhaps it was this expansion that contributed to his bankruptcy. Otherwise he would almost certainly have been a prominent shareholder in the Regent's Canal.

James Morgan also deserves to be better remembered, for the creation of the canal was largely due to his efforts. He was the company's highest paid employee and the committee placed considerable reliance on his skill and judgement. Most of the negotiations for the acquisition of land fell on his shoulders and he had to deal with the contractors and sort out numerous problems caused by building a canal through an increasingly built-up area. He was also directly responsible for overseeing both Maida Hill and Islington tunnels and many of the other works. When the company was experiencing its major financial difficulties Morgan volunteered to forego his salary in March 1817 until the works could be restarted, his payment being resumed exactly six months later.

In August 1814 James Tate levelled several criticisms against Morgan over the execution of the work, but the charges were not substantiated. Ironically, in March 1819, Tate was engaged as Morgan's assistant on a £200 salary. Morgan had an unfortunate experience in October 1818 when he had to journey to Leybourne Green, near Maidstone, to negotiate with Sir Henry Hawley over a change in the line of the canal through his land at Camden where additional land was needed. Morgan secured Sir Henry's agreement for the extra land but returning to London his coach overturned and he suffered a broken arm. The committee expressed their concern and told him not to worry too much about the company's affairs until he recovered.

On the administrative side Edmund Snee, the Minutes Clerk, took on additional responsibilities following Homer's abrupt departure. In April 1815 he took charge of the office when it was decided not to appoint a direct successor to Homer. James Price, first appointed as a messenger in the office in February 1813, was promoted to assist Snee at £70 per annum. Joseph Grimes was given the messenger's position and his wife Hester acted as housekeeper; they had to live in the office building and were paid 21/- (£1.05) per week. Snee received regular gratuities for his diligence over the company's affairs, such as £100 in June 1817. In July 1820 he was appointed the company's Accountant while remaining as Minutes Clerk and his salary was increased to £250. His son Frederick joined the company as a junior clerk in October 1817.

George Ward asked to resign as Treasurer in August 1817 as he was living in the Isle of Wight, but he was persuaded to carry on. John Edwards and James Lyon conducted the company's legal affairs, but Edwards, who lived at Colnbrook, retired in November 1818 leaving Lyon to carry on alone.

Many of the company's early meetings were chaired by Sir Thomas Bernard who was born in 1750, educated in America, and was called to the bar when he came to England. He was connected with many societies for relieving poverty; Bernard Street off Russell Square, built between 1799 and 1802 on the Foundling Hospital Estate was named after him, Sir Thomas being the hospital's treasurer at the time.[8] He died in July 1818.

From the end of October 1812 Charles Monro chaired an increasing number of meetings and he was formally appointed as the company's Chairman on 13 July 1813. He had been associated with the canal since the beginning of January 1812 when he was admitted as a subscriber for £2,000. He took a very active part in the company's affairs until he resigned as Chairman on 4 July 1816. The committee voted him £1,000 for his dedicated service and as some compensation for the heavy expenses he had incurred. He immediately re-invested the money in the canal by purchasing more shares and, despite his resignation, he remained on the committee.

George Parker, the fourth Earl of Macclesfield, who had become a shareholder, initially with 20 shares, on 31 August 1812 and was elected to the committee on the same day, succeeded Monro as Chairman. He took a leading role in getting the work on the canal restarted. Typical of his concern was during the November 1819 crisis with the Exchequer Bill Loan Commissioners when, alerted by Snee of the difficulties, he immediately returned from his country house near Watlington to take personal charge.

At the same time that Macclesfield was appointed Chairman, Colonel John Drinkwater was appointed Deputy Chairman. Born in 1762 near Warrington, Drinkwater had a distinguished military career.[9] He was involved when Gibraltar was besieged by a Spanish force between June 1779 and February 1793 and subsequently published a detailed account about it. In 1811 Drinkwater was appointed Comptroller of Army Accounts, a position he held for the next 25 years. This post seems to have allowed him spare time, as he was tireless in his work for the canal. From August 1817 he acted as the company's Superintendent, assisted by Snee in the office, and chaired many of the frequent committee meetings during the time the canal was being built.

A major advocate for the canal and an active committee member was John Nash,[10] born in 1752 and who trained as an architect under Sir Robert Taylor. Nash went into practice in 1793 and is remembered today for laying out Regent's Park, designing many of the terraces near it, and for many other works. He was involved with the canal from early in 1811 and he took a leading role in the early plans and negotiations. He, and his wife Mary Ann, were among the first, and became the largest, shareholders of the company. In June 1817 both had 50 shares, but a year later he had increased his holding to 280, by June 1819 it had grown to 483 and to 951 in June 1821, while her holding was 300 in 1820.

On top of this substantial financial stake in the company Nash undertook two other financial commitments. The Commissioners of the Department of Woods & Forests were prepared to lease land for development around the canal basin in Regent's Park, but the company was not permitted by its Act to hold such a lease. A similar problem had arisen on the Eyre Estate where the building lease had had to be held by Monro, Nash and Delafield as trustees for the company. In May 1818 Nash agreed to rent the basin land from the Commissioners and to extend the basin northwards, more than doubling its length, by widening the canal to make space for more wharves. Ultimately he was able to re-let the land at a profit to traders to develop the wharves. The company eventually agreed to purchase the land for the branch and the extended basin in March 1823, paying the

Commissioners £1,993.10/- (£1,993.50). Nash also purchased the company's surplus lands not needed for the City Road Basin and wharves; for just over 9 acres Nash paid £7,360 in December 1819.

Another prominent committee member was Harvey Combe, Lord Mayor of London between 1799 and 1800 and involved in the Woodyard Brewery, later known as Combe's Brewery.[11] Joseph Delafield was a partner in the brewery business and he also served on the canal's committee from 1812 until his death in September 1820. Henry Brooksbank, a Pall Mall banker, served from 1816 and provided several short-term loans to assist the company over difficult times. Other active committee members were Sir Culling Smith and his son Culling Charles Smith.

From the beginning, the day-to-day affairs of the canal were controlled by subcommittees that reported back to the main committee; in 1812 there were subcommittees for accounts, works and purchases. In 1815 a General Purposes Committee was also set up, but in the following year a Select Committee was formed. Its members, who were required to attend regularly, comprised the Chairman or Deputy Chairman, and two each from the accounts, works and purchases committees. The initial membership was the Earl of Macclesfield as Chairman, Harvey Combe and Henry Brooksbank from accounts, Charles Monro and Sir Culling Smith from purchases, and John Drinkwater and Culling Charles Smith from works. This group effectively managed the company's affairs through to the canal's opening.

The staff based in the office at the time the canal was opened were James Morgan – Engineer £1,000; Edmund Snee – Accountant and Minutes Clerk £250; James Lyon – Clerk and Solicitor £200 and professional fees; James Price – Clerk £100; Frederick Snee – Junior Clerk £70 and Joseph Grimes – Messenger £30. On the canal were John Golden – Inspecting Collector £130; James Maiden – City Road Toll Collector £80; Frederick Lacey – Paddington Toll Collector £80; John Lomax – Salmon Lane Toll Collector £80; and 11 lock keepers who were paid 21/- (£1.05) per week, one of them in charge at both Hawley's and Kentish Town. At the dock James Ruse – Dock Master £350; David Lewis – Boatswain £70; and two labourers paid 18/- (90p) per week.

CHAPTER FIVE

THE PROBLEMS OVER WATER

It had always been realised that one of the biggest problems facing the Regent's Canal would be providing a supply of water. In his 1802 plan, Rennie had agonised over the various options and the passage of time had made the decision no easier.

As the canal was to be, effectively, an extension of the Grand Junction Canal and a level junction between the two was envisaged, the simplest solution would have been to negotiate a supply from the Grand Junction. While this is eventually what happened it took many years to achieve and in the meantime other alternatives had to be explored.

Soon after the first notices for the new canal had been given Charles Harvey, the Grand Junction Canal Company's (GJCC) superintendent, expressed his company's concern on two counts; the viability of its extensive Paddington properties and the security of its water. The Regent's Canal was planned to join the Grand Junction at Broadwater, just over ½ mile from the end of the Paddington Branch. This branch extended on the level just over 13½ miles from Bulls Bridge at Southall, where it linked up with a 6½ mile level stretch of the Grand Junction's main line from Cowley to Norwood. This part of the Grand Junction was usually called 'The Long Level' or 'The Paddington Level' as it comprised over 20 miles of canal without locks.

Despite this length acting as a considerable reservoir, the GJCC was concerned to safeguard its supplies because north of Cowley it had major difficulties with millers who imposed severe restrictions on the use of water in the valley of the Colne. To the south, at Norwood, the busy locks down through Hanwell to Brentford and the Thames had to be supplied. Hence the threat of any of its precious water being diverted to the new canal was a serious matter.

Apart from this, the GJCC had established itself as an important supplier of water in the Paddington area. This stemmed from its seventh Act,[1] which confirmed an agreement on 22 February 1798 with the Lord Bishop of London and others for the purchase of property at Paddington. The Act also empowered it to supply 'good and wholesome' water to the inhabitants of buildings erected, or to be erected, on the land being purchased and to neighbouring streets and parishes.

The GJCC's eleventh Act provided that the water supply undertaking, which was growing in importance, should be hived-off to a separate company under an agreement of 16 January 1811.[2] As a result, the Grand Junction Water Works Company (GJWWC) was incorporated and this took over the powers under a 50 year lease with the GJCC being paid for the water supplied. The GJCC's first loyalties were to its new protégé, rather than to a concern that was likely to draw trade away from the busy Paddington wharves.

As a result, a clause in the 1812 Regent's Canal Act prohibited water being taken from the Grand Junction. To reinforce this restriction the new company had to build a stop-lock at the junction at Paddington and the water in this was to be maintained 6in higher than the level in the Grand Junction. The Regent's also had to erect a lock house for a supervisor to be employed by the GJCC, but paid by the Regent's, whose duties were to ensure that the lock was correctly maintained and operated and to refuse passage if the conditions were not met. The GJWWC was also concerned to safeguard its supplies from the canal and had its own clause inserted in the Act to confirm the construction of the stop-lock; this also specified that the stop-lock was to be supplied with water from a source independent of the Grand Junction.

Given these restrictions the Regent's Canal had to look elsewhere for its water and, in November 1810, the choice had been narrowed to three sources. The first was to take water from a stream of the Colne at Finches Allowance near Uxbridge. This was estimated to cost £21,000, with annual expenses of £1,800 for a steam engine to pump the water 21ft up into the Grand Junction's Long Level. The second was to pump water back from the Thames at Limehouse lock by lock; the cost was estimated at £25,000 with annual pumping expenses of £5,880 since a series of steam engines would be needed. The third was pumping from the Thames at Pimlico via a new heading to Paddington, the cost being £36,600 with annual pumping expenses £5,795.[3] Of the three options the last emerged as the favourite and in July 1811 James Tate made a detailed survey.

In August 1811 another plan was put forward and Tate was instructed to survey land at Finchley for a catchment reservoir and for the route of a feeder down to the summit level of the canal at Hampstead. He had prepared his plans by the end of the month and Morgan approved them, but owing to the impending Finchley Enclosure Act it was not possible to negotiate for the land. A 100-acre reservoir was envisaged, which was expected to produce 100 locks of water a day for six working days each week throughout the year.[4] By November the Finchley proposal had become the favoured option, but the deposited plans and the 1812 Act included both it and the scheme to pump water from the Thames at Chelsea.

The reservoir was to have been north of Highgate, and just east of the turnpike road to Whetstone, in Friern Barnet parish, approximately where the St Pancras and Islington Cemetery is today. A 9½-mile long feeder was proposed to carry the water on a winding course to the main canal at Chalk Farm. This was mainly on the level and involved a considerable detour eastwards towards Hackney to follow the contour. After crossing Maiden Lane the water was to drop some 60ft to the level of the canal. The estimated cost of the reservoir and feeder was £20,000.

The heading from Chelsea was planned to run in a north-westerly direction through Hyde Park to Paddington where it would feed into a small storage reservoir, while the engine house was to be close to the present-day Chelsea Bridge. An 86ft difference in level had to be overcome at high tide and the scheme was estimated at £38,000.

The purchase of the Finchley land was one of the first acquisitions made by the company. The 105½ acres for the reservoir and part of the feeder cost £9,970 including incidentals and fencing. Consideration was given to taking additional land to extend the reservoir but the decision was deferred in November 1812. Later it was agreed to take another 30 acres but the purchase was never completed. Apart from erecting fencing no action was taken to construct the reservoir and the land was let to a tenant on a short-term basis for grazing. This was because the company was still undecided just how to tackle the water supply question as evidenced by its willingness to entertain a series of approaches from aspiring inventors all offering water-saving devices and culminating in the Congreve lock experiment.

On Tuesday 18 May 1813 a group of the directors, constituting the Committee of Works and Purchases, held what turned out to be an historic meeting at the house of Colonel William Congreve where they inspected a model of a device designed to save virtually all the water normally used when operating locks.

Congreve was an inventor of some repute and perhaps best known for his rockets, which were used in the latter stages of the Napoleonic wars.[5] Earlier in 1813 he had obtained a patent for a device to be installed in the chambers of a pair of duplicate locks.[6] An inverted caisson was fitted into each chamber completely filling it and supported on a cushion of air trapped between the outer walls of the chamber and some lower inner walls, water creating a seal. A network of pipes and an air pump connected the caissons and they were so balanced that by a small amount of pumping one could be raised and the other lowered. A column of water, equal to the depth of the canal, was carried on each caisson and the fit between the caisson and the walls of the lock was so exact that hardly any could drain away. Gates were fitted which could be opened to allow boats to enter or leave the lock chamber. In theory the device, which became known as a hydro-pneumatic lock, could pass boats going in opposite directions simultaneously in a relatively short time and with hardly any loss of water.

Most of the committee were impressed with what they saw, although there was some scepticism that the structure would be able to withstand the substantial pressures involved. It was also foreseen there could be problems with water that would leak down the sides of the caissons, with damage caused if gravel, stones, or other rubbish was thrown down the sides of the lock, and in dealing with repairs. Nonetheless the idea seemed sufficiently promising to justify further investigation and £300 was voted towards a large-scale model to be constructed by Henry Maudslay & Company of Lambeth. At the time Maudslays were one of the leading engineering companies in the country.

It was decided, however, that rather than having the caissons operating side-by-side and both providing the full lift, they would be sited longitudinally, or end-to-end, with each performing only half the overall lift. By this means the massive pressures of the full lift were eliminated and the brickwork would be far less costly. Some flexibility would be lost as under the original system if one caisson was under repair the other chamber could still be used as a conventional lock, albeit with a loss of water. Under the longitudinal

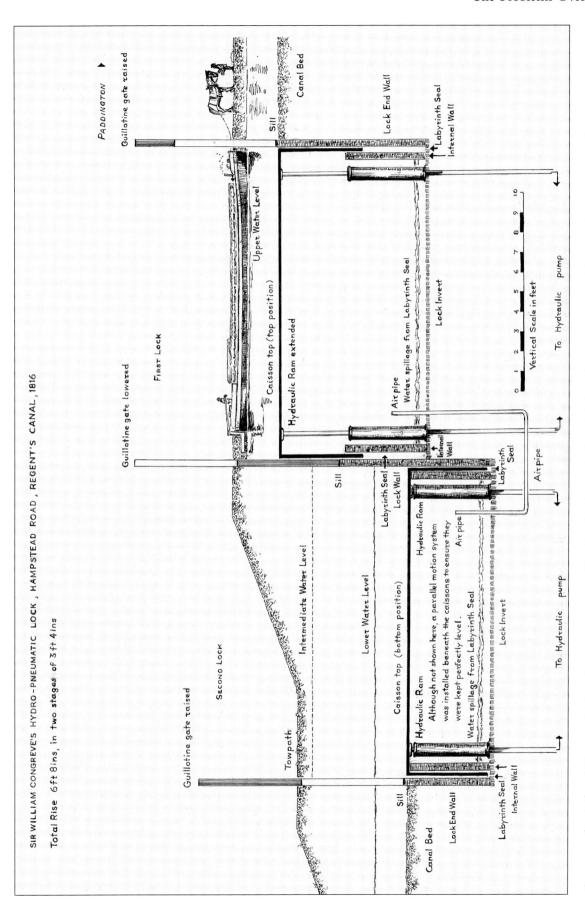

SIR WILLIAM CONGREVE'S HYDRO-PNEUMATIC LOCK, HAMPSTEAD ROAD, REGENT'S CANAL, 1816

Total Rise 6ft 8ins, in two stages of 3ft 4ins

Edward Paget-Tomlinson

Concern about the ability to obtain adequate water supplies for the Regent's Canal led to the company considering adopting Sir William Congreve's patented hydro-pneumatic lock at Hampstead Road. The trial lock had two chambers, each of which overcame a difference of some 3½ feet in level. In practice one of the main problems was that varying water levels, even as little as an inch, could upset the delicate balance between the two caissons and impose a load on the machinery that it was never designed to withstand.

system if one caisson was under repair no traffic could pass at all. Apart from this, it was felt that by having a passing place between the two caissons, boats would be able to use the lock just as expeditiously as with the parallel system.

The new model was constructed by Maudslays at a cost of £689 and was found to be perfectly satisfactory. The committee now had to consider the costs of the various options open to the company. Originally it had been planned to have 12 conventional locks with a 7ft fall, but with the caisson lock it was felt this number could be reduced to nine; six with a 10ft 6in fall and three with a 7ft fall. The machinery for each 10ft 6in lock was estimated at £3,345 and the masonry and gates at £2,600 – a total of £5,945. For the 7ft lock the estimates were £2,697 for the machinery and £2,300 for the masonry and gates – a total of £4,997. The total cost of nine locks would, therefore, be £50,661. Wooden caissons were proposed to save weight, but it was realised there could be difficulties in making them watertight. If iron was used the cost was likely to rise to £63,249 and the masonry would also need to be more substantial.

The committee had to consider the cost of the alternatives. Twelve double locks would cost £26,400; the pumping engine and heading from Chelsea £38,000 with annual running expenses £10,000 and the Finchley reservoir and feeder from Friern Barnet £31,700. As a result, on 24 March 1814 the committee recommended that a full-size 7ft trial lock should be constructed using Congreve's principle with the caisson and inner walls of iron. Morgan asked Maudslays for an estimate for such a lock and on 28 March the directors accepted his recommendation. Congreve was offered £250 per lock for the use of his patent and a contract was to be drawn up with Maudslays for the works required and for the lock to be guaranteed for 12 months.

The contract, signed on 23 June 1814, provided for the lock to be erected at Hampstead Road at the end of the level stretch from Paddington. The work was to be completed by 31 March 1815 and the company was to carry out most of the masonry work.

The contract seems to have been imprecise about what works Maudslays were required to do. In December, Henry Maudslay, and his partner John Mendham asked for an amended agreement, as they wanted the Regent's Canal Company to construct the lock house, this being essential for the installation of the machinery. They also wanted an agreement that

the water would be let into the canal when the caissons were ready, so that they could be floated into position, an undertaking that if the lock was successful they would be given the contract for the other locks, and an extension of time beyond 31 March 1815 to complete the work. Some of their requests were acceptable but the company was reluctant to see any slippage in the date. Monro and Nash were both involved in the negotiations and after a series of meetings a revised contract was signed early in February 1815. The completion date was put back just one month to 30 April but the company agreed to erect the lock house and to speed up the other masonry work.

By the beginning of March the brickwork and carpentry of the lock was nearing completion and Maudslays were busy installing their apparatus and assembling the first caisson. A month later, Morgan reported the caissons should be floated into position by the middle of April but that it would take another week to connect all the machinery together. It was still hoped the lock would be ready for the revised completion date, provided that there was good weather and the contractors made a major effort.

The deadline was not met and by the half-yearly shareholders meeting on 7 June the lock was still far from complete, although there should have been a full trial on that day. Instead there was a plaintive letter from Congreve – now Sir William Congreve – saying that there were a series of leaks round the heads of screws used in the construction of the caissons. While a way had been found to cure the problem it had caused a major delay. Eventually Maudslays had to remove both caissons from the lock chambers to complete the repairs and they were not replaced until nearly the end of November. A series of frosts then stopped the work for several weeks.

On 26 March 1816 Henry Maudslay wrote explaining that after a lengthy chapter of accidents the caissons had now been made so watertight as not to need replenishing with air for a long time and that the contract had been completed. He admitted that one important condition specified in the contract could not be met – that it should be possible to work through the double lock in three minutes. Maudslay said he had been unable to make the two shifts in less than 4½ minutes using two men, or six minutes with just one man. He went on to submit a statement of costs of £9,335 but said he was claiming only the balance of the contract price. This was £3,561 after allowing for a £2,000 payment on account made at the end of 1814. Extra costs had been incurred in having to take the caissons out to alter the gates, which was outside the contract, while the model lock had still to be paid for, although he was claiming only the agreed £300. This brought his bill up to £4,449 and, in view of the passage of time, he asked for another payment on account. He had made a similar request for a £3,000 advance in July 1815 but had been refused as the lock was then nowhere near complete.

Two days later Maudslays wrote confirming the completion of the lock and saying one of their employees was there every day to take care of the machinery and that demonstrations could be given on Tuesdays and Thursdays between 2pm and 4pm.

In his report Morgan confirmed Maudslays' timings for using the lock but pointed out that with only one man working the machinery he was so exhausted he needed a considerable time to recover afterwards. Even with two men much greater effort was needed than might reasonably be expected, especially if a succession of boats had to be worked through. He suggested that if a compressed air cylinder in the basement of the lock house was connected into the hydraulic system to the upper caisson, half of the shift could be achieved without any manual labour, although the cylinder would still need recharging regularly. Then if another air cylinder could be installed it could be used for the lower caisson. Morgan reported both caissons appeared watertight as there were very few bubbles on the surface of the water, but the lock needed to be left for several days to prove this. His report concluded that while the hydro-pneumatic principle had been established, the terms of the contract had not been fully met, as the three-minute requirement could not be fulfilled.

As constructed, the lift comprised two large caissons made of wrought and cast iron and weighing 26½ tons each. The caissons were contained in masonry lock chambers, with 36 very large cast iron plates forming a frame within which the caissons could rise and fall.[7] The caissons were supported by four wrought-iron pistons, one at each corner, and were linked by copper piping to an air pump and other machinery in the lock house. Wooden gates were installed at the ends of the caissons to enable boats to enter or leave with the loss of as little water as possible.

Following Morgan's report Congreve countered with the argument that the actual change of both levels could be performed well within the three-minute period, and it could not be expected that the time was to include the opening and closing of the gates and the movement of the boat between the two chambers. The company contended that it had always considered the three minutes to cover the time from the boat entering the lock to leaving it at the other level. The shareholders, meeting on 11 July, supported the view that the contract had not been fulfilled and, far from paying Maudslays any more money, they wanted the £2,000 interim payment refunded together with the company's own costs incurred in works for the reception of the machinery.

Mendham attended the committee on 24 July seeking a settlement. Following this, and after a full review of all the papers, it was decided that a trial of the lock should be conducted on Wednesday 28 August in front of some impartial engineers. The trials would assess if the lock achieved the saving of water stipulated in the contract and if the shifts of level could be performed in the time and with the power specified. The company invited several engineers to attend but, by mistake, Josias Jessop and William Mylne both arrived at Hampstead Road two days before the trial was due to take place.[8] Morgan happened to be in the area and the workmen operated the lock for them. The double shift of the caissons took 5¼ minutes and involved considerable effort by the men.

This preview was fortunate. The formal trial two days later was marred by a quarrel between Morgan and Congreve about what the three-minute period was meant to cover and, as this was unresolved, the contractors refused to conduct the trial. It was significant that Maudslays were in the process of installing a second air cylinder in the lock house to deal with the lower caisson and probably wanted to defer the trial until it was ready.

Congreve followed up this debacle with a letter claiming that with the air cylinder fully charged the complete double shift had been achieved in two minutes ten seconds. On the second occasion, and with the cylinder re-charged by a man pumping for three minutes, the double shift took ten seconds longer. The company replied saying that it still included the operation of the gates as part of the time allowance.

The formal trial of the lock finally took place on 10 September attended by Morgan, Josias Jessop, John Rennie junior and numerous other men of science.[9] Immediately afterwards Maudslays renewed their claim for the £4,449 and suggested arbitration if the company still objected, nominating Bryan Donkin of

Bermondsey to act for them.[10] Before deciding its next move the company asked Jessop and Mylne for a report and they inspected the lock again on 23 September. Maudslays were now becoming increasingly impatient and threatened to withdraw their employee from the site on 17 October and let the air out from under the caissons so as to leave the lock in greater security unless the company was willing to send its own lock keeper. As a stop-gap the company agreed to meet the wages of Maudslays' employee if they would leave him on the site.

In his report Jessop said a boat could travel from one level to the intermediate level in 2 minutes 56 seconds, but that there was no way it could pass through all three sets of gates in the prescribed three-minute period. The company now decided to accept arbitration and on 12 February 1817 sealed the agreement for this course, making the results binding on it.

The arbitrators were Thomas Denman, a barrister-at-law, and two engineers – Bryan Donkin for Maudslays and Charles Simpson, who had replaced Harvey as the GJCC's superintendent, for the canal company. They first met on 29 April and in June they awarded Maudslays £4,020 towards their claim. The company did not hurry to make this payment but a letter from Maudslays' solicitor in September, enclosing the key to the lock house, was successful in obtaining the money for his clients.

The arbitration award meant that the company was no nearer to a final decision about Hampstead Road Lock and the other locks on the canal. The whole episode had taken place during a period when the company was acutely short of funds and virtually no other work was being carried out on the canal. Once work resumed in August 1817 a decision became vital. It was not helped by an accident to the lock just before Christmas 1817 when, following a leak in the piping, the caissons were forced out of equilibrium causing damage to one of the pistons. As a precaution the water was pumped out of the chambers and the hydraulic system was drained to prevent any frost damage during repairs.

Congreve wrote on 30 December offering to repair the lock at his own expense and to install a small two-horsepower steam engine to charge the air cylinders. In return he wanted an agreement to use his invention at the other locks, once he had proved it could perform as he claimed. The company was not impressed and called on Maudslays to repair the damage.

In reply, Henry Maudslay denied any liability and pointed out the lock had been effectively in the company's hands since 17 October 1816 and that it had worked perfectly in the six-month period prior to that. As a favour he agreed to carry out the repairs provided the company would pump out the water. He expected the repairs to take ten days, no work on the caissons being necessary. In the event repairs were more extensive and two craftsmen were involved from 17 March to 18 April while three labourers were needed to keep the works clear of water. Tests were carried out which proved the effectiveness of the repairs but the company was still clearly reluctant to proceed with the hydro-pneumatic system.

Instead it had been actively exploring obtaining water supplies, either from the Grand Junction or from the Thames at Chelsea, in sufficient quantities to enable conventional locks to be used on the canal. Eventually, and after much debate, the general committee decided, at its meeting on 1 July 1818, that it would be neither necessary nor expedient to construct the locks on Sir William Congreve's principle. Instead, ordinary locks with side ponds were to be adopted but these were to be designed to allow for the construction of a duplicate parallel lock should trade increase sufficiently to justify this in future. Congreve was informed on the decision, paid his £250 and asked to help in disposing of the machinery in case he knew of anyone else interested in his invention. Failing this, the caissons and machinery were to be sold.

Nothing seems to have been done for some time but at the end of October an offer of £100 was received for the machinery. No decision was taken but in July 1819 the bidder was asked if he would increase his offer to £150 and remove the equipment immediately. He declined, and in October the company advertised to sell by private treaty. This produced a £225 offer for the caissons and other ironwork but not the rest of the equipment. The company, however, really wanted someone to clear the site to allow a start on rebuilding the masonry for the replacement lock.

This work was now more extensive than was at first necessary because on 28 April the company had decided to construct the duplicate locks immediately. The cost of these was estimated to be only £900 more than a single lock and side pond at each site. Two weeks later there were second thoughts and the duplication was to be confined to the five locks

A typical scene on the Regent's Canal in 1938 with an empty barge about to be locked down at what is believed to be Acton's Locks.

The Waterways Archive, British Waterways Archive, Gloucester

between Hampstead Road and City Road, where the heaviest traffic was expected. Three weeks later it was decided to extend the duplication to the remaining seven locks down to Limehouse after all.

With no acceptable offer for the redundant lock machinery it was decided to auction it off. The sale was held on site on 30 November under the auspices of the firm of Biggs & Abbott. There were 13 lots ranging from the air pump and machinery fixed in the lock house to the caissons themselves. The machinery fetched £42, the caissons £126 each and the cast-iron frames £64. The sale realised £442 and after commission and expenses the company received £405 and the long saga of the hydro-pneumatic lock was finally brought to an end after 6½ years.

In April 1814 the costs of the various options open to the company had been:

1 Congreve's Lock

Three 7ft lifts

Iron caissons and machinery at £4,061 each	£12,183
Brickwork at £2,300 each	£6,900

Six 10ft 6in lifts

Iron caissons and machinery at £4,761 each	£28,566
Brickwork at £2,600 each	£15,600
	Total £63,249

2 Chelsea Engine and Heading

Providing engine and erecting engine house	£9,000
4,642-yard heading to Paddington at £5 per yard	£23,210
2-acre reservoir at Paddington	£1,694
Land at Chelsea, sundry costs and contingencies	£4,096
12 double locks at £2,200 each	£26,400
	Total £64,400

3 Finchley Reservoir and Feeder

Cost of Finchley land: 100 acres at £90 per acre	£9,000
Estimate for additional 30 acres to be purchased	£2,700
Land for feeder	£3,000
Forming head of reservoir, cutting feeder, embankments, bridges, culverts and overfalls	£17,000
12 double locks at £2,200 each	£26,400
	Total £58,100

With the decision to experiment with Congreve's lock, no further work had been done at Finchley. In 1815, when plans were being made to forge the link with the Grand Junction at Paddington, the GJCC's Superintendent Charles Harvey raised the question of maintaining the 6in differential in the level of the stop-lock. While he stressed this would not necessarily be insisted upon, he did not want it merely to be overlooked. As a result, in the middle of August, Morgan was instructed to measure the springs at Finchley that would supply the reservoir when this was constructed. The results proved extremely disappointing and showed they would be inadequate to give a reliable supply of water for the canal.

The company then turned to various water-supply companies seeking their help. In September the West Middlesex Water Company was asked if it could deliver a supply to a reservoir to be formed in Regent's Park (as the Marylebone Park was now more usually called) and the New River Company was also approached. Both were interested but their mains were well below the summit level of the canal so pumping would have been needed, adding to the cost of the water. Another problem was the amount of water the canal would need, and the companies would have to merge to meet this demand. While both companies were willing to consider this, Parliament had different views and threw out the Bill to incorporate them together, and this killed the project.

In desperation, the company turned to the GJCC. At a meeting at the beginning of 1816 it was decided to re-examine the Chelsea scheme, but this time possibly on a joint basis. An idea was growing that if the GJCC could be released from its contract to supply the GJWWC, and if work already in hand to improve its Ruislip Reservoir could be completed, it might then be able to supply the Regent's Canal adequately from the Long Level.

To help clarify the legal position, a clause in the Regent's third Act authorised the company to supply Thames water to the GJCC if it so wished. In the meantime the GJCC was willing to do what it could to help and was able to supply sufficient water to fill the new canal from Paddington to Hampstead Road for it to be opened in August 1816, particularly as no lockage water was involved. George Clabburn was appointed keeper at the Paddington stop-lock in December 1816 at 19/- (95p) per week.

Meanwhile the GJWWC was becoming unhappy about the quality of the water it was drawing from the Grand Junction at Paddington. As a result, a series of meetings took place between Charles Simpson, Richard Robson chairman of the GJWWC, Nash and Culling Charles Smith, the latter two being given full powers in December 1817 to reach a settlement. A month later the GJWWC was asked for its terms for giving up its canal water supply in exchange of a

pumped supply from the Thames, and it replied positively. A meeting was held in Nash's house in Dover Street on 14 March 1818 to pursue the matter and by May it was apparent a worthwhile agreement would be possible.

By July 1817 the company had decided to sell the Finchley land, first offering it back to the Finchley Enclosure Commissioners, but they declined. The land was then advertised at £9,850, the effective cost to the company of acquiring and fencing it. A £3,000 offer in August was rejected out of hand. There were several slightly better offers but in May 1818, and with the prospect of an agreement with the GJWWC, Sir Culling Smith was authorised to sell the land on the best terms possible. On 22 July it was auctioned but failed to reach its £6,000 reserve. Later an agent was appointed and eventually the land was sold at a second auction on 29 August 1819 for just £5,000.

In June 1818 the company decided to pursue the Chelsea plan and Nash and Culling Smith opened negotiations for the required ½ acre of land that was owned by Lord Grosvenor. At the same time the company advertised for tenders to supply the cast-iron pipes for the heading. His Lordship did not prove very co-operative and asked for £33,000, which was 20 times more than the budgeted figure; this was for a plot of swampy land unfit for anything other than gardens. Following arbitration it was eventually bought for £2,850.

Meanwhile several tenders for the pipes had been received and a contract was awarded to Richard Salisbury & Co with delivery to be completed by Christmas 1818. By mid-November Salisburys had delivered a considerable number of pipes to Paddington and Morgan was instructed to set up apparatus to test their quality. This took considerably longer to organise than expected. By 10 March 1819 only 120 pipes had been tested, of which 24 were found to be defective.

In August 1818 the GJCC had pointed out that to authorise any water exchange an Act would be necessary, and formal notice for this was given early in September. The Act[11] confirmed a formal agreement of 26 May 1819 between the three companies. It authorised the Regent's Canal to supply the GJWWC with water from the Thames; the GJWWC to be supplied from the Thames instead of from the Grand Junction; and, in turn, the GJCC to supply the Regent's from the Long Level and any of its reservoirs and feeders.

At almost the same time the Regent's fourth Act was obtained, which included amended powers for drawing water from the Thames and included the right to cut into the river below low-water mark and lay pipes.[12] This was to be between Ranelagh Creek and floodgates on the creek that led up to wharves at Pimlico. The Act also empowered the company to pump up to 40,000 tons of water from the river every 24 hours and to erect one or more steam engines at Chelsea. These powers replaced much more restrictive conditions in the original Act, which had only permitted abstraction when the water was higher than half-flood or half-ebb tide.

With the prospect of Parliament approving the water exchange agreement the company could start making plans for the machinery that was going to be needed at Chelsea. In April 1819 the York Buildings Water Works Company had offered a steam engine, but on investigation Morgan found this would be inadequate unless the diameter of the pipeline was increased and the planned working hours of the engine extended. The Butterley Company offered a new engine at £4,300 for delivery in eight months, while Boulton & Watt offered one at £6,200 for delivery in nine months. Still hopeful, the York Company reduced the price of its redundant engine to £4,000, against its original cost of £6,200, and was willing to include two boilers in the price. After consultations with the GJWWC, who would ultimately be responsible for the Chelsea installation, Boulton & Watt were asked to supply two engines. Tenders were also invited for laying the pipeline, nine offers being received and early in June that from Daniel Pritchard was chosen, it being hoped he would be able to complete his contract within three months.[13]

Once the Act was passed the work could start but first it was agreed that William Anderson, engineer to the GJWWC, would superintend the erection of the engine house, the laying of the pipes and all the other works connected with the supply of water.[14] During all this time Morgan had been persevering with the proving of the pipes and he found that many were not of the 1in thickness prescribed in the contract and others were defective, although they could be used by being plugged to enable them to withstand the pressure.

In August 1819 Thomas Theobald contracted to supply bricks for the engine house, while Pritchard's tender to erect the engine house was accepted in September with Hunter & English providing much of

the ironwork required such as the roof and flooring together with the special curved pipes and the screw cocks. By this time the work on laying the pipeline was making good progress after a temporary delay in obtaining permission from the Treasury to lay the main through Hyde Park. Boulton & Watt were also starting to despatch the various pieces of machinery by canal from their Soho works in Birmingham for assembly on site.

Anderson, who was to receive £600 for overseeing the work, produced an estimate in October of the costs. The principal items were:

Two steam engines from Boulton & Watt	£10,000
Carriage from Birmingham and erection	£1,000
Engine house	£6,700
Suction pipe from the Thames with sluices and gratings	£3,000
Outside work at Chelsea, boundary walls, sheds, roads etc.	£2,365
24in main from engine to pipe-line	£750
Pipe-line (Salisbury & Co)	£11,031
Laying pipes, labour, lead and cartage	£2,587
Land	£1,500
Anderson's remuneration, proving pipes etc.	£1,100
Total	£40,033

At the beginning of May 1820 Boulton & Watt had nearly finished their deliveries and requested their payment of £10,000. A month later Pritchard contracted to lay the suction pipes into the Thames and to construct the road to the engine house. By the middle of July, Anderson could report the first engine should be at work by the first week in September and the second a month later. With this welcome news the GJCC agreed to a temporary supply of water to enable the new canal to be opened.

The opening only added to the urgency to complete the engines as in the middle of August it was reported the GJCC was in dispute with the Colne millers over this temporary supply. The first engine was tested on 1 September; it then ran continuously from 5 September onwards and a week later the GJCC ceased supplying the GJWWC, which then drew its water from Chelsea. The second engine came into service on 5 October.

The new arrangements, however, were not trouble-free; by the middle of October there had been several bursts in the pipeline it being claimed due to irregularities in the casting. Soon after, arbitrators were appointed – William Mylne for the GJWWC and Bryan Donkin for the Regent's – to determine the precise terms for handing over the Chelsea land, engine house and pipeline.

In December the nearby Chelsea Hospital complained about smoke from the engine. This prompted the company into accepting a tender from Francis Smith & Brunton to fit Brunton's rotary fire regulator to one of the two boilers for £525 to reduce coal consumption and smoke emission. The regulator had been installed by the end of May when the arbitrators were asked to assess its effectiveness.

Meanwhile, Telford had been called in to survey the Long Level and the company's summit level and to fix markers at Norwood Top Lock, Paddington Stop Lock and Hampstead Road Top Lock showing the water level at each site. These markers were a requirement under the 1819 Act to indicate when the company could draw water through the stop lock and setting out what was to happen if the level fell below the marks. The intention was to control the level to ensure there was always a depth of 4ft 6in over the top cill at Norwood, which should then guarantee a depth of 5ft in the Long Level. Subsequent surveys, however, showed that the cill at Norwood was 9in inches lower than calculated and this meant the requirements of the Act could not be strictly adhered to and the Long Level could be drawn down too much. In October 1821 notices were issued for an application to Parliament to alter the height of the cill at Norwood but the plan was not pursued.

In October, Donkin and Mylne reported that the fire regulator had provided a 25% saving in costs and Brunton then agreed to fit the second boiler with the device for £520. Despite this the GJWWC was reluctant for the arbitrators to proceed as burst pipes were still causing problems; it claimed 907 yards of pipe needed to be replaced at a cost of £4,354 and at the same time it complained that the pipeline extended only as far as Oxford Street, and not to Paddington as originally intended. It seems that during construction Anderson had arranged for the main to join up with an existing GJWWC main that ran to two small reservoirs at Paddington, rather than having two mains from Oxford Street. Eventually the terms of the arbitration were agreed and the GJWWC took over at Chelsea in February 1822, but not before a further dispute about the rate of interest to be allowed on the amount due to it pending settlement. The Regent's sealed the arbitration agreement on 6 March 1822.

On 5 October 1822 Donkin and Mylne awarded to the GJWWC £10,285 as compensation for taking on the liabilities at Chelsea and to the Regent's Canal £6,428 for the anticipated annual pumping costs. The GJWWC was unhappy as it considered the arbitrators had not included its claim over the defective pipeline and in March 1823 referred the matter to a barrister, William Cooke, for a preliminary opinion. Another complication arose in September when the GJWWC's solicitors pointed out that the Regent's did not have a good title to the Chelsea freehold. This was due to inordinate delays by Lord Grosvenor in executing the conveyance as he was still haggling over minor matters in an attempt to obtain a better settlement, but the problem was resolved early in October.

During this time discussions continued over the Long Level to resolve the depth question. The GJCC refused to raise its banks but was willing to consider dredging. The Regent's was also concerned that the other works it was to take over as part of the water exchange agreement were not in a proper state of repair; these included Ruislip Reservoir and the Ruislip and Brent feeders. Morgan and John Holland, the Grand Junction's engineer, carried out a joint inspection in July 1823 to try to agree on the repairs needed and in October William Anderson was appointed to arbitrate. Soon after, William Cooke was asked to arbitrate over the Chelsea business.

While both arbitrators made their awards in 1824, little happened as there were now growing doubts about the legal position. Early in 1825 counsel's opinion was taken which showed that the 1819 Act needed amendment before the water exchange agreement could be finally completed between the three companies. A new Act was obtained in 1826 specifying that the all-important water levels were to be determined solely by the marker at Paddington Stop Lock.[15]

With the new Act the Regent's was able to conclude the agreement with the GJWWC early in August by paying over £6,870 – although the conveyance was not sealed until 25 October – and soon after the GJCC handed over control of Ruislip Reservoir and the two feeders, albeit not without further discussions about yet more repairs. On 16 August, George Baker was appointed overseer at Ruislip on a £61 salary with a rent free house.

As barge traffic on the lower levels of the canal was increasing, the Regent's was still concerned about water supplies and in June 1826 examined the possibility of building a reservoir on the river Brent as a joint project with the GJCC. Powers for this had first been obtained in the original 1793 Grand Junction Act and had been transferred to the Regent's in the 1819 Act. Although a feeder had been built from the Brent at Kingsbury through Willesden to the Paddington Branch around 1810, the reservoir powers had not been exercised.

As the GJCC declined to get involved, the Regent's re-examined the plan for the Finchley reservoir by looking at a site at nearby Crouch End but this was considered unsuitable. Another plan was a supply from the GJCC's Aldenham Reservoir and an offer to lease this for £300 per annum was made in December 1826. A 40-year term was agreed in principle in March 1827, while in August the Colne millers gave their formal consent to the new arrangements which involved raising and strengthening the head bank to increase the reservoir's capacity from 2,708 locks to 3,407 locks. These works, which included a new weir, were completed under Holland's supervision in March 1828.

This covered the position for a while but during the summer of 1833 there was a drought and, by the end of September, Aldenham Reservoir had been emptied, the Brent feeder was almost dry and Ruislip Reservoir was down to 24 day's supply. Attempts to obtain water from the GJCC's Tring summit were dropped, as the costs would have been prohibitive; instead a temporary supply was purchased from the GJWWC, which had a main crossing Maida Hill Tunnel. The following year was equally dry with water again having to be purchased from the GJWWC and also from the West Middlesex Water Works Company via a temporary pipeline in Regent's Park, but both supplies were very expensive.

The water shortages prompted a new look at the Brent Reservoir scheme and in November 1833 the company decided to proceed on a site where two branches of the river, the Silk Stream from the north and the Dollis Brook from the east, met in low ground west of the Old Welsh Harp public house on the Edgware Road in Hendon. The original plan was for a reservoir of 46 acres to hold 1,400 locks, but by September 1834 another 15 acres had been added to increase the capacity to 2,100 locks.[16]

Negotiations were opened with the landowners – principally All Souls College at Oxford, Christ's Hospital and the Borough of Wandsworth – and by January 1834 the land had been staked out and Morgan had completed his preliminary plans. A month later George Trumper was appointed as the company's surveyor and valuer and by the summer he had obtained most of the land at £90 per acre.

Morgan's estimate for the construction works, which included a bridge to carry Cool Oak Lane[17] leading from the Edgware Road to Kingsbury over the reservoir, was £2,347 but the lowest tender was from William Hoof of Hammersmith at £2,747.[18] After some negotiation this was accepted and work was under way by the middle of November. By the end of 1834 most of the land had been purchased, it now being deemed that 69 acres were needed, and one-third of the works had been completed.

The total cost was now estimated at £11,000, which the company's treasurer, Francis Sapte, had agreed to lend. Soon after, Morgan recommended building-up the head bank at a cost of £500 to enable a further increase in capacity should this be needed in future. By the end of May 1835 the works were virtually complete and the reservoir had started to fill. With copious rains in the autumn it was full by early November and had already proved its worth. Hoof was paid £3,435 for his contract, which included the extra works he had performed.

Although by now Morgan had resigned as the company's engineer he continued to take an active interest in the reservoir and in December 1836 suggested increasing its capacity by purchasing more land and raising the head bank. As the water supply position was still difficult he was authorised to investigate and in April it was decided to buy another 66 acres and more than double the size of the reservoir. Morgan estimated the cost at £8,750 which included the land at £6,600, raising the head bank £1,400 and alterations to the bridges carrying the Edgware Road and Cool Oak Lane.

Hoof was approached to carry out the works, which he agreed to do for £2,124 and work started in July. A temporary causeway was needed to take the Edgware Road while the bridge was being rebuilt and it was also necessary to protect the Old Welsh Harp Inn from flooding from the increased height of the water. All this took longer to carry out and cost considerably more than expected but the works were completed on 15 December. Hoof was paid £3,414, which included £700 for building an auxiliary discharge for flood water at the dam.

The enlarged reservoir filled for the first time on 29 November 1838 giving a very important boost to the company's water resources.

CHAPTER SIX

THE EARLY DAYS

Once the canal was opened throughout traffic built up quickly. There had been some trade on the upper level when this opened in August 1816 but it had remained modest until the route to the City Road Basin and from the Thames became available.

Records were maintained from 1 August 1820; in that month just 2,801 tons passed but in October tonnage was 7,281 and in December 10,376. The monthly total passed 20,000 tons for the first time in March 1822, 30,000 in March 1823, 40,000 in July 1824 and 50,000 in March 1830. The figures fluctuated considerably, often due to the weather; in January 1830 only 14,260 tons passed as the canal was icebound for several weeks.

Toll revenue increased in line; in August 1820 £132 was earned, in October £304 and in December £598. Receipts exceeded £1,000 per month for the first time in May 1822, £1,500 in October 1823, £2,000 in March 1824 and £2,500 in September 1825. Here, too, the figures varied and it was not until 1834 that the monthly toll income was consistently over £2,000.

Year	Tonnage	Revenue
1820	33,720	£1,580
1821	157,378	£11,419
1822	266,574	£15,721
1823	351,389	£20,709
1824	436,065	£24,879
1825	504,755	£27,493
1826	470,148	£24,468
1827	451,619	£34,352
1828	494,774	£23,938
1829	485,148	£23,357
1830	496,296	£23,664
1831	557,497	£24,104
1832	575,564	£24,054
1833	600,464	£25,783
1834	610,089	£28,678

A wide variety of commodities was contained in these figures. Coal and coke were the most important and this remained so virtually throughout the trading history of the canal. Building materials and other bulk items were also important traffics.

The figures for 1825 are fairly representative:

Commodity	Tonnage
Ashes	1,245
Breeze	26,219
Bricks	34,282
Cement	848
Chalk	18,222
Coal & coke	114,826
Flints	8,172
Grain	2,892
Iron & nails	33,742
Lime	24,528
Manure	2,896
Road materials	43,319
Salt	4,882
Sand	52,679
Slates	1,233
Stone	23,706
Sundries	83,455
Tallow	2,938
Timber	24,671
Total	**504,755**

Hand-in-hand with the growth in traffics was the growth in the number of businesses establishing themselves beside the canal, led by the move of several of the Paddington traders to the company's 550-yard City Road Basin. In April 1818 the company had paid Pickfords an initial £10,000 when it took over its Paddington wharf, compensating the carriers for what they would have to spend on their new City Road premises and the £5,000 balance was paid in July 1820. In June 1818 £13,000 was paid to Sargent & Rutty, £11,500 to James Holt and £8,000 to Richard Snell. The carriers remained at Paddington until they could move to City Road Basin, Pickfords paying an annual rent of £375, Sargent & Rutty £415, Holt £376 and Snell £255. In May 1819 £2,800 was paid to Armistead Sargent & Co and in November £3,400

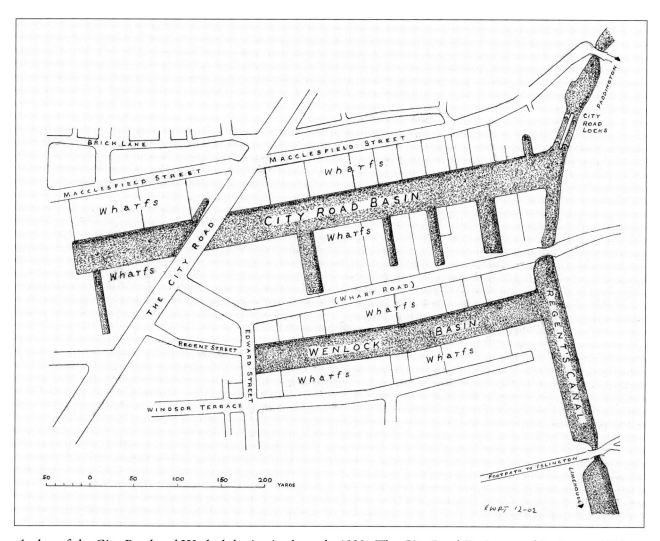

A plan of the City Road and Wenlock basins in the early 1830s. The City Road Basin opened in August 1820 with just one side dock but the other six were added over the next five years, the company's weigh dock being close to the locks. Pickfords had a wharf at the southern end of the basin but ultimately occupied almost the entire area south of the road and that part of the basin was filled in about 1930. The privately owned Wenlock Basin was opened in August 1826 and extended in 1832.

Edward Paget-Tomlinson

to Chevertons on taking over their Bulls Bridge wharves, as required by the Act.

James Holt was the first to move early in October as soon as his buildings were ready. He was followed by Snell at beginning of December, Pickfords on 16 December, and John Rutty early in 1821, considerable delays having arisen with all their building works. At the time another four wharves at the basin had been let, leaving 16 still to be disposed of, but some of those south of the City Road were still covered by excavated soil, which the company was arranging to move.

Some traffic had switched to City Road Basin even before the move. To help handle this Pickfords were allowed to pass their boats at night, when the locks would normally be closed, on payment of an additional charge. This concession was extended to the other three main carriers in September 1820. All the carriers were asked for the usual surety bond as a guarantee for the payment of their tolls. Pickfords refused, claiming they had never given a bond to any other canal company and they were then allowed the same three months' credit as on the Grand Junction.

Other carriers such as Crowley, Hicklin, Batty & Co of Wolverhampton, Whitehouse & Sons of Dudley, Morris & Carter and Joseph Nicholson followed in 1822, with Worster & Stubbs of Long Buckby early in 1823. Meanwhile Samuel and Henry Thorrington had taken the public wharf in the basin in September 1820; in February 1822 George Medhurst contracted to provide a crane on it for £220 and in March Thomas Sowter's tender to build a warehouse was accepted.[1] Several carriers went on to improve their facilities; in January 1823 Pickfords were allowed to make a side dock into their premises to facilitate the loading and unloading of their boats and they extended the dock a year later. One such dock had been built as part of the original construction and eventually there were seven side docks.

Soon after they moved, Pickfords complained about the state of the roads around the basin and in response the company agreed to provide a 35ft roadway and to open up a street serving Pittman's Buildings to provide a direct access to Old Street. This was done in conjunction with St Luke's Parish but it gave rise to a problem as to how the company was to be reimbursed for the repair and upkeep of these roads, since it had no powers to charge road users. In 1824 the company decided to apply for an Act for powers to levy appropriate rates and the usual Parliamentary notices were issued covering City Road Basin and a proposed second basin nearby. This prompted opposition from St Luke's and in May 1825 the Bill was withdrawn as St Luke's agreed to take over the upkeep of the roads. Thereafter there were gradual improvements; for instance in December 1829 the parish completed the paving of Macclesfield Street North.

In November 1820 Pickfords asked the company to provide a weighing-house at the basin so that the amount of cargo a boat was carrying, and hence the toll payable, could be determined easily. A similar weigh-dock was in operation at Paddington on the Grand Junction. In March 1821 a contract was given to Richardson & Want for the building; they were paid £855 in November. The Level Iron Works provided 36 tons of cast-iron weights for £270 and Medhurst supplied and installed two cranes for £110. By the middle of October the weigh-house and its small dock was finished, was placed under Golden's control and Jacob Booth was appointed as a labourer there at 21/- (£1.05) per week.

In March 1824 there was a disastrous fire at Pickfords wharf,[2] which disrupted their trade and later may have prompted the firm to buy back two wharves at Paddington in case of further accidents. In July 1825 Whitehouse & Sons and Richard Snell threatened to move back to Paddington complaining

about the poor quality of the canal company's lighterage service to and from the docks and the high tolls on general traffic. The company refused to reduce the tolls but hired another four barges for the lighterage service, leading to a significant improvement.

Although the company encouraged traders to move from Paddington it was also keen to find new tenants for the wharves vacated there, as it was liable to the Grand Junction for the rents. This commitment came to an end in June 1829 when the leases all reverted to the Grand Junction.

Owing to the restricted width of the canal, if traders wanted to build a wharf they normally had to excavate an indent, or lay-by, so that their barges would not obstruct the main channel. The company supervised these works very closely as initially several were poorly executed leading to water losses through leakage. The trader always had to seek permission before breaching the canal banks and usually a nominal rental for the privilege and for the water was imposed. Typical was Edward Wood & Co. who, in June 1821, were allowed to make a lay-by at Kentish Town to accommodate their coal barges with a second lay-by in March 1823. In January 1825 they made a further extension being allowed to carry the spoil away toll free.

When the canal opened, work on William Horsfall's 150-yard basin at Maiden Lane was largely completed. The company had given major assistance in building this by providing spoil dug from the nearby Islington Tunnel. It was sometimes known as Maiden Lane or Kings Cross Basin, but later more usually as Battlebridge Basin. The standard of some of the work performed did not satisfy Horsfall and he considered extra facilities should have been provided including roads round the basin. This led to a lengthy dispute and Telford was called in to arbitrate. Terms were suggested in August 1821 whereby spare land was to be conveyed to Horsfall and he was to be given short-term toll concessions on traffic to and from his basin. Even then it took some time to reach agreement but eventually the first barges used the basin in April 1822.

As early as January 1821 a major basin branching off that at City Road had been proposed, but the subsequent establishment of wharves and side docks made access to it difficult. Various alternatives were considered but in November 1825 John Edwards, who was a member of the committee, started work

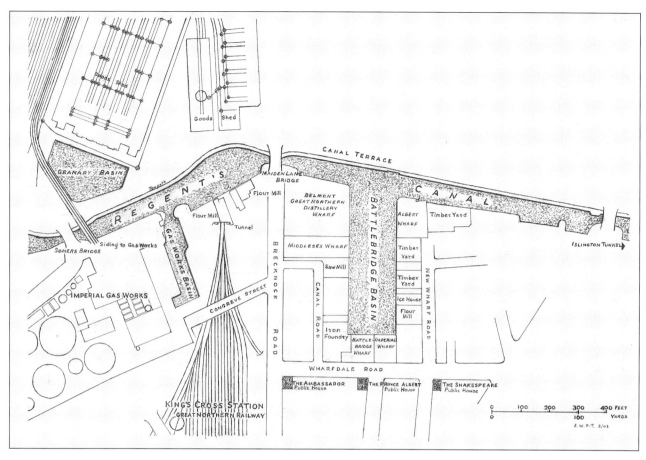

Battlebridge Basin and its immediate surroundings as shown in about 1885. Originally known as Horsfall's Basin, after William Horsfall for whom it was built, it was sometimes also called King's Cross Basin or Maiden Lane Basin. It was privately owned but was purchased by the British Waterways Board in 2000 and is now used for moorings. One of the attractions on its banks is the London Canal Museum, which was opened in March 1992. Brecknock Road is now York Way.

Edward Paget-Tomlinson

on what became the Wenlock Basin. It was opened prematurely in August 1826 when the dam across its entrance gave way, causing a 13in drop in the water level in the main canal and bringing traffic to a halt, but heavy rains soon restored the levels. In August 1832 John Edwards Vaughan, son of the original owner, extended the basin to 360 yards. It ran parallel to, and to the east of, the City Road Basin.

In March 1822 James Burton started constructing a basin near the Kingsland Road for landowner William Rhodes; it was 240 yards long and was opened in August. Robert Streather opened another basin in October 1827 at Cambridge Heath; it later became known as Northiam Basin or Gerver's Dock. Streather had purchased the land from the company in February 1824 conditional on the basin being built; subsequent owners Smith & Sharpe lengthened it in October 1837.

The earliest basin was above Hampstead Road Lock. Morgan was authorised to begin work on it in September 1815 and the basin was available when the upper-level of the canal opened. A second basin was built alongside and, once the rest of the canal opened, the company let out the wharves to three traders. A fourth trader, William Henry Whitbread, took the public wharf in September 1821. In February 1824 Nevil Smart was allowed to build a third basin immediately below the lock and he took a formal tenancy in June.

The company was less concerned with the wharves around the 2-acre Regent's Park Basin, as John Nash had leased them. Several traders were established there and a hay market, known as the New Cumberland Hay Market, was opened in 1830 taking over from that held in London's West End.[3] Thereafter the canal serving the basin became known as the

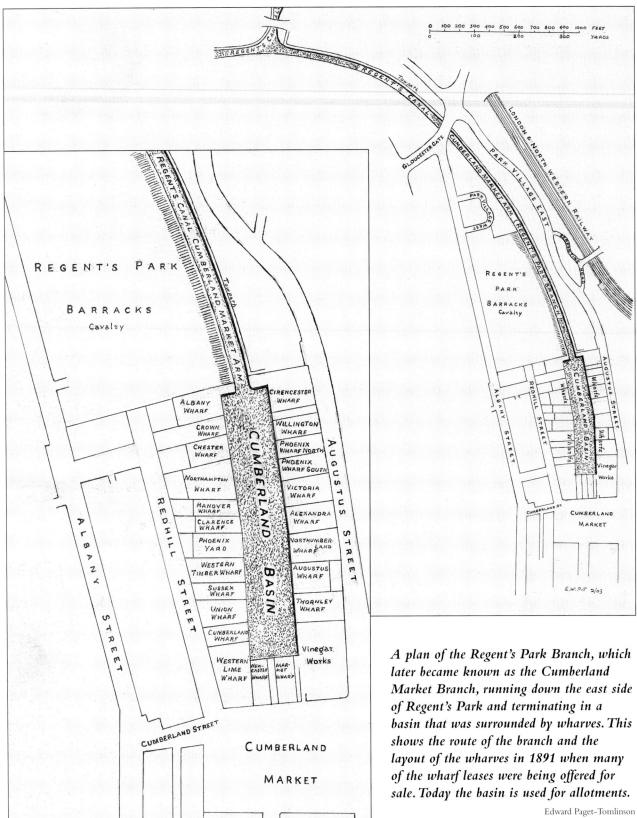

A plan of the Regent's Park Branch, which later became known as the Cumberland Market Branch, running down the east side of Regent's Park and terminating in a basin that was surrounded by wharves. This shows the route of the branch and the layout of the wharves in 1891 when many of the wharf leases were being offered for sale. Today the basin is used for allotments.

Edward Paget-Tomlinson

For many years horses provided most of the motive power to tow boats and barges on the Regent's Canal. Here three of the barge horses used on the canal were attending the London Van Horse Parade held in Regent's Park on Easter Monday 1925 (13 April) and Ophelia on the right won first prize. The Waterways Archive,
British Waterways Archive, Gloucester

Broad Walk Bridge at the eastern end of Regent's Park. The canal makes a sharp left turn here making this a difficult manoeuvre for the barges. The Cumberland Market Branch is beyond the bridge bearing round to the right. The Waterways Archive,
British Waterways Archive, Gloucester

Two important traffics handled at Regent's Canal Dock are shown in this picture dated 27 June 1911. On the far side of the jetty the steamer **Lady Ann** *is discharging 1,300 tons of coal brought from northeast collieries, whilst on the near side the steamer* **Moringen** *is discharging 600 tons of ice brought from Norway. Some of the lighters have been touched in by the photographer.*   Regent's Canal & Dock Co booklet in the author's collection

Cumberland Market Branch. In December 1825 William Leftwich approached the company to use the ice in the basin to fill an ice-well he was constructing near by, this was agreed at £10 for that winter and renewed in later years. In August 1828 a special 1/- (5p) per ton toll was introduced on ice to the basin from Limehouse, where it was imported from Norway, as this was becoming an important traffic on the canal. Ice also brought problems and the company had to adapt a barge for ice breaking in 1821 to help keep the canal open during frosty weather.

In September 1819 the Gas Light & Coke Company, which had been established in 1810 and chartered in 1812, applied for the use of a wharf in the City Road Basin. At the time it had two main works – at Curtain Road, Moorfields and Brick Lane near to the City of London – and it supplied the City,

Westminster and Southwark with gas.[4] It began to receive some of its coal supplies by barge as soon as the canal opened, its main contractor being Charles Gabriel who was established at City Road. In September 1826, and following a change in coal buying procedures, a toll reduction was agreed for Gabriel and the bulk of the traffic was then transferred to the canal. Two new contractors, Benjamin Berthron and Green & Barrett, took over in September 1827 and the toll concessions were extended to them. In 1831 the gas company established its own wharf in the basin.

In June 1821 the Regent's was advised that the Imperial Gas Light & Coke Company was to be formed to operate near the canal. Arrangements were made to have clauses inserted in its Act to prevent the new concern causing any nuisance through contaminated water, or waste liquors from the distillation process, being discharged into the canal. In June 1822 special rates were agreed for building materials passing to the new works at Gloucester Street in Haggerston and Edmund Street between Maiden Lane and St Pancras, both of which were to be served by basins off the main canal.

There was an upset when the dam blocking Haggerston Basin was removed in March 1823 without permission. Several barges entered without the legal agreement for what was initially known as Shoreditch Basin and for the toll account being completed, but this omission was speedily corrected. In October consent was given to starting the St Pancras Basin provided that a proper agreement was executed before it was opened. The work was finished by the end of January 1824 and the basin brought into use in February to facilitate the completion of the gasworks, which opened in August.

In June 1824 the Independent Gas Company applied to make a 200ft basin near the Rosemary Branch at Shoreditch, the work to be carried out by Thomas Douglas. The plans were approved early in September and by the end of October the basin was complete and in use, the gas company supplying Shoreditch and Bethnal Green. As well as delivering coal to the Independent and Imperial works, barges took away coke, tar and ammonia liquors.

In March 1830 special rates were agreed for the Ratcliffe Gas Company's coals unloaded in Limehouse Dock as a minimum of 4,000 tons a year had been guaranteed. In June 1832 even finer rates had to be conceded when the London Dock Company made a bid for the Ratcliffe's traffic. In July 1838 the Commercial Gas Light & Coke Company applied to construct an inlet into its new works at Johnson's Fields, Stepney. Permission was given and a lay-by was opened in December. Further afield the Western Gas Light Company was formed in 1844 with a works at Kensal Green, beside the Grand Junction's Paddington Branch, to supply Paddington, St Marylebone, Hampstead, Chelsea and the surrounding area. Ultimately, two basins off the Grand Junction served the Western Gas Light Company but it led to considerable tonnages of coal passing on the Regent's Canal.

The Regent's Canal benefited directly from having several gas suppliers along its course. In December 1823 George Mackintosh, who operated a small works at Limehouse, was paid £61 for erecting gas lights at Limehouse Dock and for supplying gas to them for two years. By 1827 the supply was undertaken by the British Gas Light Company. Part of the City Road Basin was also supplied with gas and considerable tonnages of coke were purchased from the various companies.

Despite the importance of the gasworks traffics there were also problems. In September 1828 the Regent's discovered that a large quantity of water had been taken surreptitiously by the Imperial works at St

The large gasholder in course of erection at the Imperial Gas Company's works at Bethnal Green. It was 200ft in diameter, 80ft high and was put up between 1856 and 1858 on a reclaimed site formerly known as Bunker's Pond. No gas was generated here but it served as a satellite gasholder station to the Haggerston Gasworks. The canal company provided a large lay-by and the barges were probably waiting their turn to deliver to a more congested site further up the canal. Malcolm Tucker

Pancras over a long period of time through means of pipes laid into the canal below water level. Drinkwater had a meeting with the gas company and William Anderson was engaged to examine the basin and that at Shoreditch where similar abstractions had been made. Anderson substantiated the claims saying 265 tons of water a day had been taken at Shoreditch over 4½ years and 950 tons a day at St Pancras over 3¼ years. He estimated that £2,841 was due, assessing the water at ¼d per ton. The gas company was clearly guilty and admitted it, but was reluctant to pay, even hinting at the need for litigation. Eventually its £1,700 offer was accepted in May 1829, and the money was paid over the following month.

At Limehouse an additional labourer and a night watchman were appointed immediately after the

dock opened and on 17 August 1820 the first ship, the *Little Mary*, entered the dock with coals for sugar refiners Craven & Bowman.[5] Drinkwater and Morgan were both present, and the event was celebrated by waiving the toll and giving the ship's crew a small gratuity.

Limehouse Dock had been built with sloping banks and to allow ships to load and unload several platforms or jetties, projecting out into the dock and to which ships could moor, had been built by McIntosh. The jetties were mostly on the west side alongside the new Horseferry Branch Road but in practice it was found they were too high to enable the coals to be discharged conveniently. Negotiations with the Commercial Road Trustees led to the new road, which governed the height of the jetties, being

The Regent's Canal Bason (sic) as constructed in 1820. It opened on 1 August and the first ship was admitted on 17 August The water area was just over 4 acres and at the time it had sloping sides, meaning that jetties had to be built out to enable ships to moor for cargoes to be landed. Initially most of these jetties were on the west side giving access to the Horseferry Branch Road.

Edward Paget-Tomlinson

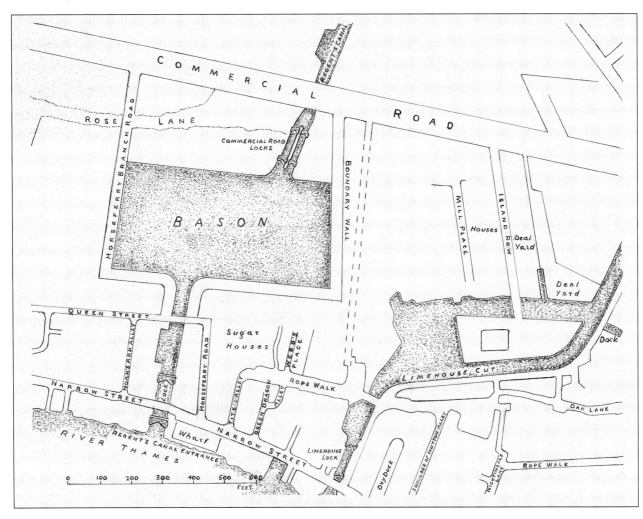

A sailing ship discharging to a group of Charringtons lighters in Regent's Canal Dock in 1938.

Waterways Archive, British Waterways Archive, Gloucester

lowered by McIntosh. There had also been a delay in placing the mooring buoys both in the river and in the dock making it difficult for ships to manoeuvre. Once these problems had been overcome the use of the dock built up steadily although it took time to alter established shipping trade patterns. In five months of 1820 just 15 loaded and 16 empty vessels used the dock, but this rose to 592 loaded and 41 empty ships in 1830, and to 670 loaded and 51 empty ships in 1835.[6]

Growth had also been hindered by the Customs House Commissioners who objected to any boats laden with foreign timber being admitted; this was largely due to the dock area not being enclosed and thus far from secure. At the same time the whole area was still being tidied up as not all of the excavated material had been moved. In September 1820 a

special toll was agreed for John Gardner to move 3,000 tons of the spoil to Hoxton. Following a meeting at the dock in June 1821 Morgan was asked to investigate lining the basin and building a wall around the site to make it secure. He estimated £13,572 for a piled brick wharf wall and £5,600 for the surrounding wall and gates. The company's finances were such that nothing was done at the time, but to improve security Thomas Parr was appointed in April 1822 as a police officer at Limehouse at 21/– (£1.05) per week.

In August 1822 Thomas Douglas's tender for a high enclosing fence at Limehouse was accepted, and the work was finished early in 1823. Even then it was not until November 1825 that it was finally agreed that ships carrying foreign timber could unload in the dock. Meanwhile several traders had offered to erect

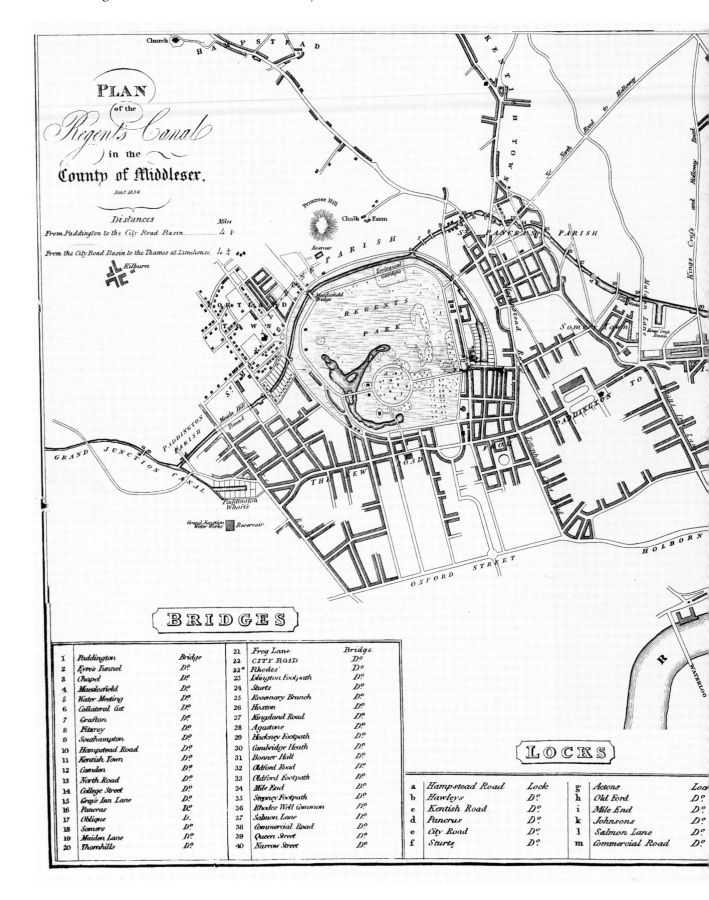

PLAN

of the

Regents Canal

in the

County of Middlesex.

Jan.y 1834.

Distances   Miles

From Paddington to the City Road Basin .... 4 ¾

From the City Road Basin to the Thames at Limehouse. 4 ¼

Kilburn

Grand Junction Water Works   ■ Reservoir

BRIDGES

1	Paddington	Bridge	21	Frog Lane	Bridge
2	Eyre's Tunnel	D.º	22	CITY ROAD	D.º
3	Chapel	D.º	22ᵃ	Rhodes'	D.º
4	Macclesfield	D.º	23	Islington Footpath	D.º
5	Water Meeting	D.º	24	Sturts	D.º
6	Collateral Cut	D.º	25	Rosemary Branch	D.º
7	Grafton	D.º	26	Hoxton	D.º
8	Fitzroy	D.º	27	Kingsland Road	D.º
9	Southampton	D.º	28	Agastone	D.º
10	Hampstead Road	D.º	29	Hackney Footpath	D.º
11	Kentish Town	D.º	30	Cambridge Heath	D.º
12	Camden	D.º	31	Bonner Hall	D.º
13	North Road	D.º	32	Oldford Road	D.º
14	College Street	D.º	33	Oldford Footpath	D.º
15	Grays Inn Lane	D.º	34	Mile End	D.º
16	Pancras	D.º	35	Stepney Footpath	D.º
17	Oblique	D.	36	Rhodes Well Common	D.º
18	Somers	D.º	37	Salmon Lane	D.º
19	Maiden Lane	D.º	38	Commercial Road	D.º
20	Thornhills	D.º	39	Queen Street	D.º
			40	Narrow Street	D.º

LOCKS

a	Hampstead Road	Lock	g	Actons	Lock
b	Hawleys	D.º	h	Old Ford	D.º
c	Kentish Road	D.º	i	Mile End	D.º
d	Pancras	D.º	k	Johnsons	D.º
e	City Road	D.º	l	Salmon Lane	D.º
f	Sturts	D.º	m	Commercial Road	D.º

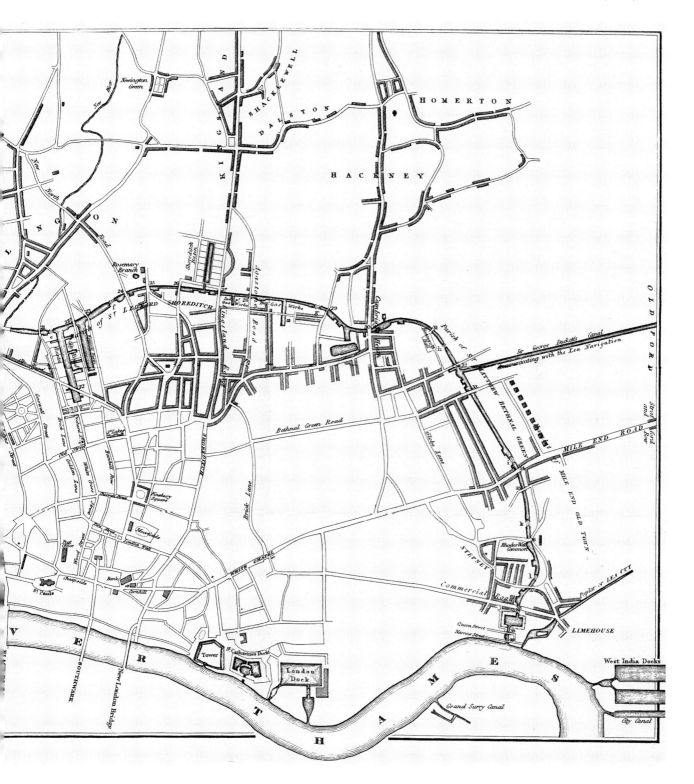

A plan of the Regent's Canal issued in January 1834. Since the canal opened Regent's Park Basin has been extended northwards nearly doubling its length, basins either above or below Hampstead Road Locks have risen to six in number, Horsfall's Basin is now named Kings Cross Basin whilst the City Road Basin now has seven side docks. A series of new basins has been created and the canal has been widened in several places to create lay-bys. Meanwhile the number of bridges has risen to forty.

unloading jetties and storage buildings. This was the start of a gradual build up in the facilities such as the first dock crane early in 1823 and, a few months, later the installation of a capstan to assist ships into and out of the entrance lock and to haul barges across the dock. David Lewis was promoted to be Dock Master's Assistant in April 1823, reflecting this growth.

In December 1822 the first of a series of extensions to the dock was made. A small piece of land that projected into the water space at the south of the Commercial Road, was excavated to give more space for barges waiting to enter the canal. A further area was excavated in August 1828. In March 1824 a major extension was proposed on the west side, but to be executed by a separate company. Morgan estimated the cost at £45,000 including the land but nothing was done.

The dock also brought its problems, not least when ships that were really too big entered, or tried to enter, the lock. In August 1824 an over-large ship damaged the East London Water Works Company's pipes that crossed the entrance channel in a siphon. The Dock Master, who had been given several warnings on the subject, was given a severe reprimand. In February 1825 the *Wilhelmina* got stuck between the walls of the outer pier and was severely damaged. This led to a lengthy dispute and eventually the company paid out £600 to settle the ship owner's claims.

Elsewhere, another early problem was over the use of Islington Tunnel. While narrowboats could pass inside, controls were soon shown to be necessary to prevent barges meeting in the tunnel. In July 1822 two men were employed to regulate the passage of craft, but even then it was a slow and tedious business to manhandle barges through. In October 1823, and following an experiment by Henry Thorrington, Morgan suggested that a small stationary steam engine working an endless chain or rope over two drum wheels could draw a 60-ton loaded barge through the tunnel in 15 minutes. Two months later a small steamboat was hired on trial to tow barges through. However, this was unsuccessful as it took 39 minutes to tow one loaded barge and Morgan still favoured his own idea.

In September 1824 an experimental boat was brought it into service. This hauled itself through by picking up a rope laid on the bed of the canal and paying it out behind. It proved reasonably satisfactory but experience showed that an iron barrel was preferable for the hauling apparatus and an iron chain was needed instead of a rope. From 1 January 1825 the company instituted a 1d (½p) per ton charge for the towing service. In May 1825 Taylor & Martineau agreed to provide a 4hp steam engine with a 1,050-yard warping chain and capstan for £595, while in January 1826 John Yates, who had provided the original boat on hire, contracted to build a new hull to contain the steam engine for £230. A test showed the new boat could haul four loaded barges containing nearly 200 tons through the tunnel in 30 minutes. Initially the steam engine was powered by burning coal – the company paid £73 to the Shipley colliery in Derbyshire for a load in August 1826 – but later coke was used, which was supplied from one of the several gas works on the canal.

The tunnel boat had a hard life and needed regular repairs. In December 1827 Horton & Ashton provided a new boiler for £150, while in June 1830 Golden reported the chain had broken in many places, had been repaired as best as its worn condition permitted, but now needed replacing. The increase in the barge trade and in the size of the barges made a more powerful engine necessary. Henry Parkes & Co agreed to provide a new chain for £123 in February 1831. A year later, Ovid Topham, who was based at Horsfall's Basin, agreed to provide a 6hp condensing steam engine for £400. Problems still arose as in January 1834 when the chain broke under load, making a hole in the boat's side 3ft below the water level, causing it to sink in the tunnel.

Even with the new towage service, signalmen were still needed at each end of the tunnel and small cabins were constructed for them at the end of 1825. In April 1831 Sowter & Dale contracted to build houses for £110 each at both ends of the tunnel for these men, the work was completed in August.

One commitment the Regent's Canal Company could have done without was the provision of additional bridges over the canal. Several landowners had reserved special powers for this in the Act and the company had a duty to maintain established rights of way. Lord Camden had the right to three such bridges but only one was built. This was for a new road from Camden Town to Holloway. Sowter & Dale contracted to build the 60ft wide, 30ft span structure for £1,776 in April 1825 and it was completed in August.

In June 1825 Lord Southampton's trustees demanded that two bridges be built at Camden as a prelude to housing development. Sowter & Dale tendered £965 for the first and £1,075 for the second as it involved a skew arch. Work started on the straight-arched Grafton Bridge in May 1826 and was completed in October but the company asked the trustees to pay the £110 difference for the skew Fitzroy Bridge. Once this was agreed work started in July and was completed in February 1828.

Not all the landowners insisted on the bridges reserved to them in the Act being built. One example occured in April 1821 when Morgan obtained an agreement releasing the company from its liability for a bridge on Sir Henry Hawley's land. And some bridges did not involve the company in any expense. In September 1829 James Rhodes was allowed to proceed with a new bridge to take Wharf Road, running between the City and Wenlock basins, northwards over the canal.

One new bridge was not on the Regent's Canal at all but on the Grand Junction at Paddington where it gave access to the Regent's Canal towpath; this horse bridge was built in iron by George Day in 1822 with John Dickson doing the masonry work. Elsewhere Thomas Morris's tender for a new footbridge over the canal at Salmon Lane was accepted in May 1821.

Another improvement was the provision of vertical rag-stone walling to reinforce the canal banks and increase the cross-sectional area of the waterway. As early as November 1820 rag-stone had been used near Horsfall's Basin to protect the towpath, but in April 1824 Morgan recommended its more general use particularly in cuttings to prevent recurrent slippages of the soil. In 1832 a rolling programme was started with the work concentrated on areas where slips were preventing barges from passing, such as at Rhodeswell, Grays Inn Lane and Kentish Town. The problem was aggravated by the increasing amount of trade on the canal and the use of larger barges.

In August 1834 several parts of the Cumberland Market Branch were reinforced as there had been a succession of slips there, and a year later work started on parts of the main canal through Regent's Park, although Morgan had recommended against this. In time the work was extended to cover the entire course of the canal, making a major improvement in the width and depth of water and reducing the need for regular dredging work.

One problem that the opening of the canal did nothing to resolve was the long-running dispute with William Agar. On October 1820 he claimed £3,000

for the extra land he alleged the company had taken for its works, for its failure to lay down pipes to supply him with canal water as had been agreed and for various other breaches of the agreement. A month later he began formal proceedings for a trial in the Court of Exchequer. Drinkwater, accompanied by Nash,[7] consulted Pollock, the company's barrister, and it was decided to defend the action and to attempt to include all the other points still in dispute in the same hearing.

At the end of January 1821 Agar's solicitor rejected the company's move but it persisted and, following the formal hearing on 14 June, the court decided that all the matters in dispute should be settled by arbitration. Not content with this decision, Agar tried to have the judgement set aside and the arbitrator dismissed but the court rejected his attempt.

The arbitrator, Judge Edward Alderson, had a difficult task and he took his time. In July 1823 Lyon reported several meetings with him, but Agar was now claiming there were yet more matters outstanding that could lead to further contention and was seeking a meeting with the committee. As such meetings had proved a fruitful source of the continuous litigation over the last ten years the committee wisely turned down his request.

Not daunted, Agar put forward his proposals to end the dispute. Fundamentally, he wanted the company to use its Parliamentary powers to compulsory purchase the freehold of the leasehold land he occupied on both sides of the canal. He undertook to acquire the land so purchased and to cover all the costs but he was adamant that without this he would never allow any wharves to be built on the land through his estate. If the company agreed to this, he would also allow the side pond at St Pancras Lock to be converted into a second chamber. However, he wanted any land claimed by the company released and he wanted its consent to his making two short cuts through the towpath to serve his estate, with he providing swing bridges.

At first the company felt that such action on its part would be an abuse of its Parliamentary powers and declined to act. It also pointed out it did not need Agar's permission to deal with land that had been conveyed to it for the duplicate lock. In February 1824 Agar came back with identical proposals but as Alderson had still not made his award the company was unwilling to make any moves that might prejudice the situation. Instead, Pollock was asked to contact Alderson to try to hurry things up.

Meanwhile the company was starting to experience problems as the single lock at St Pancras was proving to be a bottleneck for traffic at times. Lyon was now asked to bring pressure to bear on Alderson but even then it was not until 26 December 1824 that the award was published. It was a long and comprehensive document.

Four points were decided in Agar's favour:

for the delay in supplying and installing five regulating water pipes specified in a May 1818 agreement the company was fined £100;

for failing to cover parts of the banks of the cuttings and embankments with top soil and vegetable mould £95;

for making the slopes of the cuttings and embankments steeper than specified £95, and

for failing to grant Agar the sole fishing rights through his estate before a specified date a nominal sum of 1/- (£0.05).

This made a total of £283.1/- (£283.05), which the company was to pay within two months.

Against this, the award provided that the company could bring the duplicate lock at St Pancras into use. Agar also had to accept the grant of the fishing rights that had belatedly been made the day before the award was issued and his claim for damages and expenses for trespass on his estate and for another eight petty grievances were all thrown out. Lyon was instructed to pay over the fines immediately, hopefully to settle the dispute once and for all.

Despite two approaches Agar's solicitor refused to take the money, Agar being unwilling to do anything to suggest he accepted Alderson's award. Acting on the award, however, the company instructed Morgan to remove the obstructions and bring the second chamber of the duplicate lock into use immediately but great care was to be taken to ensure that no damage whatsoever was caused to Agar's property. The lock keepers were also instructed to be extremely careful to maintain the correct level of water on either side of the lock. On 13 April Morgan reported the duplicate lock was complete and in working order.

Three months later Agar started a fresh action citing 17 breaches of his agreement with the company. These related mainly to the water pipes and the company carried out some minor works to try and pacify him.

Early in 1828 some settlement was discovered in the approaches to the skew bridge on Agar's estate. Remedial works were carried out and while these were in progress gates were made in the wing wall of the bridge next to Agar's house. He actually thanked the company for this in September 1832 when he renewed his request for the purchase of the freehold but the company resolutely declined to discuss his proposal until he accepted Alderson's award. Agar visited Harvey Combe at his brewery to press his case and tried to claim that his new grievances had all arisen since the award, but the company was unmoved.

On 24 October 1832 the solicitors reported that Agar was at last willing to settle the action by accepting the award and they were told to make the payment immediately. Two weeks later the committee was told the long-running dispute had been settled.

Agar had still not got what he really wanted, but he was now proposing to make wharves along the canal on his estate provided he could first acquire the freehold. The company was now willing to look more helpfully on his plan provided the wharves were used solely in connection with the canal. Agar had also had discussions with the Prebendary of St Pancras and in December an agreement was reached whereby the company paid £1,900 for the copyhold interest in the land. It involved a 120-yard wide strip containing 13 acres on the northeast or towpath side of the canal and 24 acres on the other side. Agar then purchased the land from the company for the same sum and met all the expenses.

In retrospect the dispute seems barely credible. Agar took his claims to absurd lengths in his self-appointed role as professional litigator. While the company was not entirely blameless at times, it was dealing with an individual who was unreasonable and motivated by greed; an experience it could well have done without.

Another thing that opening the canal failed to do was to ease the company's financial problems. Despite the additional £105,000 in shares raised at the end of 1819 there was still insufficient to complete the canal. At the General Assembly on 6 June 1821 the shareholders were told that to finish all the works and to cover continuing interest and capital repayments to the Exchequer Bill Loan Commissioners, a further £64,500 was needed.

An approach was made to the Commissioners for a larger loan, but restrictions in their Act on the amount of money they could advance prevented them from assisting. To surmount the problem the company sponsored an Act authorising the Commissioners to lend a further £100,000 if required and the same Act also empowered the company to raise another £200,000 in shares or on mortgage.[8] With the additional £200,000 in the 1819 Act, this brought the total authorised capital up to £1,000,000.

Once the legal difficulty was removed, the Commissioners met on 24 July and agreed to make a further £50,000 loan with interest at the same 5% as on the original advance. Equally important, however, was their agreement to postpone capital repayments for five years, leaving the company merely having to cover interest; this was under the powers of an Act,[9] which permitted a moratorium to be granted providing it did not increase the original term of the loan. Allowing for capital repayments that had already been made on the original loan, this left the combined debt at £235,000. The annual interest charge was £11,750, which was still a burden to the company as revenue took time to build up.

In 1822 the company was instrumental in promoting another Act for the Exchequer Bill Loan Commissioners which reduced the interest rate from 5% to 4%, thus saving the company £2,350 each year.[10] Despite this the interest repayment was still a major commitment and in 1824 the committee applied to the Treasury for a further reduction in the rate. There was a meeting between Drinkwater and the Chancellor of the Exchequer but the request was turned down. Out of the approach, however, came an Act giving discretionary powers to reduce the interest rate where the works were considered to be of national importance.[11]

The Regent's Canal Company was still finding it difficult to meet the interest payments and by the middle of 1824 £16,000 was still outstanding for interest up to 31 December 1823 and the company had other debts of £10,000. The company's main argument with the government was that the rate charged to the company was more than the government incurred in providing the funds. The government was, therefore, making a small profit on the transaction and this can hardly have been what was intended when the scheme was set up. By the end of 1825 increasing revenues had eased the situation somewhat and the arrears had been reduced to less than £5,000.

On 5 September 1826 the five-year moratorium on capital repayments expired but this coincided with a drop in revenue that aggravated the company's position. The loan had originally been intended for repayment over a 20-year term and this would mean the company would have to find another £11,750 each year on top of the interest. On 30 September 1826 interest owing was £6,082 making the total debt outstanding £241,082. At the same time the company was finding the control imposed by the Commissioners increasingly irksome as all decisions involving major expenditure had to be referred to them for approval.

Once again negotiations were opened with the Commissioners and in 1827 the government offered a £25,000 abatement on the debt due to the alteration of the original line of the canal through Marylebone Park and for making the branch canal to the basin. The committee estimated this figure more or less equated to the difference between the 4% charged to the company and the cost of the money to the government and recommended acceptance of the offer, which was conditional on the loan being repaid in full. Calculated to 31 October 1827 the interest arrears were £10,885 making the debt £220,885 after allowing for the £25,000 rebate. It was agreed half was to be paid on 31 October and the balance, with additional interest, on 25 March 1828.

To provide these funds the company turned once again to its long-suffering shareholders who were asked to provide £223,000 by the issue of three new shares of £25 each for every four shares held; £2 payable on application, £11 on 17 October and the balance of £12 on 8 March 1828. In the event 9,124 new shares were issued raising £228,100 and bringing the issued share capital up to £726,025 represented by 2,541 original shares of £100 each and 18,877 shares of £25 each. With these funds an initial payment of £110,442 was made to the commissioners at the end of October and the balance of £111,786 in March 1828 thus liberating the company from government control.

During all this time the tonnage and revenue had been building up to more respectable levels with the result that at the General Assembly on 3 December 1828 it was agreed that in future a dividend was to be declared out of the net annual income to 31 March. The shareholders patience was finally rewarded on 3 June 1829 when a maiden dividend of 12/6d (62½p) was declared, payable on 20 July at the company's offices. On the 21,418 shares in issue, this absorbed £13,386; a small enough return but at least it was a start.

Regent's Canal Construction Costs

1812 Prospectus	Estimate	Actual to March 1829	Cost
87 acres of land, 5 houses, deal yard & wharf at Limehouse	£55,000	120 acres with costs & redemption of Land Tax	£181,738
Excavation & puddling	£38,984	Excavation, puddling, resoiling & relaying pipes	£114,562
2 tunnels – 1,045 yards	£31,350	3 tunnels – 1,285 yards	£72,058
29 bridges	£11,600	37 bridges	£51,152
12 locks	£13,125	12 locks	£55,021
Chelsea engine & reservoir	£38,000	Chelsea engine & main	£54,978
Limehouse barge basin & tide lock	£12,314	Limehouse ship basin & ship lock	£48,624
Culverts, fences, towpath	£7,662	Culverts, fences, towpath & damages	£15,857
Paddington wharfingers	£40,000	Paddington wharfingers	£61,617
Contingencics	£31,965	Parliamentary costs, City Road Basin, salaries, repairs &c	£215,734
Collateral Cut & wharf land	£120,000		
Total	*£400,000*	*Total*	*£871,341*

It was also a time to assess what the works had cost to date and the figures showed only too clearly why the company had such a long and drawn-out struggle before it could achieve its first dividend.[12] See the table above.

There was a significant development on 18 June 1823 when the engineer Francis Giles informed the company that Sir George Duckett was planning a canal from the river Lee to link up with the Regent's Canal near Old Ford Bridge. Duckett owned the Stort Navigation and saw the new canal as a means to divert trade between this navigation and the Thames away from the Limehouse Cut and Bow Creek while making a useful link with the Regent's and hence with the Grand Junction Canal.

In October the Regent's Canal Company approved the plans but with restrictions on the abstraction of water and including the requirement for a stop lock at Old Ford. In February 1824 protection clauses were agreed for the Bill.[13] The canal was to be nearly 1¼ miles long dropping through three locks to the Lee; it was known as the Hertford Union Canal, or sometimes as the Lee Union Canal.

Duckett was authorised to raise £50,000 to finance the work but he had major difficulties in finding the funds until he managed to borrow £20,000 from the Exchequer Bill Loan Commissioners in 1829.[14] As a result, construction proceeded only slowly and it was not until February 1829 that Giles submitted detailed plans for the works at the junction at Old Ford. These involved a bridge over the entrance to the new canal taking the Regent's towpath and a 14ft wide roadway that gave access to surrounding land. A

The rather unassuming entrance to the Hertford Union Canal at Old Ford is through the towpath bridge on the left. The former Twig Folly Wharf, which included Tomlin's barge repairing yard, was almost opposite this entrance.
Author – 30 May 1984

A pleasure boat heads westwards on the Hertford Union Canal past former timber yards. Old Ford Upper Lock is in the distance. Author – 30 May 1984

stoppage was agreed to construct the junction but the works overran causing considerable delays to traffic on the Regent's Canal.

Meanwhile, Duckett was negotiating with the Regent's Canal Company over the scale of charges and the figures were published in January 1830 with the new canal to be opened on 1 March 1830. Its works were incomplete, however, and the Regent's agreed to provide a temporary supply of water until Duckett's steam engine and pump were installed.

Trade was slow to develop and Duckett was constantly badgering for toll concessions to stimulate traffic; in June 1830 he applied to join the Regent's board but met with a cool response. This was partly due to the delay in commissioning the steam engine. It had been promised for May but in October was still far from complete. The steam engine did not come into service until the spring of 1831 when Duckett agreed to supply water to the Mile End pound from May to October each year in exchange for drawing water from the pound during the winter months. In March 1833 Giles had to apologise for failing to provide enough water to the Regent's as he had been unable to obtain much from the Lee because the service reservoir, from which the steam engine

operated, had proved too small to store sufficient during the neap tides and was to be enlarged.

Part of the reason for the low usage of the Hertford Union Canal may have been due a fear about it being under the control of a single individual. To overcome this Duckett proposed transferring the canal to a new company and issuing 500 shares of £100 each but nothing came of the idea. Another reason was the unattractive toll structure and the refusal of the Regent's Canal to co-operate on measures to overcome the problem. Duckett even declared his canal toll-free for a three-month period from 1 January 1831 but to no lasting effect.

In 1832 Duckett was declared bankrupt and this prompted the Lee Trustees to consider applying to Parliament for powers to purchase his canal. They decided to go ahead in June 1833 after the canal had been advertised for sale by Duckett's assignees. Sir Culling Smith then suggested the Regent's should consider purchasing, but the idea was not pursued. The Lee Trustees also decided not to proceed. Desultory negotiations continued with Duckett and with Peter Giles, who was now managing the canal in place of his father, aimed at trying to amend the toll structure and encourage trade. But it was to be another 20 years before matters were finally resolved.

A formal notice issued on behalf of Sir George Duckett announcing the opening of the Hertford Union Canal and setting out the scale of tolls.

The Waterways Archive, British Waterways Archive, Gloucester

NOTICE

Is hereby given, that the New Canal between the Regent's Canal & the River Lea, will be navigable for Barges after the 1st of March, 1830.

TOLLS.

Upon every Barge Containing above
25 Tons or Chaldrons . . . . . £1 0 0 } Per
From 15 to 25 Tons or Chaldrons . 0 15 0 } Barge.
Under 15 Tons or Chaldrons at the rate of 9d. a Ton or Chaldron, but no Barge to pay less than 7s. 6d. a Barge.

Any Person using a Spiked Instrument against the Banks or Works of the Canal, will be immediately Prosecuted, and any Lock Keeper permitting such Instrument to be used, and not informing against the Party, will be forthwith dismissed.

[BINGHAM, Printer, 84, Mount Street, Grosvenor Square

CHAPTER SEVEN

THE RAILWAY AGE

The Regent's Canal formed an arc around the north of London and, therefore, became heavily involved with railways as they tried to establish termini as close to the centre of the capital as possible.

The first project appeared in February 1825 when a notice was published for a railroad from Paddington either to the East and West India Docks, to the Isle of Dogs or to Blackwall. As the line would cross the canal at the tail of Salmon Lane Locks, Lyon was instructed to petition against the plan in order to protect the canal company's position. The Bill was thrown out for non-compliance with Standing Orders but re-appeared unsuccessfully in different formats over the next few years.

The first successful scheme to affect the Regent's Canal appeared in January 1831 for the London & Birmingham Railway (L&BR). Originally it was to start at Paddington but the terminus was moved to Maiden Lane near Horsfall's Basin and then to Chalk Farm just north of the canal and west of the Hampstead Road where Lord Southampton was

willing to sell the railway 25 acres. The company opposed the plans, which would have interfered with wharves on the canal and with the Brent feeder at Willesden and protective clauses were secured in the L&BR's 1833 Act.

Towards the end of 1834 the L&BR applied to Parliament to extend its line southwards across the canal to a new terminus at Euston Square. The canal company tried hard to have the extension restricted to passenger traffic but had to be content with protective clauses governing the bridge.[1]

Many of the bricks and other materials needed for building the line were delivered to Camden by canal with reduced tolls and concessions to unload onto the canal's banks agreed for the contractors William and Lewis Cubitt. The company also agreed to supply water to the L&BR's locomotives both at Chalk Farm and from the Brent feeder at Lower Place.

The line opened from Euston to Boxmoor in Hertfordshire on 20 July 1837.[2] It involved a steep gradient from the terminus up to the canal and this was

This watercolour, purporting to be in 1838, shows the London & Birmingham Railway's new bridge over the canal at Camden. A sailing barge and a canal boat are apparently unloading constructional materials by the bridge although this section of the railway had been opened to traffic in 1837. The locks on the canal were big enough to take small sailing barges, but the numerous bridges meant such craft were normally horse hauled with the mast being re-stepped during cargo handling.
The Waterways Archive,
British Waterways Archive, Gloucester

The entrance to the former London & North Western Railway transhipment dock at Camden. When the railway company built a siding to link the dock to the railway the towpath, which formerly ran round behind the dock, had to be diverted to the more usual position beside the canal, thus necessitating the towpath bridge.

Author – 19 May 1984

initially worked by stationary winding engines sited just north of the bridge. The route to Birmingham was opened throughout on 17 September 1838. An early traffic was ale transhipped into barges at Camden for destinations on the Thames and revised canal tolls were introduced in May 1848 to stimulate traffic between the railway, City Road Basin and the river.

The opening of the L&BR prompted Pickfords, the largest long-distance carriers on the canal, to start diverting some of their trade to the railway. This led to a major rift with Joseph Baxendale, one of the firm's partners, who was also a director of the Regent's Canal Company. The dispute was patched up when Pickfords purchased land on the south side of the canal just west of the railway bridge at Camden Town in March 1839 and built a basin and depot where railway traffic could be transhipped to and from canal craft. The new depot was opened in December 1841 with a bridge over the canal to connect it to the railway goods yard on the north bank.

In December 1840 the L&BR acquired from John Semple and Thomas Hubert their leasehold interest in two wharves and two small basins on the north bank of the canal at Camden. In January 1845 it agreed to purchase the freehold from the canal company, together with some land at the rear, for £3,000 with a view to extending one of the basins up to the railway to serve as a transhipment depot.

Previously the towpath ran behind the basin, and the work involved a new path alongside the canal and a bridge to carry it across the mouth of the basin. Branson & Gwyther's £1,335 tender for the masonry and towpath works and J. Deeley & Co's £574 tender for a cast-iron bridge diagonally across the canal were accepted in July.

The sale of the land to what had now become the London & North Western Railway (LNWR) was not completed until February 1847; detailed plans for the extended basin were agreed in July and it was completed in April 1848 although in August the LNWR decided to roof it in. The railway also acquired land on the south side of the canal and the work included a siding across the canal to connect up with these new premises.

The second railway to cross the canal was the Eastern Counties Railway (ECR) which was projected to build a 5ft gauge line from Shoreditch to Norwich. The Regent's Canal Company reviewed the plans for the bridge at Mile End in February 1836 and protective clauses were included in the Act. The first section of the line from Devonshire Street, near the canal, to Romford was opened on 20 June 1839 with extensions westwards across the canal to Shoreditch and eastwards to Brentwood on 1 July 1840.

In April 1841 there were problems at Devonshire Street with water leaking to a basin being built by the

ECR and in May 1842 it applied to construct a lock to link this basin to the canal. The Regent's refused, fearing water would be lost to the canal but suggested a lay-by would meet the ECR's needs and plans for this were approved in June. The ECR was converted to standard gauge in 1844.

Back at Limehouse plans had re-emerged for a line to Blackwall. In November 1835 the London & Blackwall Railway was projected to pass over the Commercial Road Locks and the canal company's land north of the dock. As this would have prevented the extension to the dock that was then being planned, an objection was lodged and the route was moved northwards to cross the canal near Salmon Lane Locks. In January 1836 the promoters of a rival Commercial Railway (COR) produced plans for a line from Minories to Blackwall that again crossed land at the Limehouse dock. The London & Blackwall plan disappeared, but negotiations with Sir John Rennie for the COR led to an agreement on 12 July whereby the railway would be built on a viaduct across the land, the canal company would have exclusive use of the arches under the line, and the COR would build a wharf wall parallel to the line from the Commercial Road Locks to the western end of the dock as the first stage in the 1½-acre dock extension.

The COR obtained its Act immediately afterwards but before starting to build the viaduct asked to move its line further south from the Commercial Road. This led to a revised agreement on 15 August 1838 whereby the COR now also agreed to contribute half the cost of excavating the dock extension. Soon after, and on obtaining powers to extend its line westwards to Fenchurch Street, the COR changed its name to the London & Blackwall Railway. Meanwhile, as a first step towards clearing the site, the company started to move the spoil heaps left from the original construction by using them to ballast empty vessels leaving the dock.

Railway construction work started at Limehouse in February 1839 and involved demolishing the lock keeper's house at the entrance to the canal. The cable-operated 5ft gauge line opened from the Minories to Blackwall on 6 July 1840 crossing the company's land on three 87ft arches, one over the Commercial Road Locks, with a series of smaller arches to the east.

The new quay wall was started in July 1839 after the toll keeper's house was demolished and whilst work was suspended over the winter months owing to poor weather, it was completed in July 1840. In October John Hart's £4,320 tender was accepted for the excavation work. Three jetties and two cranes had to be moved before he could start. Much of the excavation had been completed when, on 18 July 1841, a high tide overtopped part of the clay stank that had been built round the extension, thus flooding it. The remaining work had to be undertaken by a steam dredger and was largely completed by 19 November.

In the meantime a new barge basin, which was part of the extension lying to the north of the London & Blackwall and accessed through two of the wide viaduct arches, had been opened on 22 September. The final part of the work was building a new toll office and lock house at the joint expense of the two companies, James Gerry contracting for this in October at £369.

In 1847 the London & Blackwall was planning a line from west of the dock to cross the canal on a high-level bridge north of Salmon Lane Locks and link up with the ECR at Bow. At the same time it wanted to convert to standard gauge and introduce locomotives. The Regent's, fearing that sparks from the engines could set fire to goods and shipping in the dock, petitioned and protective clauses were included in the Act. Despite this a major fire alert in February 1849 led to demands for the line alongside the dock to be roofed in. After proceedings in the House of Lords, the London & Blackwall reluctantly agreed in May to cover in the western section of its line beside the dock and, a month later, to extend this to the eastern section.

The next project to involve the canal was a line that became the Great Northern Railway (GNR) from London to York. From a terminus at King's Cross, it was to tunnel under the canal at Maiden Lane and the company petitioned to secure protective clauses in the Act. Joseph Cubitt, the GNR's engineer, submitted outline plans for an aqueduct to carry the canal over the railway in August 1848 but nothing was done. Instead, when the GNR opened to Peterborough on 7 August 1850 it was from a temporary terminus, just north of the canal.

New plans for the aqueduct were produced in February 1851 and two months later the contractor John Jay started work on the site,[3] a formal agreement between the Regent's Canal Company and the GNR was signed on 14 May 1851. Much of the clay dug from the cutting and the tunnel was barged to the Thames with sand and ballast for the works providing

The Great Northern Railway's granary warehouse and basin that opened in April 1851. The two centre arches allowed canal craft to access the main warehouse whilst those of the left and right served transit sheds, one handling incoming and the other out-going traffic.
Illustrated London News, 28 May 1853

Inside one of the Great Northern Railway's transit sheds showing goods being exchanged between railway wagons and canal craft. The scale of the drawing is suspect as the height of the building to the crossbeams was actually only 20ft.
Illustrated London News, 28 May 1853

a return cargo. The GNR was allowed to erect a temporary wooden bridge over the canal to carry earth from the site to the south that was being cleared for the terminus. The aqueduct was built in two stages. The canal was opened over the first part in October 1851[4] and over the second in March 1852. The line to the new terminus opened on 14 October 1852.

In the meantime the GNR had decided to build two canal basins, one serving a large warehouse for general traffic, the other for coal and stone. In May 1850 the canal company approved plans for the basins, both of which involved towpath bridges, and agreed a special toll for the coal traffic.

The stone and coal basin, which had two arms, was situated immediately downstream of St Pancras Lock and came into service soon after the opening of the line to Maiden Lane. The second basin, situated a further 300 yards from the lock, was probably opened at the same time, although the warehouse was not completed until April 1851. Known as the Granary this six-storey building was equipped with hydraulic lifting gear. Two branch canals from the basin led into its basement so barges could enter.[5] On each side of the Granary a goods transit shed was built, one to handle in-coming rail traffic, the other out-going traffic. Each shed was served by a further branch canal from the basin enabling railway wagons to load or unload directly to canal craft. The transit sheds incorporated extensive stabling for the GNR's delivery horses, the manure being taken away by barge.

As part of its goods yard the GNR had erected coal drops north of, but not connected to, the canal. With significant growth in the volume of coal handled, the GNR purchased land on the south side of the canal midway between the two basins and promoted a Bill to develop this land as a coal depot. This involved occupying several canal wharves and building a bridge to carry a connecting siding and, as protective clauses were at first refused, the Regent's petitioned. A settlement was reached and in January 1866 the plans for an iron bridge over the canal were approved. The GNR then erected the new coal drops in conjunction with the coal merchant and mine owner Samuel Plimsoll, and these incorporated facilities to discharge into barges.[6]

Prompted by the canal company's refusal to reduce its toll on coal, at the end of 1866 the GNR promoted a Bill to construct another siding across the canal to the Imperial Gas Works at St Pancras. Protective clauses were agreed in March 1867, plans for the

bridge were approved in August and the line opened in 1868 leading to a marked reduction, but not to the cessation, in the delivery of coal by barge to the gasworks.

One line that affected the canal, but did not cross it, was the grandly named East & West India Docks & Birmingham Junction Railway, which became the North London Railway (NLR) at the beginning of 1853. The line was incorporated in 1846 to run from the LNWR at Camden to the docks with a junction to the London & Blackwall at Bow. As the route ran largely parallel to the canal, the Regent's petitioned and received £8,000 in compensation. The line opened throughout in February 1851 prompting a plan for a transhipment basin at Camden, but no action resulted. The NLR, and its parent LNWR, was also anxious to gain more direct access to the City and promoted a line to a proposed new terminus at Broad Street. The NLR obtained its Act in 1861 and the line opened in November 1865 after a lengthy dispute with the Regent's over land needed for the canal bridge at Haggerston. Thereafter most of the LNWR's traffic to the docks was lost from the canal.

The next arrival was the Midland Railway (MR), which had had access to London since 1858 by using the GNR from Hitchin but was anxious to establish an independent route into the capital. It produced plans for a line from Bedford to a terminus at St Pancras crossing the canal 150 yards west of St Pancras Lock and secured its Act in 1863. Much of the line was still under construction when the MR opened a large goods depot just north of the canal in January 1865 accessed via the NLR and GNR. Work on this depot involved straightening and deepening a short section of the canal under plans approved in September 1863 and confirmed in a formal agreement in October 1864 that also involved an exchange of land. William Winn, one of the contractors for the depot, used his barges to carry away the earth excavated from the site.

The MR went on to build a five-storey warehouse on the south side of the canal to store ale and grain. The first ale delivery from Bass's Burton-on-Trent brewery arrived on 16 March 1865.[7] The warehouse, reached by a siding across the canal 300 yards west of the proposed main line crossing, was equipped with hydraulic hoists enabling barges lying alongside to load barrels for onward distribution.

The line from Bedford was opened across the canal, for goods traffic only, on 9 September 1867, the

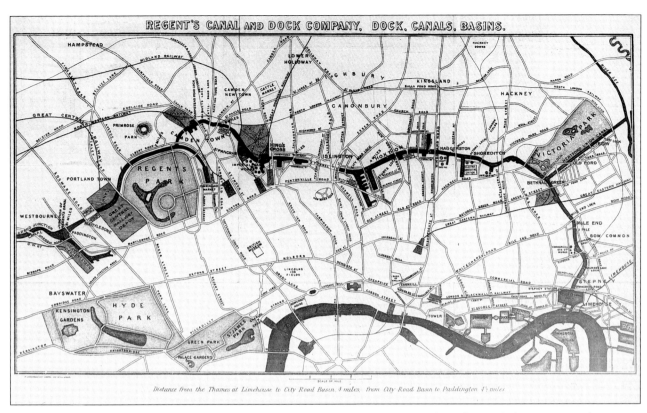

REGENT'S CANAL AND DOCK COMPANY, DOCK, CANALS, BASINS.

Distance from the Thames at Limehouse to City Road Basin, 4 miles; from City Road Basin to Paddington, 4½ miles

In 1911 the Regent's Canal & Dock Company issued a publicity booklet, which featured the various railways that crossed the canal, most of which had transhipment facilities. Regent's Canal & Dock Co booklet in the author's collection

terminus being incomplete. To prevent a steep drop down from the canal crossing to the Euston Road the station was built on arches; it opened on 1 October 1868. The area that the station and the goods depot covered had been Agar Town, a notorious slum named after William Agar who had caused the Regent's so much trouble in its early years.[8] During the works the contractors, Waring Brothers, were allowed to erect a temporary bridge across the canal and to use canal water for brick-making purposes. Much of the excavated material was barged to a dump on the Hertford Union Canal, the company giving a toll concession provided that a minimum 2,000 tons a month was carried.

The MR works included a branch leaving the main line north of the canal and tunnelling under the waterway to link with the Metropolitan Railway (MET). The line opened in July 1868. Plans for a canal basin and coal drops had been approved as early as September 1863 and, once the terminus was complete, Waring Brothers started on these and completed the work by January 1869. When water was admitted to the basin it leaked into the MET branch

tunnel below. The canal leaks were cured by lining the tunnel with engineering bricks, enabling the transhipment basin to be opened early in the autumn. The coal drops were accessed by a separate bridge over the canal. The MR's line also involved crossing the Brent reservoir at Hendon. The plans were agreed in July 1865 and the viaduct was built by Joseph Firbank.

In 1864 the Metropolitan & St Johns Wood Railway was authorised to build a line from the MET at Baker Street northwards to Swiss Cottage. This opened in April 1868 crossing the canal west of Park Road Bridge which carried the Finchley Road. Another line was promoted by the Great Eastern Railway (GER) to run from Bethnal Green northwards to Hackney Downs; it was opened in May 1872 crossing the Regent's Canal at Cambridge Heath. Neither of these two lines had a major effect on the canal.

The last main line to cross the canal was an extension into London by the Manchester, Sheffield & Lincolnshire Railway using the MET's route from Buckinghamshire and then an independent line through St Johns Wood to a new terminus at

A series of barges lie alongside the Great Central Railway's Regent's Canal Wharf near Marylebone Station in 1911. The covered wharf was equipped with hydraulic cranes enabling goods to be transhipped efficiently between railway wagons and barges. A considerable tonnage of goods was despatched by barge from this wharf to the London Docks for export.

Regent's Canal & Dock Co booklet in the author's collection

Marylebone. The company petitioned against the first Bill in February 1891 and against the second a year later, but despite this and strong local opposition an Act was obtained in 1893 for what was to become the Great Central Railway (GCR). The line was to cross the canal immediately to the west of the MET's Baker Street line bridge and the GCR planned a large goods depot just south of this crossing.

Firbank, the GCR's contractor, was allowed one-third off the normal canal toll for materials for the new line, which opened for passengers in March 1899. A temporary bridge had been erected across the canal for spoil excavated from the works but strong competition led to much of this being taken away by rail rather than in barges. The goods depot opened on 11 April and on the following day the first barge loaded using the new transhipment facilities that comprised a long covered wharf equipped with hydraulic cranes including one capable of handling up to 25 tons.[9]

Apart from its new transhipment depot, which was accessed by a separate bridge over the canal, and which was advertised as 'Regents Canal Wharf', the GCR also used canal water to supply its locomotives. In 1902 the company collaborated by agreeing a special toll to

enable the railway to capture some of the coal traffic to Kensal Green Gasworks on the Grand Junction Canal.

The importance of the Regent's Canal's route through north London was recognised at an early stage by railway promoters and the canal company was soon receiving a succession of proposals to convert the canal into a railway. The first came as early as February 1835 while in January 1836 a plan for a London & Grand Junction Railway appeared with a line from Camden to Skinner Street at Finsbury. The promoters proposed buying the canal but the company petitioned and secured several improvements in the Act. An amending Bill was promoted in the following year and was thrown out by the House of Commons and the scheme died. In 1842 the Thames Haven Dock & Railway Company planned to convert the canal from Camden Town to the Thames into a railway, but the idea was dropped.

In September 1845 a group of promoters calling themselves the London Junction Railway offered £725,000 to buy the canal's 21,418 shares at £33.17/- (£33.85) each with a view to constructing a railway on its course. The bid was rejected but an increased offer of £1,000,000 was accepted, half of

Drawing of the covered way to take the proposed railway from Paddington to Limehouse beside the canal through Regent's Park so as to cause as little disturbance as possible.

which was to be paid before the canal was taken over, and the balance within three years. A general meeting on 29 September approved the arrangement and an application was made to Parliament. The venture was now styled as the Regent's Canal Railway Company but the promoters were unable to raise the necessary £2,250,000 capital and the scheme collapsed.

In July 1846 William Radford[10] the canal company's acting engineer, was told to investigate constructing a railway along all or part of the canal as a counter to the proposed East & West India Docks & Birmingham Junction Railway. James Rendel,[11] the engineer of the neighbouring Lee Navigation, was called in to assist. The plan was for a line from the Great Western Railway at Paddington, passing under the Grand Junction, to join the Regent's Canal at Lisson Grove, intersecting with the LNWR and the proposed GNR and then continuing to Limehouse, with a branch to the West India Docks. The cost was

estimated at £685,000 and a Bill was deposited in Parliament to authorise the work.

It was realised that the passage of a railway through Regent's Park would be a sensitive issue and a model was made showing that it was proposed to achieve this in a covered way. Despite this, Her Majesty's Commissioners of Woods & Forests petitioned against the Bill and, in the face of this and other petitions and as negotiations with the LNWR had broken down, the plan was withdrawn in May 1847.

The idea did not die and the company continued to receive suggestions but no action resulted until June 1859 when a plan to convert the canal to a railway and build a branch line to the City was launched by the Central London Railway & Dock Company, which offered to pay £30 per share and to take over the company's debt. Its offer was agreed but as a safeguard a £10,000 deposit was requested. This was refused but the company still supported the approach to Parliament where there was considerable opposition on Standing Orders. This led to the Bill being withdrawn, the promoters refusing to pay the company's considerable legal expenses.

The plan re-emerged later in 1860 for a line from Kings Cross to the dock at Limehouse with a branch to the Cattle Market at Copenhagen Fields. While the company was willing to resuscitate the matter, the promoters were unable to raise the funds required and this second attempt was also abandoned.

During 1865 the company had drawn up its own contingency plans for a railway either on or beside the canal from King's Cross to Limehouse so that it would be ready should a suitable opportunity arise in the future. No further action was taken but in 1872 influential outside interests opened negotiations for a railway that would involve the canal, which would be taken over on a guaranteed fixed rental. The initial plans proved over optimistic but in October 1874 a more modest scheme emerged for a double line from the MR and GNR alongside the canal to the Thames with an enlargement of the dock. The estimate was £800,000 on top of which the promoters offered to purchase the canal for £1,080,540. A formal agreement was signed on 16 December 1874 and on 19 April 1875 an agreement was signed with the Lee Conservancy Board for a new entrance for the Limehouse Cut as the original entrance would have been affected by the proposed dock extension. Later a connection with the GER was included in the plans.

The promoters – the Regent's Canal & Dock Company – submitted a Bill to Parliament and the Regent's Canal Company petitioned against this, both in the Lords and in the Commons, to obtain the protection clauses it deemed necessary. Despite this and other petitions the Act was obtained on 11 August 1875.[12] The Act authorised raising £2,290,540 of capital but the promoters experienced difficulties in obtaining the money and tried to get the Regent's Canal shareholders to accept ordinary or loan stock in the new concern instead of the cash payments scheduled in the Act. Extensions of time were allowed but to no avail and in June 1876 the sale agreement was declared void. The promoters sought an Act for an extension of time, which the Regent's Canal Company opposed despite a part-cash part-preference stock offer and eventually a dissolution Act received the Royal Assent on 6 August 1877.[13]

In the autumn of 1880 another group of promoters led by James Forbes, the chairman of the London, Chatham & Dover Railway, opened negotiations to buy the Regent's Canal and on 2 March 1881 agreed to pay £1,170,585, this being £130 for every £100 of stock. This agreement was included in the Act establishing the Regent's Canal City & Docks Railway Company, which was passed on 18 August 1882.[14] The new company took over the canal on 31 March 1883 and the original company was then wound up (see Chapter 8).

Meanwhile, in February 1838 an important property at Limehouse owned by the London & Blackwall Railway and occupied by Charles Turner had been offered to the Regent's for £8,650. It comprised a wharf fronting onto the river to the east of the ship lock and a warehouse. The company offered £6,500, which was refused and the property went to auction and was seemingly sold for £5,500. It came up for auction again in February 1842 when the company secured it for £6,085. An attempt to obtain Customs permission to use the warehouse as a bonded store was abandoned when it was found that the building needed considerable repair; instead it was demolished and the land was used as an open wharf.

By the early 1840s, traffic was increasing to such an extent that Radford was becoming concerned about congestion at the river entrance. To overcome this he proposed a separate entrance for barges through the new river frontage with a major extension of the water space. This proposal was adopted in March 1845. Additional land would be needed, principally Richardson's timber yard, an extensive site immediately east of the dock. The Marquis of Salisbury had bought this in July 1843 and he now agreed to sell it for £25,000 in cash and £5,000 in shares. The purchase extended the company's boundary to the Limehouse Cut and included a bonding yard for timber and deals, which business the company continued. Other land was acquired from John Boulcott, Joseph Adams and the City of London.

The company arranged to borrow up to £30,000 for the new works and in July 1847 tenders were invited for the barge lock. These ranged from £25,568 to John Knight & Son's offer of £15,584, which was accepted on 18 August.[15] The work went ahead uneventfully and the new lock was opened on 30 May 1849[16]; it was 79ft long and 14ft 9in wide compared with the ship lock that was 125ft long and 31ft wide.

In this 1930s view, barges occupy both chambers of the Commercial Road locks at Limehouse, whilst another waits its turn below the lock. Note the use of hydraulically powered capstans on the central island to manoeuvre the craft to and from the chambers.

Waterways Archive,
British Waterways Archive, Gloucester

Once the barge lock was open the Knights started excavating the large dock extension to the east, most of which was on the land acquired from the Marquis of Salisbury who had become a director of the company in 1847. By March 1850 the Regent's Canal Company had found that the bonding business was not profitable and decided to close it and sell off the remaining stocks. This was completed in November and most of the site was then incorporated into the new extension.

At first the Knights' work was financed from the sale of the excavated material for brick making and other constructional purposes but this meant progress was somewhat slow. To meet the demands of the increasing trade Radford was anxious to speed up the work and tenders were invited for an accelerated programme. Seventeen offers were received ranging up to £11,560 but that of Jonas Gregson for £2,950 was accepted in October 1850. Gregson soon ran into financial problems but managed to complete his contract by the middle of 1852 when his creditors moved in to sell off his plant and equipment. The extension added nearly 4 acres to the water space. During 1850 and 1851 the company issued extra shares to finance its capital expenditure and to reduce borrowings.

With many colliers using the dock the company was interested in any means to speed up the discharging process. The first suggestion for machinery came from a trader as early as January 1832. In 1846 the dock traders started to campaign for better facilities and in December 1850 Radford was ordered to prepare plans for machinery to unload coal ships. James Rendel was consulted and supported Radford's plans,[17] and on 21 May 1851 William Armstrong of Newcastle contracted to supply a 15-ton and a 6-ton hydraulic crane, 20 coal cranes and two vibrating coal hoists for £8,700.[18] It was not until April 1852 that John Jay's tender was accepted for the hydraulic engine house on the west side of Commercial Road Lock, his contract included laying the hydraulic pipes around the dock, providing jetties for the cranes and installing the hydraulic pumping machinery provided by Armstrong.

The work made good progress spurred on by a report in August 1852 that a new 550-ton iron-hulled screw steamer had been unloaded by machinery in the West India Dock in only 18 hours. The installation was complete by the end of December but was prevented from working as water in the dock, from which the input to the hydraulic system was taken, was polluted by effluent from the Commercial Gas

Left: *The original Gloucester Avenue Bridge over the Cumberland Market Branch shown here in July 1876. The bridge was built in 1814 but in 1835 footpaths were added, one on either side of the road, being carried on the segmental brick arches, the work being supervised by James Morgan, the bridge's designer. The growth in London's road traffic meant that a much wider bridge was needed and it seems preparatory work on this is about to begin.*

Camden Local Studies Library

Below: *William Booth Scott, the Chief Surveyor of the St Pancras Vestry, drew up the design for the new Gloucester Avenue Bridge. His Royal Highness the Duke of Cambridge opened the bridge on 8 August 1878 and it still stands today, albeit the branch canal under it has been filled in.* Camden Local Studies Library

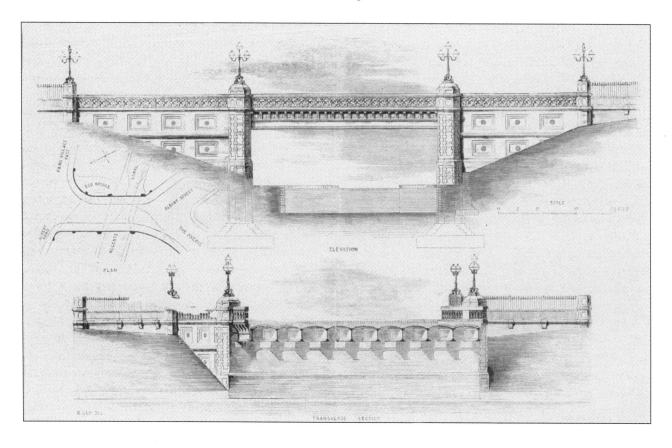

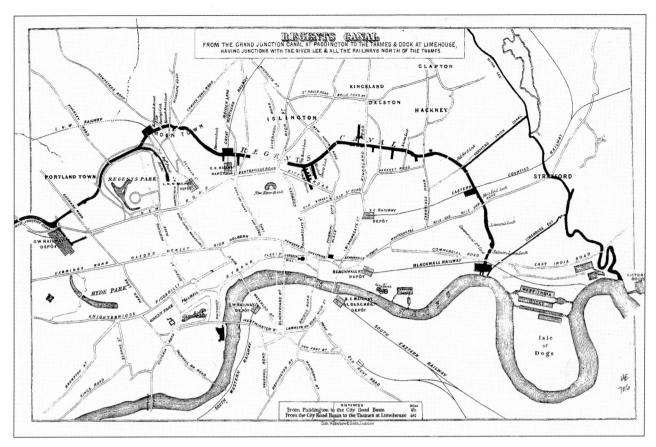

A plan of the Regent's Canal issued in 1855 to accompany a schedule of tolls and charges. This shows most of the principal basins along the canal and also shows the four railways that crossed the canal at that time.

Company. This was soon overcome and the machinery was in operation in early January 1853.

The eastward extension of the dock prompted ideas to form a link with the nearby Limehouse Cut giving access to the Lee and Stort navigations. Radford first reported in April 1846 and the River Lee Trustees supported the idea but little happened until the summer of 1850 when Radford and Rendel got together to draw up detailed plans.[19] These included a short cut from the dock to near the western end of the Island Lead Works on the Limehouse Cut and a stop lock on that cut at the Commercial Road Bridge. On 8 December 1852 an agreement between the company and the trustees was signed for the Lee Junction Cut to go ahead.

In February 1853 George Myers' £8,624 tender was accepted; it included not just the new stop lock, which became known as Britannia Lock, but also taking down and rebuilding the Commercial Road bridge over the Limehouse Cut. It appears that the new link was opened on 7 December 1853, or soon afterwards. On 1 January 1854 the company took

charge of the entrance lock on the Limehouse Cut, which was effectively made redundant by the new connection, and of the Limehouse Cut south of the new Britannia Lock.[20]

The Lee traders were unhappy with the Lee Junction agreemen. Although this allowed a certain tonnage to pass through the dock without paying toll the traders enjoyed toll-free navigation on the tidal part of the Lee. They also wanted a separate entrance to the Limehouse Cut. Matters came to a head when the company decided to seek powers to construct a large ship lock into the dock to accommodate the new steam colliers that were coming into service and were too large for the original lock. The plans included deepening and extending the water space, creating new wharves particularly on the south quay, widening the entrance to the Lee Junction Cut and closing the river entrance and lock on the Limehouse Cut.[21] In November 1863 a Bill was introduced into Parliament but the Lee traders petitioned against it. Counsel then advised the company that the 1852 agreement with the Lee

(24)

REGENT'S C

OPEN

1st November, 1855.

The Locks on the Canal admit Barges 78 Feet Long, an

N.B.—The Rates stated below are for G

The Rates for Goods in BOATS are—to Islington Tunnel 1d. per ton less—b

CANAL.

	To or from Grand Junction Canal, at Paddington, also London and North Western Railway, and			F G. J. and L. Rail the Ri (Via He Canal at Lin and T
	Any Point short of Pancras Lock.	*Beyond Pancras Lock, & short of Islington Tunnel.*	*Beyond Islington Tunnel, to Hertford Union Canal & short of the Dock at Limehouse and Thames.*	
	Per Ton.	Per Ton.	Per Ton.	Per
	s. d.	s. d.	s. d.	s.
1. Bricks, Clay, Gravel	0 5	0 6	0 6½	0
2. Coal Tar, Coke, Empty Casks, Malt Liquor, Iron, Nails .	0 6	0 9	0 9½	0
3. Cement-Stone, Chalk, Cokebreeze, Firebricks, Guano, Hay and Straw, Refuse-Ashes, Cullet, Soda and Soda Ashes, Sand, Tiles, Vegetables	0 6	0 8	0 8½	0
4. All other Articles	0 6	0 9	0 11½	0

	To or from Thames and Dock at Limehouse, and		To or from Thames & Dock at Limehouse, Hertf. Union Canal, River Lee, and any point			F the T and at Lin Hertfo C and Ri to b Eyre's & to G
	Any Point short of Mile End Lock.	*Beyond Mile End Lock, to Hertford Union, River Lee, & short of Old Ford Lock.*	*Beyond Old Ford Lock, & short of Acton's Lock.*	*Beyond Acton's Lock, & short of Islington Tunnel.*	*Beyond Islington Tunnel & short of Eyre's Tunnel.*	
	Per Ton.	Per Ton.	Per Ton.	Per Ton.	Per Ton.	Per
	s. d.	s. d.	s. d.	s. d.	s. d.	s.
1. Ballast, Sand	0 6	0 8	0 8	0 8	0 9	0
2. Bricks, Flour, Grain, Malt Liquor, Vegetables, Gas Liquor, Manganese Liquor, and Lime Water .	0 6	0 9	0 9	0 9	0 10	0
3. Cement-Stone, Chalk, Firebricks, Guano, Cullet, Iron of all sorts, Nails, Pottery-flints, Road Materials, Stone	0 6	0 10	0 11	0 11	1 1	1
4. *COALS, †Coke, Coke-breeze, Coal Tar . .	0 6	0 9	0 9	0 9	0 9	0
5. Asphalte, Cement, Cheese, Empty Sacks, Lime, Oil Cake, Slates, Tiles, Timber, Whiting, and all other Articles	0 6	0 10	1 1	1 2	1 3	1

SP

* COALS (*whether in barges or boats*) from GRAND JUNCTION CANAL, CAMDEN STATION, and GREAT NORTHERN RAILWAY, to any part of the Regent's Canal, Hertford Union Canal, River Lee, or the Thames

—— From Great Northern Railway, not towed or passing a Lock . . . .

—— (*whether in barges or boats*) from EASTERN COUNTIES RAILWAY to Hertford Union Canal, River Lee, or the Thames . . . .

———————————————————— to any point short of Islington Tunnel .

———————————————————— beyond Islington Tunnel . .

ALL ARTICLES, (*whether in barges or boats*) carried, or to be carried, on the GREAT NORTHERN RAILWAY, from or to the Hertford Union Canal, River Lee, or the Thames, or any part of the Regent's Canal . . . .

Barges to be charged for

WILCOCKSON.

This table, dated 1 November 1855, was issued by the company setting out the tolls payable on all kinds of traffic on the canal.

Author's collection

AND DOCK,

NIGHT.

not exceeding 30 *Feet Beam, can be admitted into the Dock.*

all Barges being **Towed** by the Company.

nel 1½d. per ton less—*upwards* beyond Eyre's Tunnel 2d. per ton less.

DOCK.

ssels with Cargoes of **100 Tons and upwards** are permitted to enter the **Dock** to discharge into Craft for the Canal free from the Transhipping and Docking and Undocking Charges.

ssels with Cargoes under **100 Tons** will not be allowed to enter the Dock on the above terms, except into Boats, and in special cases, at the discretion of the Dock Master.

e working time of Vessels, landing, loading, or transhipping Cargoes, is computed as follows:—

Colliers, at 49 tons	
Coasters, at 50 tons per register	
Timber loaded Ships at 30 tons, per register	per working day.
Vessels loading Scrap Iron at 10 ditto	

Police Rate of 3s. is charged on each Vessel entering the Dock.

Ships or Vessels remaining in the Dock beyond the time above specified, are charged 1d. per ton, register, per week: not less than Five Shillings to be charged.

ps, &c. notwithstanding the above regulation, to leave the Dock when required by the Dock-Master, or in default thereof to be subject to a charge of 6d. per ton, register, per day.

ps, &c. leaving the Dock with the whole or part of Cargoes, to pay 3d. per ton., and the Docking and Undocking Charges.

ges, Lighters, or other Craft, passing to or from the Canal, and remaining in the Dock more than 48 hours will be charged 1s. per day until removed.

ges loading or discharging Cargoes, to be allowed *four* working days, and will be charged One Shilling per day, for each day above four.

ges, notwithstanding the above, to leave the Dock as soon as loaded or discharged, or be charged 1s. per day until removed.

CRANAGE.

	s.	d.	
OALS, *Parties providing their own labour for filling, guiding, and tipping the tubs*	0	4	per ton.
OAD MATERIALS—Ditto. ditto.	0	2	,,
TONE—In blocks under 5 tons	0	7	,,
,, 5 tons and under 10	0	10	,,
,, 10 tons and upwards	1	3	,,
RON—In pieces under 5 tons	0	10	,,
,, 5 tons and under 10	1	1	,,
,, 10 tons and upwards	1	6	,,
IMBER, Rafting	0	3	per load.
,, Transhipping	0	3	,,
,, Landing	0	9	,,

xtra Charge for use of Cranes after 7 P.M. 1d. per Ton.

Quantities under 5 tons to be charged as 5 tons.

WHARFAGE.

	s.	d.	
All Articles remaining on Dock Wharfs, under seven days	0	3	per ton.
Seven days and above, per week	0	3	,,

TRANSHIPPING.

	s.	d.	
Coals into Craft for the Thames or River Lee	0	3	per ton.
All other Articles	0	6	,,

SHIPPING.

	s.	d.	
Iron, in scrap	1	0	,,
All other Articles for the Thames or River Lee	0	6	,,

LANDING.

	s.	d.	
Coals	0	4	,,
All other Articles	0	6	,,

DOCKING AND UNDOCKING.

hips and Vessels entering the Dock to land or load Cargoes at Wharf, under 150 tons register	15s.
Ditto ditto ditto 150 tons and upwards	21s.
ighters having Ballast on board for any Vessel	10s. 6d.
essels entering the Dock to load Manure from Craft brought down the Canal	10s. 6d.

ES.

	PER TON.
& COKEBREEZE (*whether in barges or boats*) from GAS WORKS on the Regent's Canal to any point	0s. 6d.
—— (*as back carriage*) ditto . ditto . ditto	0 4
avel from the Hertford Union Canal, River Lee, or the Thames, to any part of Regent's Canal	0 6½
ES *short* of Cowley Lock, to or from any point beyond Pancras Lock, not to be charged less than	0 6

	IN BARGES.	IN BOATS.	
ES to or from any point *beyond* Cowley Lock, not to be charged more than	9d.	6d.	
nd Breeze, and Salt, to or from any point *on the Regents Canal*	5d.	3d.	
e, Clay, do.	8d.	6d.	PER TON.
Do. (*as back carriage*) do.	4d.	3d.	
s, proceeding or returning, upon which the full Tonnage has been charged	2d.	1d.	
s loaded or unloaded in the *Waterway*, to pay, in addition	3d. Per Ton.		

(*except as back carriage*).

ROLLS BUILDINGS.

Trustees was invalid, resulting in the trustees also petitioning. This left the Marquis of Salisbury, who was now the Chairman of the Regent's Canal Company, with little option but to resign as he was also Chairman of the Trust.

A House of Lords committee then decided that a separate barge entrance should be provided for the Limehouse Cut east of the dock and that the Lee Trust should either pay part of the cost or reduce the amount that could pass the Lee Junction Cut toll free. As a result the Bill was withdrawn for the ship lock. With the 1852 agreement being deemed at an end, notice was given to charge all articles passing through the Lee Junction Cut at 5d (2p) per ton. The Trust objected, protesting that it was not responsible for the withdrawal of the Bill, but the company then

By 1864 Regent's Canal Dock had grown in size with a major extension to the north (1841) following on from the opening of the London & Blackwall Railway; a new wharf wall on the northwest quay (1841) and a new wharf wall and shed on the south quay (1843), both later equipped with hydraulic unloading machinery; the building of a new barge lock (1849) and a major extension to the east (1848–1851), a link (the Lee Junction Cut) with the Limehouse Cut (1853), and a series of jetties around the dock (from 1820). This plan also shows further extensions that were being proposed including a new ship lock to the east of the barge lock, a dock extension to the south and a further extension to the east; and a new entrance with double locks for the Limehouse Cut.

Edward Paget Tomlinson

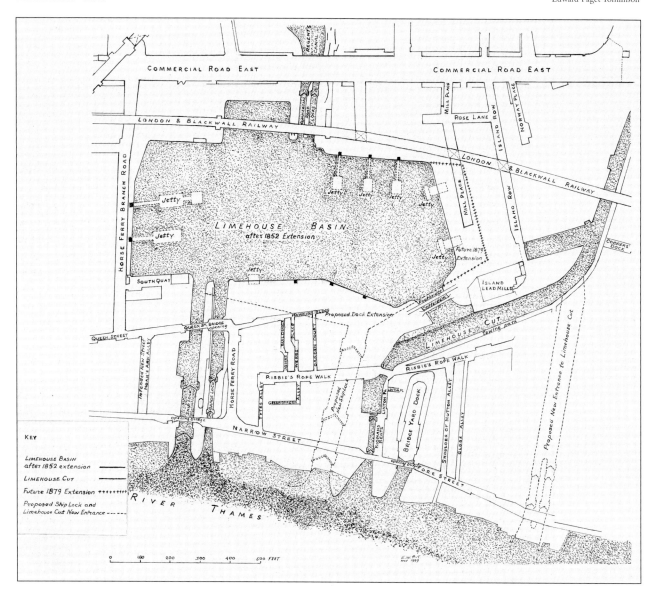

decided to sever the junction by building a cofferdam across it to prevent any loss of water and this was completed by 15 June at a cost of £359.

In October 1864 there was a meeting with the Marquis of Salisbury to try and resolve the differences and new plans were drawn up which involved not only the company's new ship lock and dock extension but a new entrance with double barge locks for the Limehouse Cut nearly 200 yards further east, new roads and a new wharf on the river.[22] With the Lee Trust agreeing not to oppose the Bill, the company decided to try again, the works being costed at £161,108. In the event the Lee Trust did petition against the Bill in February 1865 on the grounds there had been insufficient time to revise the agreement and arrange protective clauses.

To save the Bill, all the clauses relating to the new Limehouse Cut entrance were abandoned and opposition from the Limehouse District Board of Works resulted in the plans for some of the new roads also being scrapped. Amended plans were then prepared with the site of the ship lock being moved 200ft westwards, away from the Limehouse Cut. The Act then received Royal Assent in July 1865; becoming known as the Limehouse Basin Act.[23]

It was estimated that £180,000 would be needed to finance the work and the company started acquiring the land it needed around the dock such as in Mill Place, Island Row, and Narrow Street; these purchases included the Union Wharf and both the King's Arms and Crown public houses in Narrow Street. The land cost £69,257 against an estimate of £54,000.

Tenders for the works were invited in March 1867 and a £91,300 offer was accepted from Mansfield Price & Co who had been contractors to several railway companies. They were called on to start the work by 22 May but failed to do so and repudiated the contract. To prevent any delay Edwin Thomas, who had taken over from Radford as engineer in 1853, began the work by using direct labour and sub-contractors. A month later W.G. Armstrong & Co's £22,415 tender for the Narrow Street Swing Bridge, the lock gates, sluices and hydraulic machinery was accepted and on 16 October the canal company's chairman, William Parker, laid the foundation stone at the new entrance.

To provide power for the new lock and for the swing bridge it was necessary to increase the hydraulic capacity and in November 1868 work started on a new engine house in Mill Place, north of the dock. Armstrong tendered £4,474 for the steam engine and accumulator. The building work was not without incident as the owners of the neighbouring Volunteer public house in Mill Place complained that the octagonal accumulator tower and chimney adversely affected their property. This led to a protracted wrangle and eventually the company was forced to purchase the property for £3,595 in 1871.

In May 1869 William Shelbourne & Son undertook to deepen and extend the dock by dredging and on 2 August the new ship lock – 350ft long and 60ft wide – was opened by William Parker and Salisbury Baxendale, the Deputy Chairman,[24] the company having issued new shares to finance the works. Meanwhile an agreement had been reached with the Lee Trustees to sell to them for £1,350 land needed to improve the entrance to the Limehouse Cut. The Trust promoted its own Bill in 1868 to authorise the alterations.[25]

In April 1870 the river wharf east of the new ship lock was ready for use and was advertised to let – it was known as Victoria Wharf. A warehouse had been provided and, in July 1878, R. Moreland & Son contracted to erect a galvanised-iron roof over the wharf for £2,115. Soon after, a second wharf was opened on the river, west of the barge lock and across the entrance to the original ship lock; later this became known as Chinnock's Wharf.

With the new land the company had acquired there was enough room for a further increase in the dock's water space at the extreme eastern end and in July 1877 Thomas was ordered to investigate what was to be the final extension. Excavation started in February 1878 and water was let into the new space on 2 July 1879; it was less than ½ acre in extent but it increased the area of the dock to its maximum size of 10 acres.

Earlier in 1879 the Volunteer public house, along with some other property in Mill Place, was sold to the London & Blackwall Railway for £7,200 in preparation for a new east–north connection that became known as the Limehouse Curve. By now the line was operated by the GER, which asked for the roof covering the line alongside the dock to be removed. After reference to the House of Lords the covering east of the Commercial Road Locks was taken off but that to the west remained. The company's original fears were justified when on 26 July 1881 the roof of its fitters' shop was damaged by a large quantity of burning coal thrown out by one of the engines.

The opening of the new ship lock prompted a series of improvements to the facilities at the dock. In September 1869 a warehouse on the north bank of the Limehouse Cut was repaired and adapted as a granary at an estimated cost of £1,270; it was subsequently let to a tenant. Then, in January 1870 work estimated at £1,280 started on a timber-built warehouse on the newly created south quay. This became known as the Liverpool shed after the London & Liverpool Steam Shipping Company, which started to use the dock in September 1870.

Elsewhere traffic on the Hertford Union Canal continued at a very low level, seemingly confined to trade to and from Bishops Stortford. Despite continuing approaches from Duckett and his trustees the company saw little benefit in offering further concessions and in March 1848 it issued a warning notice that the canal must be maintained to its correct Parliamentary level or else its entrance would be closed off. The trustees replied saying they considered they could not continue to operate the navigation and, as the water level had not been restored, Radford put in a clay stank on 22 March closing the canal.

In May 1851 the Hertford Union was advertised for sale and Radford was asked to report on the position. He recommended against purchasing, no doubt influenced by the plans for the Lee Junction Cut. The purchase was considered again in February 1854 and rejected but in July the canal was advertised for sale by auction and this caused a change of heart. Negotiations were opened and in August the company agreed to take it over for £6,850. The money was paid over on 20 September and the company took possession and started re-instating the canal, the work costing another £1,650.

A Bill was promoted in Parliament to authorise the acquisition of the Hertford Union and this was approved in June 1855.[26] Under new owners the canal saw a change in its fortunes. New wharves were established along its banks and nearby land was acquired and let out for commercial use; all of which brought it increased traffic. Typical was the purchase of 4½ acres of land, known as Bird's Field, near the top lock for £7,750, which was then let out for brick making, but Victoria Park occupied most of the northern side of the canal.[27]

The company continued to carry out improvements to the main canal. The biggest work was the continuation of the rag-stone retaining and facing walls to protect the banks of the canal and increase its cross-sectional area. By the early 1840s most of this work had been completed. James Morgan had been unhappy about the need for some of this work and, as his advice was not heeded, he tendered his resignation in September 1835 deeming his services were no longer necessary. His resignation was accepted but he undertook to see the works at the Brent Reservoir through to their completion.

Other works on the canal included building Great Cambridge Street Bridge at Haggerston. Grissell & Peto's tender for £931 was accepted in March 1839 although the final cost came out at £1,315.[28] Another bridge needing attention was the Oblique Bridge on Agar's estate where complete re-building became necessary; Knight & Son's £1,634 tender was accepted in March 1851. At the eastern end of Regent's Park a suspension bridge designed by a Mr Dredge was erected for the Commissioners of Woods & Forests in about 1845 but it seems its foundations were inadequate, as it had to be replaced in 1864.[29]

Another development was in July 1836 when R. Woodcock & Son contracted to construct offices and a boardroom for the Regent's Canal Company on its land at City Road Basin for £580. The building was finished early in 1837 enabling the staff to move from the offices in Great Russell Street in March. The first board meeting in the new location was held on 12 April. Later, a carpenter's shop and a company store were erected nearby. The new offices followed from a review to cut expenditure and several clerks were made redundant with the move.

Assisted by the improvements carried out, particularly at the dock, traffic on the canal had increased significantly (see the table on page 89).

With this continued increase in traffic, the company was still unhappy that its water resources were adequate to cope with demand and in October 1848 it attempted to purchase at auction 37 acres of land adjoining Brent Reservoir, but its price limit was exceeded. There was a meeting at Brent Reservoir in June 1850 when Radford was asked to report on the possibility of enlarging the reservoir and in October it was decided to try and add capacity for another 5,000 locks at an estimated cost of £24,611. This was to be achieved by extending northwards along the Silk Stream and eastwards along the Dollis Brook.

James Rendel was called in to advise and supported the plans but such a major extension needed Parliamentary sanction. In December 1850 a

Regent's Canal Traffic 1854–1880

Year	Tonnage	Receipts	Expenses
1854	1,497,468	£58,283	£23,835
1856	1,419,276	£56,577	£23,473
1858	1,514,130	£58,727	£25,755
1860	1,558,990	£67,552	£34,866
1862	1,514,166	£69,657	£36,312
1864	1,706,602	£73,883	£39,629
1866	1,796,100	£77,041	£43,913
1868	1,669,319	£69,780	£36,345
1870	1,648,684 (est.)	£68,580	£32,016
1872	1,997,965	£72,287	£30,398
1874	2,095,629	£84,408	£39,667
1876	2,186,077	£88,710	£43,705
1878	2,053,368	N/A	N/A
1880	2,174,642 (est.)	£88,246	£32,690

Bill was promoted and this was passed in June 1851. The Act cost £855 and Rendel was paid £155 for his services.[30] The company then set about acquiring the land needed, the main owners being All Souls College of Oxford and St Pauls Cathedral. The works included raising the Edgware Road Bridge by 4ft together with 370 yards of the road on either side to prevent it being flooded, specific conditions being laid down as to how this was to be carried out. The Edgware Road's northern bridge needed no alteration but the Cool Oak Lane Bridge needed to be raised by 3ft. With the use of boards on the main overflow weir, it was intended to raise the water level to give 6ft of additional depth.

On 21 April 1852 John Jay's £9,937 tender was accepted for the works but almost immediately it was decided that without going beyond the limits of deviation allowed in the Act, the head bank could be

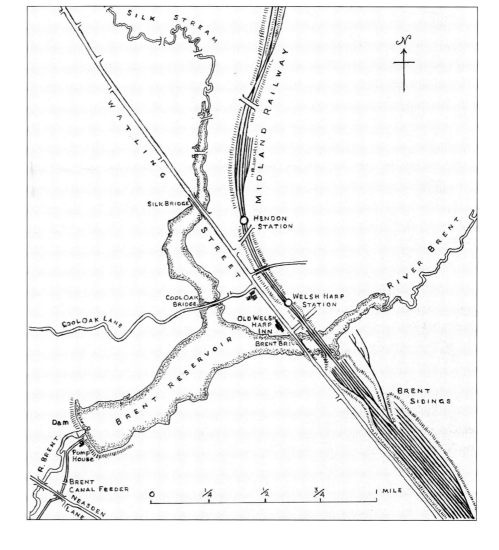

The Brent Reservoir showing it after its final enlargement in 1853 with one arm stretching northwards up the Silk Stream valley and another stretching westwards along the Dollis Brook. Welsh Harp Station on the Midland Railway opened for passengers on 2 May 1870 but closed on 1 July 1903. It handled large crowds who came to the lake, the Old Welsh Harp Inn and its associated pleasure gardens. Edward Paget-Tomlinson

Water spills over the dam of the Brent Reservoir in the 1890s. The reservoir was built on the course of the river Brent and supplied water via a 3¼-mile circuitous feeder to the Grand Junction Canal and hence to the Regent's Canal at Paddington.

London Borough of Brent, Cricklewood Library & Archive

raised still further to accommodate another 450 locks. The additional cost was some £1,700, which included the purchase of another 8 to 10 acres of land. Very wet weather during the winter delayed the work, but by the middle of 1853 the reservoir could hold another 1,000 locks and by the end of the year construction was virtually complete with capacity up to its envisaged maximum of 10,000 locks. With this extension the company felt confident enough to give up its tenancy of Aldenham Reservoir from the end of 1859.

Among property acquired in the reservoir enlargement was the freehold of the Welsh Harp Inn on the Edgware Road. It seems some alterations had to be carried out to the building before the company advertised the 'New Welsh Harp' for letting in December 1853. The first tenant proved unsatisfactory and the sheriff had to be summoned in February 1857

to evict him. His replacement was William Warner who went on to develop the inn, making it into a popular venue.[31] He held the tenancy until his death in 1889 and his widow carried on until the expiry of the lease in 1899.

In 1862 a well was sunk near the reservoir's head bank with a view to tapping local springs. A supply of four locks a day was expected, but the results were disappointing. In 1864 the company explored a 1,500-lock increase in the reservoir's capacity by the purchase of a relatively small piece of land on the banks of the Silk Stream. Another Act would be needed but investigations revealed that the land comprised a large number of individual holdings making its acquisition complicated and expensive and the idea was dropped.

The reservoir gave the company problems at times; in January 1841 part of the embankment was carried away following a rapid thaw.[32] The water caused major flooding in Southall and Brentford and several drownings, giving rise to a series of compensation claims. The breach was repaired, using eight thicknesses of brick, and in August 1842 William and Thomas Stewart's £1,695 tender for new waste weirs was accepted and the work was completed by the end of the following January. There was a similar flood in April 1878.

During a long drought in 1864, when the Regent's Canal Company was forced to buy water once again from Aldenham Reservoir and from the Grand Junction Water Works Company, the possibility of pumping water from the Thames was suggested. In October the cost of five engines and pumps to take water up to the Mile End pound was estimated at £4,800 with a further £900 for alterations and improvements to the lock houses at Salmon Lane, Johnson's and Mile End locks. Cuthbert Russell tendered £2,690 in April 1865 to provide the engines and pumps and these were installed by early in 1866. Tests showed, however, that their performance was not up to the specification. An arbitrator was appointed to settle the matter.

In July 1868 it was decided to extend the pumping up to the summit. Six pumps were hired from Easton & Amos with eight engines and another two pumps from Henry Sykes to pass the water round the eight locks involved. These solved the problem until the drought had eased and the hiring was then discontinued, although four of the pumps were purchased from Easton & Amos for £597.

The opening of the Grand Junction's Slough Branch on 19 October 1881 prompted a long-running dispute with that company about water being lost from the Long Level through leaks in the new canal.[33] Tests in 1887 showed that over the past 5½ years more than 19,000 locks had been lost, and this was after nearly 2,500 locks had been introduced by the Grand Junction in compensation. The dispute was still rumbling on in 1889 but eventually the leaks were cured and the matter was settled.

The dispute arose because the management of the water in the Long Level continued to be a very sensitive matter between the two companies. Under an agreement made in January 1869 either side could enter into arrangements to supply water to third parties. The agreement laid down minimum charges, provisions for metering and that the proceeds should be divided, 25% being paid to the other company. As a result both sides maintained a very close watch on water levels and the supply position, as it was crucial to both canals.

To fund the developments at Brent Reservoir and at Limehouse Dock the Regent's adopted a mixture of short-term loans, often from insurance companies, and additional share capital. Between 1850 and 1851 5,600 shares were issued at £16 producing £89,600 while from 1865 to 1868 9,000 shares were issued at £20 producing £180,000. This brought the total

Mile End Lock with its lock keeper's cottage was always an important location for the Gardner family who were leading barge traders on the canal and later amalgamated with Charringtons.

Author – 30 May 1984

number of shares issued for various amounts to 36,018 but to simplify matters these shares, with a nominal value of £25 each, were converted into £900,450 of stock in 1874.

The dividend was maintained at a steady but modest rate reaching a peak of 29/- (£1.45) per share in 1866. From 1874 the dividend had to be expressed as a percentage of £100 of stock and this peaked at 5% in 1882.

In March 1842 the Earl of Macclesfield, who had been the Regent's Canal Company's chairman since 1816, died. John Elliott Drinkwater Bethune, Colonel John Drinkwater's son, succeeded him but had to resign in February 1848 on his appointment to the legislature of the Supreme Court in India. The Marquis of Salisbury was approached and agreed to join the board and take over the chairmanship and he served until the disagreement with the Lee Trustees forced his resignation. William Parker, the Deputy Chairman, then took over in May 1864 until his resignation in April 1877 after serving on the board for 36 years. His deputy, William Richard Bingley, succeeded him and remained in the chair until the end of March 1883. Colonel Drinkwater resigned as deputy chairman in June 1836, remaining actively involved until the end. He died in June 1844 near Leatherhead.

On the administrative side, clerk and secretary Edmund Snee died on 25 October 1864 after an unrivalled 52 years service and the company awarded a £120 annuity to his two unmarried sisters. Snee's son, Frederick, had retired on health grounds in July 1862 after 45 years service. On 2 November 1864 John Frederick Abbott, who had joined the office staff in January 1862, was apppointed to replace Snee as clerk and secretary on a £500 salary. Another long-serving officer was James Lyon who had acted as the company's clerk and solicitor since 1812. He resigned in June 1856 and Keith Barnes, a partner in the firm of Lyon Barnes & Collis took over the legal work and Edmund Snee was appointed the company's clerk.

After James Morgan resigned in 1835,[34] it seems the company managed without a full-time engineer until William Anderson was appointed in January 1841. He suffered from poor health and effectively acted as a consultant to the company until his death in March 1844. In June 1841 William Radford was appointed superintendent of works at £250 and served until resigning in the autumn of 1853. His replacement was Edwin Thomas who was appointed engineer in November and who went on to serve the canal for almost 44 years.

At the dock, James Ruse had to resign in August 1821 due to ill health and was replaced by Matthew Bowles who served until April 1830 when he too had to give up for health reasons. His assistant, David Lewis, then took over as Dock Master but he died at the end of 1840 and James Wells took the position from 1 January 1841. Wells lasted only 16 months as he was in poor health. John Bigg, his assistant, took over in April 1842 until his death in 1859. John Chambers became Dock Master in October but was dismissed in July 1863 when Henry Braine was appointed on a salary of £210.

CHAPTER EIGHT

TOWARDS THE GRAND UNION

From the 31 March 1883 a new era opened for the canal. Under its Act, the Regent's Canal City & Docks Railway Company could raise £8,100,000 in £10 shares and borrow up to £2,700,000. The Act set out 12 separate sections of railway line starting from the Great Western at Paddington and running alongside or close to the canal, crossing Kingsland Basin to reach Old Ford and then running alongside part of the Hertford Union Canal before branching off to the Royal Albert and Victoria docks. There were connections to both the Midland and the Great Northern railways and a branch from Islington to Cripplegate.

Like its predecessors, the new company experienced difficulties in raising the considerable sums of money needed and a series of Acts followed modifying its plans. In August 1883 the canal became a separate undertaking with a capital of £1,500,000,[1] while the expensive branch to Cripplegate became a separate City Lines undertaking.[2] In July 1885 powers were given to establish further separate railway undertakings and to pay interest on capital.[3] In May 1887 an extension of time to build the lines was granted,[4] with a further extension in August 1890.[5] In June 1892 plans for the City Lines were abandoned, further time was allowed for the rest and the company was renamed the North Metropolitan Railway & Canal Company with its railway capital reduced to £4,291,800.[6]

The seal of the Regent's Canal City & Docks Railway Company, which was established in 1882 with ambitious plans to build a series of railways linking in with the canal. It took over the canal from the original 1812 company on 1 April 1883.

The Waterways Archive, British Waterways Archive, Gloucester

On 27 June 1892 the Regent's Canal City & Docks Railway Company changed its name to The North Metropolitan Railway & Canal Company and it continued to operate the canal until 1900.

The Waterways Archive, British Waterways Archive, Gloucester

Finally in July 1900, by which time the powers for the remaining railways had lapsed, a further Act renamed the company The Regent's Canal & Dock Company and allowed three debentures to be consolidated into one stock.[7] The company's railway aspirations were finally at an end.

Some involvement with other railways remained, not least the spread of underground lines through the capital. The first was the City & South London Railway, a section of which opened in November 1901 passing under City Road Basin close to the City Road Bridge.[8] In June 1899 the company agreed a special toll for 120,000 tons of spoil carried from the excavations to the river Lee and also for 15,000 tons of iron segments for lining the tunnel. Special staging was erected in the basin to handle these traffics. The railway, now part of London Underground's Northern Line, was charged an easement of £250 for passing under the basin.

In June 1902 the Whitechapel & Bow Railway, now part of the District Line, opened passing under the canal at Mile End and paying a £400 easement for the two tunnels involved. The Great Northern & City Railway opened under the canal at the New North Road Bridge at Hoxton in February 1904; during its construction a special toll was agreed for 70,000 tons of spoil removed from the tunnel. The railway erected an electricity generating station nearby that was

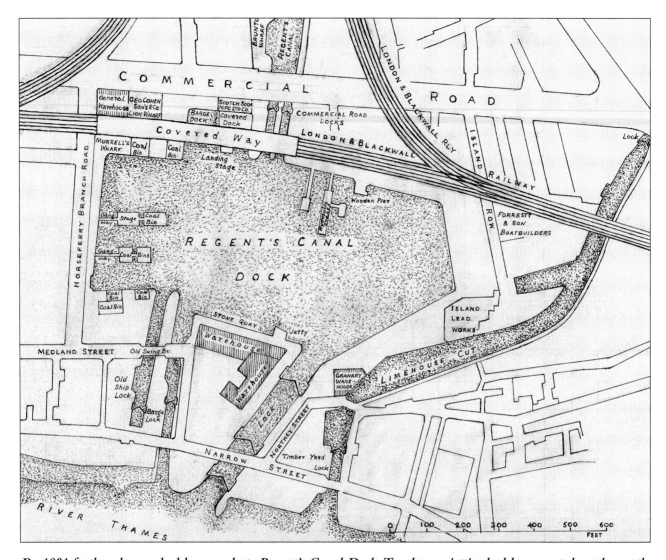

By 1891 further changes had been made to Regent's Canal Dock. Two longer jetties had been erected on the north quay (one in 1878); the London & Blackwall Railway's Limehouse Curve had opened (1880), the southern (1869) and eastern (1878) dock extensions had been completed; the new ship lock had been opened (1869); the Granary Warehouse had been developed in the southeast corner (1869), the Liverpool Warehouse had been erected on the south quay (1870); the New Warehouse had been built beside the ship lock together with a small jetty on the south quay (1884); the river entrance to the old ship lock had been closed off and jetties had been erected on the west side equipped with hydraulic unloading machinery (1870). Edward Paget-Tomlinson

supplied with condensing water from the canal and with coal brought in barges. For a time it was part of the Northern Line.

The Great Northern, Piccadilly & Brompton Railway, now the Piccadilly line, opened in December 1906 passing 64ft under the canal in two steel tubes just west of Maiden Lane Bridge and the Charing Cross, Euston & Highgate Railway, now the Northern Line, opened in June 1907 passing 27ft under the canal in two tunnels at Kentish Town

Bridge; special tolls had been agreed for the spoil and for bringing in the segmental lining plates. Then, in January 1915, the Baker Street & Waterloo Railway, which became known as the Bakerloo Line, was extended to Kilburn passing under the canal at Warwick Avenue and paying £234 for an easement for the twin tunnels.

While these underground lines had little effect on canal traffic, the company maintained close links with those main line companies with which it was

St Pancras Locks and the Great Northern Railway's Kings Cross Goods Depot in 1911. The railway had two links to the canal; this one originally served a stone and coal depot and was opened in December 1850. The bridge carrying the towpath over the entrance still stands today. Regent's Canal & Dock Co booklet in the author's collection

connected. In July 1911 it issued an illustrated publicity booklet entitled *The Regent's Canal & Dock Co*, which outlined the dock facilities that could be provided at Limehouse and the transhipment facilities that existed at Marylebone with the Great Central Railway, at Camden Town with the London & North Western, at St Pancras with the Midland, at King's Cross with the Great Northern and at Devonshire Street with the Great Eastern.

One place where transhipment was not possible was with the former London & Blackwall Railway at Limehouse. In April 1850 the Central Gas Company had proposed a siding at Limehouse to enable coals to be raised from ships in the dock into railway wagons for taking to its works. The Great Eastern Railway leased the London & Blackwall from the beginning of 1866 and was interested in pursuing the

idea for a connection, submitting two proposals in September 1870 but nothing was agreed.

In October 1921 the canal company looked at the possibility of providing sidings, either at high-level by extending the viaduct or at low-level with a lift up to the railway, as part of a project to improve the north quay of the dock but it was deterred by the expense. The Great Eastern's successor, the London & North Eastern Railway, was still trying to achieve a connection at Limehouse in August 1928 when it suggested a loading dock projecting from the parapet of the viaduct on which a crane could be mounted to discharge from ships straight into wagons. The once-intensive passenger traffic to Blackwall had been withdrawn in May 1926 and the line was now confined to goods traffic, but still no action was taken.

Elsewhere in Limehouse Dock a rolling

The coal-unloading jetty on the west quay of Regent's Canal Dock in 1911. Regent's Canal & Dock Co booklet in the author's collection

programme of improvements continued. In July 1884 Whitford & Company contracted to erect a corrugated-iron shed on the south quay at the east end of the Liverpool shed for £1,750. It was known as the New Warehouse, was served by a small jetty and equipped with a hydraulic crane provided by Sir W. G. Armstrong & Co. Then in November 1889 Whitfords agreed to add a corrugated-iron extension to the Liverpool shed for £945. Both the Liverpool and the New warehouses were occupied by the London & Liverpool Steam Shipping Company until it stopped using the dock in October 1894, as the Regent's was unable to provide it with additional facilities that it needed.

Another development was the erection of a new jetty in the southwest corner of the dock to cope with an anticipated large increase in the gasworks coal traffic. John Mowlem & Co agreed to construct the new jetty in July 1891 for £3,200 and Sir W. G. Armstrong Mitchell & Co agreed to provide hydraulic cranes for £2,480.

In June 1894 John Wolfe Barry, an eminent engineer, reported on the condition of the dock and suggested a series of improvements within the company's existing boundaries. These involved:

reconstructing 400ft of the north quay which was settling forward into the dock,
underpinning, strengthening and paving 225ft of the east and 400ft of the southeast quays,
extensive dredging to give 28ft depth at high water of ordinary spring tides,

building a new transhipment jetty in the northeast corner,
replacing the old Medland Street Swing Bridge with a fixed structure, and rebuilding Salmon Lane Bridge and widening the canal there.

At the same time a new pumping station was to be sited in the old ship lock to draw water from the Thames with a series of pumps and pipelines to supply the upper levels of the canal.

The enabling Act was passed in August 1896,[9] and on 23 March 1897 Henry Lovatt's tenders of £70,412 for the dock improvements and £8,392 for the pumping station were accepted. Shortly after, the larger of the two hydraulic engines on the north quay failed and, as the smaller one could not cope, a temporary supply had to be taken from the London Hydraulic Power Co Ltd. Wolfe Barry was called in and recommended setting up new plant in the old ship lock alongside the new pumping station at an estimated cost of £19,000 and then moving the existing plant there from the north quay. In June 1897 Armstrongs' £11,750 tender for the two steam pumping engines with two accumulators in a steel-framed house was accepted while Tangyes Ltd of Birmingham contracted to supply two boilers for £1,064.

Work on the improvements went ahead uneventfully; the new bridges at Salmon Lane and Medland Street were opened early in May 1899 and the Chairman, James Staats Forbes, ceremoniously laid the final coping stone for the quay refurbishments on 20 June. The new coaling jetty was brought into use on 8 November but it was not until the end of February 1900 that Wolfe Barry was able to report that the dredging and other improvements were complete. In March the new hydraulic plant became operational but soon after it was decided not to move the old engine from the north quay, as it would cost £5,000. Instead it was retained for emergencies.

The number of ships using the dock was substantial. Coal was the largest traffic although tonnages fluctuated somewhat, particularly after the opening in

1870 of a large gasworks alongside the river Thames at Beckton.[10]

Year	Ships	Dock tonnage	Canal tonnage	Total tonnage	Dock revenue
1890	1,112	781,822	992,187	1,774,009	£17,947
1892	1,156	818,397	1,149,991	1,968,388	£22,915
1894	1,149	836,779	1,020,726	1,857,505	£21,394
1896	1,122	810,576	1,124,178	1,934,754	£21,063
1898	955	794,572	1,041,506	1,836,078	£19,846

Regent's Canal Dock in 1911. Changes since 1891 include the northwest quay being developed with a new warehouse (1905); two of the small jetties on the north quay had been removed (1898) to be replaced by a long jetty in the northeast corner (1899); the Alexandra Warehouse had been built on the east quay (1905); the old Granary Warehouse in the southeast corner had been demolished (1897) with the Edward Warehouse erected partly on its site (1902); the Liverpool Warehouse on the south quay had been partly destroyed in a fire (1910) but a further warehouse had been built beside the ship lock; part of the old ship lock had been filled in to house a pumping station (1898); one of the jetties on the west quay had been removed (1905) and the other had been rebuilt (1892).

Edward Paget-Tomlinson

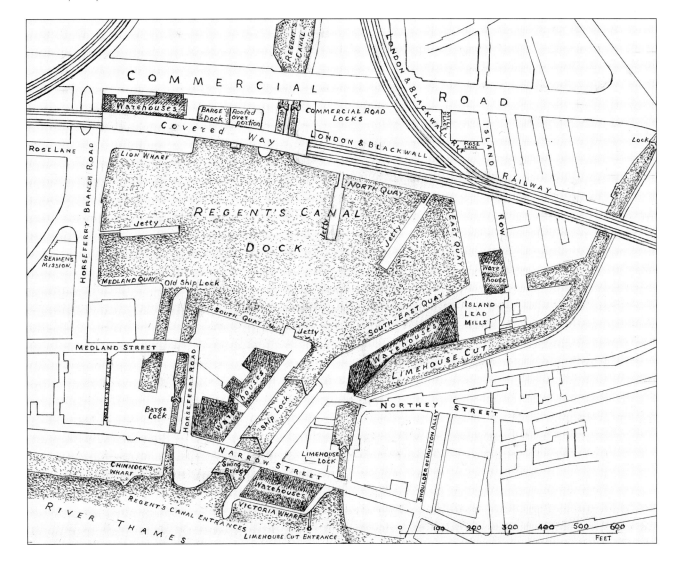

Canal craft alongside the Bergen Wharf in Regent's Canal Dock in 1938. Waterways Archive, British Waterways Archive, Gloucester

In April 1898 the Lee Granary on the southeast quay was demolished as it was in poor condition. In the space created a new single-storey brick warehouse roofed with sheet copper was erected, Watts Johnson & Co's £6,157 tender being accepted in February 1902. The building, which was in three sections and extended to the south side of the Island Lead Mills, was completed on 14 October and named the Edward Warehouse after King Edward VII. In December 1903 Sheffield Brothers' £2,595 tender was accepted to build a new warehouse on the nearby east quay and immediately to the north of the lead mills. This was another single-storey brick building that was completed on 2 May 1904 and named the Alexandra Warehouse after Edward VII's queen.

Up to the First World War there was few other developments and during the war little was possible, although Rees & Kirby's tender to erect a new warehouse on the south quay for £2,552 was accepted in November 1914. This was known as the West shed and Armstrongs supplied two one-ton mobile cranes for it at £1,300. The ending of the war, however, prompted thoughts of further improvements, particularly on the southwest and west quays. Sir Robert Elliott Cooper was called in to advise and drew up plans for a large warehouse backing onto Medland Street and another onto the Horseferry Branch Road. Space had been created for these as the company had closed and dismantled the coal jetty in the southwest corner in 1919; its cranes being unable to work fast

enough to attract the steamers. The jetty's revenue had fallen from £1,424 in 1914 to £595 in 1918.

In July 1920 tenders submitted jointly by Sir W. G. Armstrong Whitworth & Co Ltd and Armstrong & Main Ltd of £13,992 for the Medland building and £27,815 for the Horseferry building were accepted.[11] The British & Netherlands Wharf Co Ltd agreed to take the Medland Wharf for its Dutch and German steamer services in August while Bergenske (London) Ltd., a subsidiary of the Bergenske Steamship Company, agreed to take the Horseferry Wharf for its Scandinavian traffic and for fruit and vegetables from Spain. The wharf was thereafter known as Bergen Wharf.

The two-storey steel-framed corrugated iron Medland Warehouse had a narrow quay alongside the barge entrance and a 12ft open quay fronting onto the dock. The Bergen Warehouse was of similar construction but was built on a 230ft by 54ft concrete raft that projected over the water where it was supported on concrete piles; it had a 20ft open quay.

Apart from the building, the Regent's undertook to equip the Medland Wharf with machinery such as two 2-ton electric travelling cranes from Armstrongs at £4,780 each, but the Bergenske company equipped its own wharf, albeit working in liaison with the canal company. Construction took much longer than expected; Bergen Wharf was not completed until 21 August 1922 and Medland Wharf on 23 October. Both also cost considerably more than the estimate,

The Regent's Discharging Company's mechanised jetty in the northeast corner of Regent's Canal Dock, shown here in 1938.

Waterways Archive, British Waterways Archive, Gloucester

partly due to extra facilities provided – the Medland building cost £21,023 but with the equipment the total was £71,144. The Bergen building cost £35,285 with a further £42,000 spent on equipment by the Scandinavian concern.

These developments strained the Regent's Canal & Dock Company's finances despite the generous credit terms allowed by Armstrongs, and to try and overcome this, the Regent's Dock Development Co Ltd was registered in December 1921. The intention was for it to carry out the work the company was authorised to do but did not have the funds to carry out. Under a post-war measure the Treasury was prepared to issue guarantees through a Trades Facilities Advisory Committee to enable capital projects to go ahead. The new company initially sought a £40,000 guarantee to extend the northwest quay at an estimated cost of £26,216, to do the same for Chinnocks Wharf at £6,032 and some other smaller works. The Trade Facilities Advisory Committee queried the application claiming that the 1896 Act did

not cover the works proposed and, on the objection being sustained, the request had to be withdrawn.

With the expectation of increased traffic from the new wharves and from increased traffic at the north quay there were problems at times with coal barges causing congestion in the dock and with the dust produced during discharge from colliers. Added to this, the northeast jetty was getting into a poor state and revenue was falling due to competition.

Year	Tons handled	Revenue	Rate charged
1919	205,179	£6,762	1d to 8d per ton
1920	239,556	£10,480	8d to 1/– per ton
1921	227,056	£10,600	10½d to 1/– per ton
1922 (10 months)	157,349	£5,901	9d per ton

As a result, the company gave notice that the jetty would close on 31 March 1923 and be dismantled. The main users were Charrington Gardner Locket & Co Ltd on behalf of the Chartered Gas Light & Coke

An aerial view of the Regent's Canal Dock in its heyday in 1938 showing a cluster of ships and canal craft occupying the water space. Waterways Archive, British Waterways Archive, Gloucester

Company and their response was to form the Regent's Discharging Co Ltd as a joint venture between the two to erect and equip a new jetty alongside the old one.[12] A nominal rent was agreed but construction did not begin until 1 April 1925. By the middle of December work was sufficiently advanced for the Regent's Canal & Dock Company to invite tenders to demolish the old jetty and John Shelbourne & Co's £663 offer was accepted. The new jetty was completed early in 1926 and Shelbournes completed the removal of the old structure on 24 March, well ahead of schedule and thus earning themselves a £50 bonus. The main destination for the coal transhipped at the new jetty was to the Kensal Green gasworks on the Grand Junction Canal just west of Paddington.

In September 1918 the company had authorised a start being made on filling in the barge basin under the railway arches and to the north of the railway line, this being a prelude to building a new wall from the northwest quay to the Commercial Road Locks. With the shortage of money, the project had to be deferred but in December 1924 Armstrongs agreed ten-year credit terms to cover the estimated cost and this enabled the work to start. It could not be hurried as access was still needed to the premises of a tenant of part of the barge basin and a 30ft gap had to be left in the new wall. When the lease expired at the end of June 1926 the gap was closed off, the quay wall completed and the last part of the barge basin filled in, Armstrongs' work costing £13,518.

Another project was to make the channel to the former barge lock into a lay-by. In April 1924 Armstrongs contracted to build a wall across the lock's river entrance on a day-work basis as it involved fitting in with the tides – the estimated cost was £3,656. This would also allow an extension to be made to Chinnocks Wharf. Armstrongs also contracted to build a wall across the head of the barge lock and raise the wall around the lay-by. In July 1928 it was decided that the lay-by should be roofed in to protect the company's craft and tugs that were moored there. A suitable structure was ordered but then the plans were changed and it was erected elsewhere.

With the opening of the Chartered Gas Light & Coke Company's large new gasworks at Beckton there was a reduction in demand on the older works and they were gradually closed down. For instance,

A crowded scene showing a large number of loaded barges, many carrying small power station coal, in Regent's Canal Dock awaiting dispersal.
Waterways Archive,
British Waterways Archive, Gloucester

the Independent Company's old works at Haggerston were closed in 1900 and the Imperial Company's old works at St Pancras followed in 1907.[13] The Commercial Gas Company at Stepney ceased using barges to lighter its coal up from the dock in 1912, bringing it instead by steam wagons from its riverside Wapping works.[14] The loss of the gasworks coal traffic, however, was largely made good by the erection of a series of electricity generating stations on the banks of the canal. Not only did they use barges to bring in coal but they also made use of canal water for condensing purposes, providing the company with an additional source of income.

The first project was by the County of London & Brush Provincial Electric Lighting Company, which agreed to take land on the west side of the City Road Basin just north of the City Road in May 1894 and went on to develop a generating station there. It used water from the basin for condensing but in 1906 this led to problems for the nearby London Hydraulic Power Co Ltd, which was unable to take its full supply from the basin as the water temperature was too high. Eventually, what was now the County of London

Electric Supply Company arranged to discharge into the nearby Wenlock Basin.

The Borough of St Pancras was next, building an electricity generating station beside the canal and entering into a water agreement in May 1898. Shoreditch Borough followed with an electric lighting station at Whitson Street, alongside Haggerston Basin. The council had applied for land from the company in April 1899 and entered into a water agreement in January 1901. In 1911 a major extension was planned but it was not carried out until after the First World War; it was completed in 1922.

In February 1899 the company agreed that the Central Electric Supply Co Ltd could build a basin into its proposed works at Grove Road, St Johns Wood but it is not certain if it had been built when the generating station opened in 1902; the company became part of the London Power Co Ltd in 1926. In 1904 the Great Northern & City Railway's generating station opened at Hoxton while in 1906 St Marylebone Borough's generating station opened on the opposite side of the canal to the Grove Road undertaking.

Despite the changes, traffic remained healthy:

Regent's Canal Traffic 1888–1905

Year	Canal tonnage	Dock tonnage	Canal dues	Dock dues	Rents &c	Total receipts	Expenses
1888	1,009,451	663,508	£41,095	£17,946	£14,205	£73,246	£27,425
1898	1,041,506	794,572	£44,921	£19,846	£20,225	£84,992	£40,973
1905	1,045,184	N/A	£40,502	£22,089	£29,471	£92,062	£38,605

St Marylebone Borough Council established its electricity generating station beside the canal in 1906 and it was served by canal craft delivering coal and taking away the ash. Here two wide boats operated by H. Sabey & Co Ltd of Paddington are involved in loading ash whilst ahead a pair of narrow boats can just be seen, which had probably delivered a load of coal from the Warwickshire coalfield. The canal also served the vital function of supplying cooling water, providing a useful source of revenue as most of the water was returned to the canal, albeit somewhat warmer than when it was taken. The Waterways Archive, British Waterways Archive, Gloucester

The First World War had an adverse affect on the figures and by 1923 the canal tonnage had fallen to 595,556 before recovering slightly to 706,926 tons in 1924 and 732,862 tons in 1927. Traffic handled in 1924 included 291,921 tons of coal and coke, 86,924 tons of timber, 46,679 tons of gas liquor and coal tar, 42,281 tons of oils, 35,667 tons of bricks, stone, cement and marble and 31,867 tons of strawboard.

Soon after the 1892 Act was passed a long-running dispute began with solicitors Higginson & Vigers over their professional charges in promoting and obtaining the Act incorporating the company. After many delays an action brought by the solicitors, who were shown in the accounts to be owed £10,342, was heard before Mr Justice Charles on 16 June 1894

and he gave judgement for the plaintiffs. The company appealed and on 28 November 1894 the Lords Justices of Appeal unanimously reversed the previous judgement. The solicitors then appealed to the House of Lords but on 18 May 1896 the appeal judgement was upheld.

Another problem arose as several of the bridges over the canal were proving to be too weak and too narrow for the demands of the increasing road traffic. As early as 1864 Islington Vestry wanted the Caledonian Road Bridge widened and it carried out the work in 1868 and the Regent's Canal Company widened the canal as part of the scheme. In the 1890s there were a series of demands from London County Council for bridges to be rebuilt, such as those at the

Rosemary Branch and at Acton's Lock, but the company argued that it was not liable to do this, as the bridges had not been designed for the weight and volume of modern traffic. Usually it agreed to make a contribution to the work providing that it was relieved of future maintenance, but sometimes it donated the extra land needed instead. The spread of tramways only aggravated the problem, for instance in 1908 the company agreed to the London County Council replacing the brick arch of Camden Road Bridge with girders as part of a tramway electrification project. Other weak bridges had to be protected by weight-restriction notices, such as in 1921 when the company had to forbid the London General Omnibus Company from using Park Road Bridge. Marylebone Borough Council rebuilt the bridge in 1928 with the company paying £500 towards the cost.

In March 1895 Edwin Thomas reported that the pumping installations at Mile End, Johnson's, Salmon Lane and Commercial Road locks needed repairs. A decision was deferred but Wolfe Barry was called in to review the company's water resources. He reported in July 1896 that it would be uneconomic to enlarge Brent reservoir; instead he recommended installing new equipment with two centrifugal pumps at Limehouse pumping up to the Mile End pound through a 1,700-yards long 33in diameter pipeline and with new permanent pumps being installed at City Road, St Pancras, Kentish Town, Hawley's and Hampstead Road locks. On 10 November, Tangyes agreed to provide the pumping equipment and pipeline for £18,330, sub-contracting the laying of the pipeline to John Aird & Sons for £825. All the work was to be completed by 15 April 1898.

In February 1897 the plan was amended with the Kentish Town installation pumping past Hawley's and Hampstead Road locks through a 280-yard long 24in diameter pipeline. Tangyes agreed to this alteration to their contract for an additional £1,820, but £500 would be saved on the buildings and annual operating costs would be lower. On 23 March 1897 Henry Lovatt's

£8,392 tender for the Limehouse pumping station building was accepted as was his £3,003 tender for the engine houses at City Road, St Pancras and Kentish Town on 7 September. The need for action was highlighted in December when a series of portable pumps again had to be brought in due to a serious water shortage.

The City Road engine, where it seems the earlier temporary plant was retained, started pumping on 30 December 1897. A month later the main pipeline to Mile End was almost complete and in March 1898 Tangyes were able to carry out a full steam trial of the main machinery in Birmingham prior to its installation at Limehouse. The St Pancras engine started pumping in April and that at Kentish Town on 4 May while three days later the high duty pumps from Limehouse began working to Mile End and the low duty pumps, drawing from the Thames, started shortly afterwards.[15] This introduced saline water into the canal, which caused problems for some users such as the London Hydraulic Power Company who had to seek alternative sources at times.

In September 1898 it was found necessary to provide duplicate portable engines at Old Ford, Acton's and Sturt's locks prompting a suggestion for permanent plant at all three locations. In November 1898 the company decided to install permanent plant at Old Ford, pumping round Old Ford and Acton's locks via a 1,550-yard pipeline, and also at Sturt's pumping via a 675-yard pipeline round Sturt's and City Road locks.

On 10 January 1899 Tangyes contracted to provide the necessary machinery for £7,840 and on 7 February Lovatt's £5,060 tender for the two pumping station buildings and his £9,000 tender for the pipelines were accepted. Work on both was virtually complete by September when Old Ford was expected to start pumping at the end of October and Sturt's a month later. Pressure of work at Tangyes, however, led to delays but both new pumps were ready by 1 March 1900.

One of the powers given under the 1900 Act was to consolidate the existing

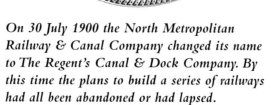

On 30 July 1900 the North Metropolitan Railway & Canal Company changed its name to The Regent's Canal & Dock Company. By this time the plans to build a series of railways had all been abandoned or had lapsed.

The Waterways Archive, British Waterways Archive, Gloucester

A well-laden timber barge entering one of the twin City Road Locks in 1938. The City Road pumping station, by then redundant, is shown behind.

The Waterways Archive, British Waterways Archive, Gloucester

debenture stocks. The original company had first issued debentures in 1874 to refinance existing mortgages and loans with £60,685 at 4% and £200,000 at 4¼% being outstanding when the new company took over in 1883, much having been incurred to fund the on-going programme of improvements at the dock. In 1896 a new 3% debenture began to be issued and by 1900 £113,900 at 3%, £101,852 at 4% and £200,000 at 4¼% was outstanding, making £415,752 in all. Under the new Act these were consolidated into £533,036 stock at 3% with £33,951 of extra stock being issued to the holders of the 4% stock and £83,333 to the holders of the 4¼% stock so that they did not lose any interest, the overall charge to the company being unaltered.

The new company's original capital had been £1,275,000 but in 1893 a further £83,100 was issued to meet the costs of the series of applications to Parliament, bringing the total to £1,358,100. The

shareholders continued to receive a regular dividend except between 1915 and 1917 when traffic was seriously disrupted due to the war. Initially this dividend was at 4% and was effectively an interest payment but as the railway plans failed it soon reverted to the more normal payment based on the canal's profits. The highest dividend was 3% in 1892 but this gradually declined up to the war and only started to recover in the 1920s.

The outbreak of the First World War on 28 July 1914 had little immediate effect on the Regent's Canal but all new capital expenditure was deferred and the company agreed to pay dependants one-half of the normal wages of all those called up. After a while, however, the war started to force up costs and war bonuses had to be paid to employees to boost their earnings. Trading patterns were also disrupted, both in the dock and on the canal, leading to a loss of traffic, which caused a drop in profits and the cessation in the payment of dividends from the second half of 1915. Despite this a request from the Chancellor of the Exchequer to support the issue of 5% War Loan to meet the costs of the hostilities led to the company investing £5,000 in stock and starting a savings scheme for its employees.

One decision taken early in the war was to allow sea planes to be tested on the waters of Brent Reservoir and in July 1917 the testing of machine guns was also allowed there. Less drastic, was agreeing to allow men serving with 20 Squadron Armoured Cars based at Dollis Hill to bathe in the reservoir but the company laid down strict conditions as to their conduct.

On 1 March 1917, and under the powers of the 1914 Defence of the Realm Regulations, the canal came under the control of the Board of Trade's Canal Control Committee. Under this arrangement compensation was to be paid for the loss of profits and in January 1918 the company's gross revenue to 31 December 1913, the last full year before the war started, was agreed with the committee at £80,930, expenses at £39,012 giving a net profit of £41,918.[16]

For the ten months to 31 December 1917 receipts fell to £57,381 while expenses were £40,239 and compensation of £18,000 was paid enabling payment of a small dividend to be resumed. In 1918 revenue was £66,514, expenses £52,989 and compensation £28,393 while in 1919 £25,097 was received and in the eight months to 31 August 1920, when government control came to an end, compensation was £13,501.[17] The Canal Control Committee monitored all the outgoings very carefully, having to sanction any increases in wages and war bonuses and it also disallowed any increase in canal tolls, but dock dues were increased regularly in line with those of the Port of London Authority.

In March 1918 the War Office Salvage Department issued notices to requisition some of the railway arches and open space on the north quay, one of the warehouses on the south quay and the Edward Warehouse on the east quay. The intention was to bring in waste material from the war and distribute it throughout the country by canal. This duly took place but with the ending of the war on 11 November 1918 the War Office was able to scale down its activities and by April 1919 it had vacated the dock, allowing the company's tenants to resume their normal usage.

The Grand Junction Canal had been negotiating the purchase of the Warwick & Napton, Warwick & Birmingham and the Birmingham & Warwick Junction Canals since June 1924. Prompted by this and partly by Wilfred Curtis, the Regent's Canal Company chairman who had also been a member of the Grand Junction's Select Committee since January 1923, discussions were started early in 1926 between the two companies for a possible merger.[18] In June six directors of the Regent's with their manager inspected the Grand Junction from Braunston to Brentford and in turn directors from the Grand Junction inspected the dock and the Regent's Canal to Old Ford on 9 August and the Hertford Union Canal and the rest of the canal to Paddington two days later. By the end of November the provisional plan was for the company to buy the Grand Junction, less its Paddington estate, and on 22 March 1927 officers of the two concerns and their financial advisers met to try to agree terms. At the same time an actuary was appointed to prepare a draft for a superannuation scheme for the staff and overtures were made to the Oxford Canal with a view either to purchasing it or to obtaining running powers between Braunston and Napton in order to obtain complete control over the canal route to Birmingham.

Parliamentary agents were appointed in April and soon afterwards the Grand Junction agreed terms to buy the Warwick canals for £149,100. This included £1,000 compensation for the members of their joint committee and £3,000 compensation for the manager, William Salt, but £15,595 was to be set aside to overcome arrears of maintenance. In October, however, it was decided that for legal reasons the Regent's should buy the Warwick canals direct and a price of £136,000 was agreed with a further £4,000 for the compensation payments.[19] Two Bills were then deposited in Parliament to authorise the purchases.

The Bill for the Warwick purchase was unopposed and had an easy passage, having its third reading in the Commons on 11 May 1928 and in the Lords on 23 July. The Grand Junction Bill attracted five petitions against it but eventually passed the Commons committee with various alterations on 19 May and had its third reading on 5 June. It then passed through the Lords receiving its third reading on 23 July and both Bills received the Royal Assent on 3 August.[20] The purchase agreement required the Regent's Canal & Dock Company to change its name to the Grand Union Canal Company.

The purchase involved paying £62,258.15/- (£62,258.75) for the Warwick & Birmingham Canal,

£8,641 for the Warwick & Napton Canal and £65,104 for their jointly-owned Birmingham & Warwick Junction Canal making a total of £136,003.15/- (£136,003.75), the odd £3.15/- (£3.75) being to even up the fractional payment. After the Birmingham & Warwick Junction money had been split between the two concerns the Warwick & Birmingham's amount was £100,968.15/- (£100,968.75) giving its shareholders £67.6s.2.4d (£67.31) per £100 share and Warwick & Napton's was £35,035 giving its shareholders £35.15/- (£35.75) per £100 share.[21]

To finance this acquisition the Regent's had asked its bankers, the National Provincial Bank, for a short-term loan prior to making a new share issue early in 1929. The bank made difficulties over the request and as the Warwick canals and the Grand Junction all banked with Lloyds Bank, the company transferred its account and was granted the facility it needed

Meanwhile the Grand Junction Canal Company, which remained as a property-owning concern, received £285,709 of Grand Union 5½% debenture stock for giving up its canal assets. The Grand Junction's shareholders received £760,536 of capital stock that had been agreed as at 1 January 1926 together with a further £40,906 in respect of capital transactions in 1927 and 1928 making £801,442; equivalent to £70.18s.6d (£70.92) for each £100 share of the £1,130,000 capital.[21] The issue increased the Grand Union's capital to £2,159,542 and early in March 1929 £250,000 of a new 6% preference stock was issued to repay the company's borrowings.

Between 1883 and 1928 five directors had served as Chairman of the Regent's Canal & Dock Company. First was James Staats Forbes who resigned due to ill health in March 1901 and was succeeded by Thomas James Waller. He retired at the end of 1913 with Walter Hunter taking over in February 1914 but his tenure was short as he died in September and was replaced temporarily by Thomas Spooner Soden. He stepped down in February of the following year to become Deputy Chairman with Wilfred Henry Curtis, elected to fill Waller's place on the board in 1913, taking over.

On the administrative side John Frederick Abbott remained as secretary on a temporary contract until the company terminated it in March 1885 when Frederick Coole was appointed at £450. He retired due to ill health at the end of 1895 receiving a £225 pension and his place was taken by Elkanah Clarkson at £400.

He had first joined as a clerk in July 1883 and went on to serve the company for over 40 years, being awarded an MBE in 1920. He retired in March 1924 with a £450 pension but died in February 1929. Edward Parker Abbott, John Abbott's son, took his place at £800, having first joined the company as a junior clerk in July 1881, but he retired at the end of 1926 with a £650 pension having served for over 45 years. Leonard Bygrave now took over as secretary and accountant at £700 he having joined in August 1901 at £40.

Henry Braine died in 1896 having served as Dock Master for 30 years and John Joseph Clark was then appointed. Failing eyesight led to his giving up in June 1906 after 43 years with the company in various roles. William Candler took over until his retirement at the end of 1915; Stephen English then held the Dock Master's position until the end of 1921 when Henry White was appointed.

On the engineering side Edwin Thomas retired due to ill health on 1 August 1897 after 44 years service. He was awarded a £500 pension but died in November 1897 at Bournemouth aged 70. The board agreed to continue a reduced payment to his wife Anne. Initially no replacement was appointed but John Glass, who had been appointed Traffic Manager on the day Thomas retired, took over much of the running of the canal. Glass had joined the company as a stores clerk in December 1864 and worked his way up. He retired at the end of April 1911 on a £350 pension; Glass died at Buxton in January 1919.

To replace Glass, William Henry Smith was appointed General Manager at £800 but he resigned in July 1914 when Clarkson took over much of the duties of running the canal. In July 1915 Gordon Thomas, the Grand Junction's engineer, was appointed as the company's consulting engineer but the arrangement did not last long – a year later he was dismissed by the Grand Junction for suspected embezzlement. To replace Thomas, Alexander Wilkie was appointed Outdoor Supervisor in June 1916 with George Henry Wood as Inspector. A year later Wilkie was promoted to Superintendent at £240 and in March 1924 to Manager at £750, with Wood as Chief Inspector at £400. By the beginning of 1927 Wilkie had become Chief Officer at £1,000 and in November he was serving as Traffic Manager for both the Grand Junction and the Regent's companies. He reverted to being Chief Officer from October 1928 with his salary increased to £1,250 in preparation for his enlarged role with the Grand Union.

CHAPTER NINE

THE GRAND UNION DAYS

From controlling a canal whose main line with its three branches was just less than 11 miles long, the Grand Union Canal Company was now in charge of a waterway stretching from London to Birmingham, which, with a series of branches including a major one to Leicester, totalled 240 miles. And from 1 January 1932 nearly another 37 miles was added when the three navigations taking the route northwards from Leicester, down the river Soar valley through Loughborough to the river Trent and then up the river Erewash valley to Langley Mill on the Nottinghamshire and Derbyshire border were acquired.

During and immediately after the First World War the volume of traffic on the Regent's Canal had fallen but a recovery then took place and at first this continued after the merger. The new company, however, was experiencing increased competition from both road and rail transport and it realised that it

Four pairs of narrowboats owned by Associated Canal Carriers being loaded by overside discharge from a ship in Regent's Canal Dock in the early 1930s.

Tony Smith collection

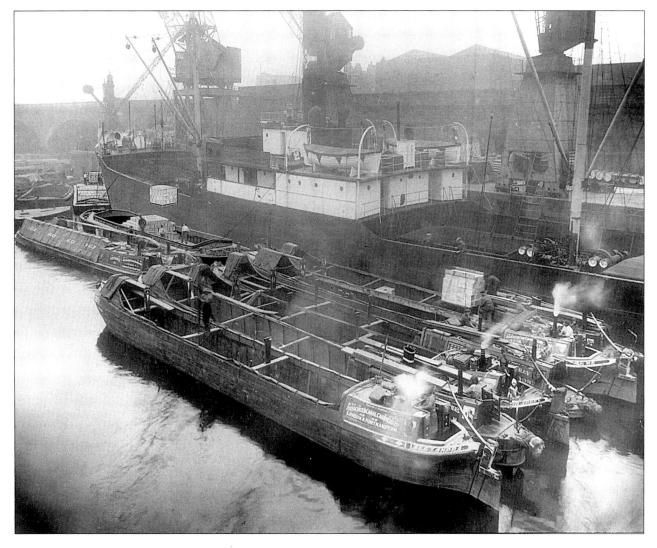

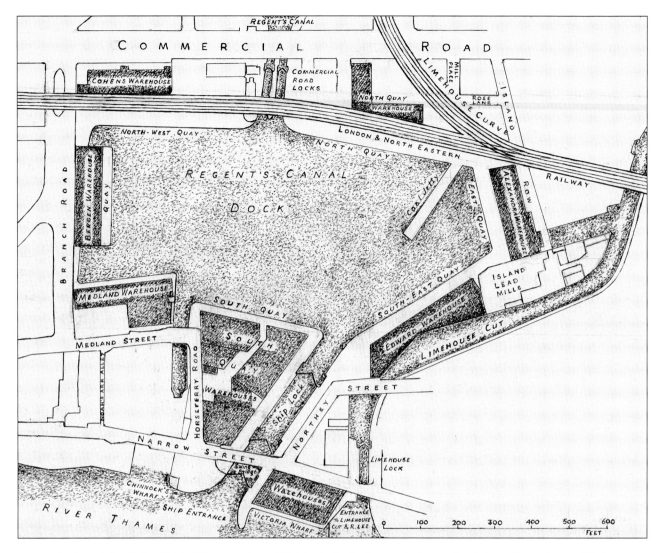

Regent's Canal Dock in 1934. Changes since 1911 include the barge dock north of the railway being filled-in (1918-1927) with the northwest quay being extended across its entrance (1927); the coal jetty on the north quay had been demolished (1912) and warehouses had been developed there (from 1912); the northeast coal jetty had been replaced (1926); the Alexandra Warehouse had been extended northwards (1919); a small jetty on the south quay had been removed (1917); the warehouses had been extended on the south quay (from 1915); the river entrance to the barge lock had been sealed off (1924) with the lock site being redeveloped and the channel into the dock being converted into a lay-by (1921); Medland Warehouse had been erected on the southwest quay (1922); the former coal jetty in the southwest corner had been demolished (1919) and the Bergen Warehouse now occupies the west quay, extending out over the water space (1922).

Edward Paget-Tomlinson

would have to take action if it was to maintain and improve its position. To this end all new barges being built for use on the Regent's section could carry 100 tons and work started to extend this standard to the Long Level and further north if possible with a major dredging programme.[1]

At Regent's Canal Dock, Stothert & Pitt Ltd completed the erection of a 10-ton electric gantry crane costing £4,730 on the north quay in February 1929 and in November 1931 Edward Green & Son contracted to extend the warehouse on this quay for £1,728. Stothert & Pitt was awarded a £19,500 contract to install five electric cranes around the dock in October 1937 replacing some of the older hydraulically-operated equipment. In the same month H. Bradford & Sons Ltd contracted to build new offices on the pier head for the Grand Union Canal Company; these cost £2,703. A second

Nine pairs of narrowboats, mostly from the Associated Canal Carriers fleet, are waiting to be loaded in Regent's Canal Dock in the mid 1930s.

Tony Smith collection

contract for offices followed in March 1938; these cost £1,739 and were built on a concrete raft over the old barge lock entrance.

Even before the merger an experimental pair of narrow boats designed to carry an increased payload had been ordered in July 1928 from the Steel Barrel Co Ltd of Uxbridge. They were delivered in early February 1929 at a cost of £1,177 and were named *George* and *Mary*, after the reigning king and queen. Their hulls were steel but Bushell Brothers of Tring provided wooden cabins and the motorboat was fitted with a 22hp Kromhout engine. In March 1929 Arthur Harvey-Taylor, a carrier based at Aylesbury, agreed to take the boats on free trial for six months in order to assess their carrying capacity and running costs. If they were found satisfactory, the intention was for him then to purchase the pair over a five-year term.

In August 1930, Associated Canal Carriers Ltd, a small carrying concern based at Northampton, was purchased for £750, with a further £609 owed for rent and tolls being written off, and soon afterwards it took the *George & Mary* on hire and ultimately

purchased them from the parent company in August 1936. In the meantime the Grand Union Company injected funds into its new subsidiary enabling it to purchase further boats from other carriers and, in February 1931, to order six new pairs of a similar design to the experimental pair. In February 1934 the subsidiary was renamed the Grand Union Canal Carrying Co Ltd (GUCCCo), a new manager was appointed in June and a major expansion was authorised with orders placed for further new boats to increase the size of the fleet to 186 pairs.[2]

At the same time there was a major investment programme on the Warwick section. Fifty-two narrow locks were replaced by 51 wide ones of an improved design, a series of bridges were rebuilt giving full navigational width, several miles of concrete bank protection were installed which also increased the cross-sectional area of the waterway, and much dredging was carried out.[3] Later, new terminals were established at Tyseley and at Sampson Road, Birmingham. Work was also carried out on the Grand Junction section with many miles of bank protection being installed and a channel-deepening programme instituted up to Berkhamsted.

The company then actively set about finding traffics for its new fleet and for its modernised waterway. The most significant event was on 14 October 1935 when the SS *Dona Isabel* transhipped 1,250 tons of continental steel to narrow boats in Regent's Canal Dock for delivery to Birmingham and destinations in south Staffordshire. The action brought the company into conflict with the railways, which contended that the new traffic contravened an agreement between them and the Canal Association. A lengthy dispute followed with the railways threatening a rates war but the company held its ground and steel developed into a regular traffic

To assist in obtaining and organising the steel traffic, John Miller (Shipping) Ltd was appointed as the company's continental agent in Belgium, France and Holland for a three-year term from the beginning of 1936 on a fixed annual £300 fee and commission payments on traffic secured. This then led to John Miller, the agent's Managing Director, joining the company's board on 21 October 1936 and the GUCCCo board six days later. This followed a major review into the GUCCCo's affairs that led to an abrupt halt being called to its expansion programme, the resignation of its manager and Miller's appointment as its Managing Director. The GUCCCo was never able to find enough crews to operate its full fleet, with the result that many boats had to be laid up. From the end of 1937, however, spare craft began to be hired out to other carriers and from the end of 1939 older boats began to be sold off.

There was a major development in September 1937 when the Grand Union set up a shipping department and acquired a small steamer for £8,000. It renamed the vessel *Marsworth*, another two ships were hired on time charter and a weekly service was started from Regent's Canal Dock initially to Antwerp and soon after also to Rotterdam. Initially the GUCCCo operated the ships but in November 1937 a new subsidiary company, Grand Union (Shipping) Ltd, was formed with a capital of £15,000. The new service was promoted as the Regent's Line.

In September 1938 the shipping company obtained the agency for the Oranje Line, which provided a fortnightly direct service from London to the Canadian and United States Lakes using four steamships and visiting such ports as Montreal, Toronto, Detroit and Chicago. The St Lawrence River, which gave access to the lakes, was frozen during the winter months and the ships then operated only to the east Canadian ports. In December 1939 a 1,738-ton steamer was bought for £9,250 and renamed *Blisworth*. Between September 1937 and August 1939 the ships brought 57,592 tons into the dock of which 12,152 tons went on up the canal.[4]

The development of the shipping business, however, brought the company into conflict with various competitors, who claimed it had no powers to operate ships, and in February 1939 the Attorney General served a writ on it as the first step in legal proceedings. Affidavits were sworn on both sides and the case was due to come to trial but the outbreak of the Second World War caused the case to be deferred.

In October 1941 the Grand Union instructed its solicitors and Parliamentary agents to begin work on a Bill to modernise, consolidate and extend the financial and administrative provisions of its existing Acts. The Bill was deposited in the House of Lords in the autumn of 1942 and received its first reading on 20 January 1943. There were several petitions against the measure including from the Chamber of Shipping and from some local authorities concerned about possible sales of land around the Brent Reservoir. A Lords' Select Committee considered the Bill over three days from 16 March and it was then read for the third time on 6 April and received its first reading in the Commons on the same day. The Chamber of Shipping lodged a further petition and, supported by several shipping concerns, opposed the Bill before a Commons Select Committee during a three-day hearing from 1 June. Despite this the committee approved the measure with slight drafting amendments and the Commons gave a third reading on 29 June and the Act received the Royal Assent on 6 July.[5]

For some time the company had been experiencing difficulties with the tenant of Bergen Wharf. By 1936 SLA Ltd had taken over from the original Bergenske concern and in April it was allowed concessions estimated at £500 off the dock dues for its Norwegian steamers and off the charges levied for the dock police. The measures were unavailing as a year later SLA gave notice of its intention to close down Bergen Wharf on 15 May and transfer its ships to the East India Dock.

The company's response was to set up the Grand Union (Stevedoring & Wharfage) Co Ltd (GUS&W) in June 1937 as a subsidiary company with an initial capital of £5,000 to take over operations at the wharf. The Norwegians had spent some £42,000 equipping the wharf and warehouse but SLA agreed to surrender its two leases, which were not due to expire until 1943, if the company would pay £7,000, forego £3,000 for outstanding rent, and pay £500 per annum for the next six years for revenue derived from other ships running between Norway and the dock. These terms were agreed and GUS&W took over on 24 June. A month later Sir William Arrol & Co Ltd's £4,056 tender for a new electric travelling crane for the wharf was accepted.

The Bergen take-over was the prelude to a major development as the largest trader in the dock, Roland-Argo Wharves Ltd, which occupied wharves on the south quay along with the Alexandra, Edward and Medland warehouses, had been experiencing similar difficulties. This resulted in Roland-Argo giving up all of its leases and GUS&W taking over (see Chapter 10).

At the same time as GUS&W was formed, Grande Union Belge De Transports SA. was established at Antwerp in Belgium to develop the continental trade; it was registered as a Grand Union subsidiary with a capital of three million Belgian francs.

The stevedoring and wharfing work soon became very profitable, enabling GUS&W to provide considerable cash sums to its parent concern. At the end of November 1938 its capital was increased to £50,000 and it purchased the shares in the shipping company for £15,000 and in the Belgian company for £20,517 from its parent. On 25 March 1938 it had taken over Chinnocks Wharf, using it for the shipping and Belgian companies' operations and in February 1939 H. Bradford & Sons Ltd's £1,476 tender for a new warehouse there was accepted. Building work started two

months later and was completed by September 1940 at £2,711, which included the cost of the cranes. A final expansion came from the beginning of 1941 when GUS&W took over the north quay at the dock, the previous tenant, whose trade had mainly been with Germany, having to give up due to the wartime disruption.

The Grand Union Canal Company established a series of other subsidiaries such as Thomas Clayton (Paddington) Ltd, which operated rubbish disposal contracts on the Long Level; Grandion Ltd, which took over running the lido that had been established on the reservoir at Ruislip; and Grand Union Warehousing Co Ltd but none of these affected the Regent's Canal to any significant degree.

During the 1930s the size of the Brent Reservoir reduced to 144 acres with considerable amounts of land sold off profitably for development. At the dam the company could increase the water level by inserting stop planks on the weir. This practice, however, was deemed unsafe and likely to cause flooding. On 22 July 1936 Holst & Co Ltd contracted to install five iron siphons at the dam for £4,424. They were set at various levels and were designed to come into operation, one by one, as the water level rose. Once installed the weir could again be built up to its full height with a masonry wall. Today the need for the reservoir's water for canal purposes has reduced; instead it provides an important amenity for west London and is popular for fishing and sailing.

The outbreak of the Second World War on 1 September 1939 had an immediate effect on the

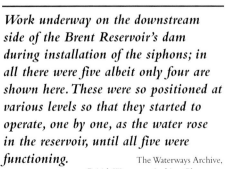

Work underway on the downstream side of the Brent Reservoir's dam during installation of the siphons; in all there were five albeit only four are shown here. These were so positioned at various levels so that they started to operate, one by one, as the water rose in the reservoir, until all five were functioning. The Waterways Archive, British Waterways Archive, Gloucester

In 1936 five siphons were installed at the Brent Reservoir's dam to help discharge floodwater to the river Brent. To enable the works to take place the level of the reservoir had to be lowered, as shown here. The control gear for the sluices at the dam is housed in the cabin built out over the water. The Waterways Archive, British Waterways Archive, Gloucester

The downstream face of the dam of the Brent reservoir showing the five siphons encased in concrete.
Author – 11 February 1999,

A busy summer scene at Ruislip reservoir in the late 1930s. Originally the reservoir was an important source of water for the Regent's Canal but the establishment of the Grand Union Canal Company in 1929 enabled the water supply arrangements to be simplified and the leisure potential of the reservoir could then be exploited. In May 1951 Ruislip Lido was purchased from British Waterways by Ruislip & Norwood Urban District Council for £37,500.

The Waterways Archive,
British Waterways Archive, Gloucester

canal and dock. In anticipation of the hostilities Kent & Sussex Contractors Ltd had provided three air-raid precaution shelters at the dock accommodating up to 375 people. They cost £1,125 for the basic structures but the company budgeted another £458 to provide ventilation, seating and toilets.

The tonnage through the dock was badly affected at first; in the first eight months of 1939 453,552 tons were handled against 425,827 tons in 1938 but for the next three months it was only 84,602 tons against 178,460 tons in 1938. Later traffic started to recover.

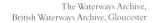

Year	Dock Tonnage
1936	877,766
1937	802,345
1938	722,467
1939	642,500
1940	359,797
1941	408,387
1942	426,960
1943	545,688

On 7 September 1940 the dock experienced its first enemy bombing with damage caused to property on the northwest quay. By the end of October warehouses on the Medland, Edward and South quays had been hit and the engine room and pump house in the old ship lock were also very badly affected; it was estimated repairs would cost £15,307.

To try to minimise the problem of incendiary bombs six men were employed each night as firewatchers to patrol the area. Then in July 1944 flying bombs caused further extensive damage.

On 1 July 1942 the dock, the canal and the subsidiary companies came under the control of the Ministry of War Transport and thereafter it maintained strict control over all toll rates and outgoings, especially salaries, wages and capital expenditure but paid out compensation for loss of profits. Regent's Canal Dock, GUS&W and the shipping company, all of which were profitable, were released from this Canal Control Order on 15 March 1943.

Throughout the 1930s there had been a series of complaints about the lack of dredging in the dock and small schemes were carried out such as removing 1,600 tons of mud in early 1936 for some £350, but in July 1937 the engineer estimated that £4,140 would need to be spent on dredging every year for the next ten years to restore the dock to its proper depth of 20ft. With the outbreak of the war and the resulting slackness in the dock, the company authorised further small dredging schemes but in March 1944 the Tilbury Contracting & Dredging Co Ltd offered to remove an estimated 80,000 cubic yards at 6/6d (32½p) per cubic yard. The contractors also offered deferred payment terms and work started in April and was completed on 28 September at a cost of £31,667, the quantity removed being nearer 90,000 cubic yards.

Another development affecting the dock was the purchase of the SS *Eskwood* by the shipping company in January 1944, its capital being increased by 10,000 shares to £75,000 to finance the purchase. The vessel was subsequently renamed *Kilworth*. In January 1945 a new diesel ship of 1,100 dead-weight tons was ordered at a basic price of £53,700 from the Burntisland Shipping Co Ltd. It was delivered in June 1946 and named *Knebworth* and a sister ship, *Bosworth*, was delivered three months later.

While some minor repairs to damaged dockside property had been carried out prior to the imposition of government control it was not until the war had ended on 2 September 1945 that major reparations could start. £5,600 was authorised in that month for repairs to the Medland, or 'B' warehouse as it was now known. This wharf had also suffered subsidence and Holst & Co Ltd was awarded a £15,674 contract to deal with the problem in August 1946. War damage repairs were also needed to the 'C' (South Quay), 'D' (Edward) and 'E' (Alexandra) warehouses with only the 'A' (Bergen) and 'F' (North) quay premises escaping major damage. Due to the post-war shortage of bricks it was to be several years before all the damage was repaired and the warehouses could be brought back into use.

During the war one section of the Regent's Canal was closed – this was the Cumberland Market Branch. As early as March 1929 the Commissioners of Woods were planning to redevelop the western side of the terminal basin for housing, the wharf leases being due to expire in 1930. The Commissioners wanted to use the basin as a playground area for the new houses but the company declined to sell, as there was still some traffic on the branch. By the end of December 1933 the situation was different and the company was considering applying to the Ministry of Transport for a closure order under Section 45 of the 1888 Railway & Canal Traffic Act.

During 1934 the branch was inspected several times by surveyors acting for the Commissioners and in October 1936 a provisional agreement was reached for them to buy the branch for £6,000. The company's shareholders authorised initiating abandonment procedures on 31 March 1937 but it was not until 12 June 1939 that a formal agreement was reached with the Commissioners and an application could be made to the Ministry.

On 3 May 1940 the Ministry issued a notice for the Warrant of Abandonment and this advertised by the company in *The Times* and the *London Gazette*. The Abandonment Order was then made on 3 July.[6] In October the company was quoting terms for receiving material to be tipped into the branch from war-damage debris clearance and filling in then started. In January 1941 the first section had been completed and the Commissioners paid over the first of three £2,000 instalments. The sale of the branch was completed in November 1942 and the company received the final instalment and a further £1,433 from the tipping receipts less expenses. Today the site of the former basin is used for allotments.

The remaining short stub of the Cumberland Market Branch in use by a floating restaurant and for moorings. The remainder of the arm was filled-in with rubble from the blitz between 1940 and 1942 and was then sold to the Crown Commissioners.

Author – 19 May 1984

In financial terms the 1929 merger proved to be disappointing for the Grand Union Canal Company's shareholders. An initial dividend of 12/6d (62½p) on the ordinary shares was paid on 4 September 1929 but after 1930 the rate dropped and ceased altogether after April 1934. It was not resumed until April 1946 by when the company had been brought under government control. Even the holders of the preference shares suffered; the 6% payment was maintained until August 1936 but then stopped and was not resumed until the end of 1944 when a backdated 3% was made for both 1942 and 1943 and the full rate then resumed.

Government control came to an end on 31 December 1947 but from 1 January 1948 the entire undertaking of the Grand Union Canal was nationalised to become part of the British Transport Commission. The canal and the dock came under the south-eastern division of the Commission's Docks & Inland Waterways Executive, trading as British Waterways.

Just before nationalisation the company had received an offer from George A. Tom & Co Ltd to acquire the shipping company for £120,000 with a further £35,000 to repay a loan from GUS&W. The offer was accepted in principle but could not be completed until after the British Transport Commission took over. The shipping company remained in business, *Marsworth*, a new diesel vessel joining the fleet in 1949, and it continued to make some use of the dock until about 1965 when it became part of the General Steam Navigation Co Ltd.[7] Trade at the dock soon resumed pre-war patterns; for instance, in the autumn of 1949 two ocean-going ships of the Norwegian Fjell Line delivered cargoes from ports on the Great Lakes.

From 1 January 1950 the dock was administered as a separate entity within the Docks & Inland Waterways Executive with the Managing Director of GUS&W as Dock Manager. Traffic was still fairly buoyant; in the first 24 weeks of 1951 293,636 tons of imports and 53,041 tons of exports were handled at its six general cargo quays where ships of up to 3,000 tons could be accommodated. In addition colliers, each carrying up to 2,800 tons, could be dealt with at the northeast jetty where two transporter cranes with 5-ton grabs could tranship the coal to barges. Some of these barges worked up the canal but many went out onto the river on short local journeys to gas works and electricity generating stations.

From 1 October 1953 the Docks & Inland Waterways Executive was replaced by a new Board of Management, which then commissioned a review of its waterways by a committee set up on 8 April 1954 and chaired by Lord Rusholme, a member of the British Transport Commission. This committee, known as the Board of Survey, reported on 29 November 1954 and its main recommendation was that the inland waterways should be separated from the docks and come under a new organisation with a general manager in charge.

The British Transport Commission had already decided to act on this and on 1 January 1955 British Transport Waterways was created with Sir Reginald Kerr as the General Manager. The Board of Survey also recommended that Regent's Canal Dock, along with two other docks, should be returned to be administered as part of the canals and that the dock, the Regent's section and the canal up to Berkhamsted should be improved.

Following on from this, early in 1956 the British Transport Commission announced that it was to spend £5,500,000 modernising its main commercial waterways and of this sum £1,396,000 was earmarked for the southern section of the Grand Union, which had carried 736,150 tons of traffic in 1954. More details of this expenditure were given by Sir Reginald Kerr on 8 October 1957, the main aim being to widen and deepen the canal up to Berkhamsted in order to handle 90-ton craft. Work on the Regent's section was limited but at Hampstead Road Lock the towpath was to be carried across the mouth of the dock immediately below the lock so that horses and towing tractors could pass under the bridge rather than having to cross the busy main road. Regulating weirs were also to be installed at the locks to avoid the towpath being flooded.[8]

The Board of Survey report had included plans to abandon many of the canals in the country and this attracted much criticism, particularly as it was an internal enquiry. On 1 February 1956 the setting up of an independent enquiry was announced in Parliament headed up by Leslie Bowes, later Sir Leslie Bowes, who was Managing Director of the Pacific Steam Navigation Company. This committee reported on 28 July 1958 and recommended the refurbishment and maintenance of the main system of waterways with government money. Some of the committee also favoured setting up a separate waterways authority, removed from the British

The trip boat **Jason** *turning at Little Venice before making for the Warwick Avenue Bridge, which marks the entrance to the Regent's Canal. John James first established trips in* **Jason** *in 1951 as part of the Festival of Britain celebrations.*

Author – 19 May 1984

Transport Commission. The report also placed the commercially-used waterways in a special category, recording that Regent's Canal Dock had earned £462,797 in 1954 with expenses of £431,619 and £468,620 in 1956 with expenses of £467,852.

The new separate authority did not appear until 1 January 1963 when, following the demise of the British Transport Commission, the independent British Waterways Board was set up. One of its first acts was to issue an interim report in January 1964 entitled *The Future of the Waterways* which concluded that only the Regent's section and the canal up to Uxbridge had any real commercial prospects. A second report – *The Facts about the Waterways* – followed in December 1965 outlining various options but making it clear government money was needed whichever was chosen.

In a White Paper in the summer of 1966 the government accepted the concept of an amenity network of subsidised cruising waterways and a further White Paper – *British Waterways Recreation and Amenity*

– was issued on 7 September 1967 setting out which waterways would make up a commercial category and which an amenity category. By now commercial traffic on the Grand Union had declined dramatically and the whole canal was confined to the cruising network, established by the Transport Act 1968.

The shift from the Regent's Canal being solely a commercial waterway to becoming an amenity waterway could be said to have started on 5 May 1951 when as part of the Festival of Britain celebrations the actress Beryl Reid inaugurated a trip boat service from the western portal of Maida Hill Tunnel through Regent's Park to Hampstead Road lock and back.[9] The service was operated using the narrow boat *Jason* owned by John James and it proved extremely popular, introducing large numbers of people to a little-known part of London. It was kept on after the festival had ended and remains in business today. Later other trip boats started, including the *Jenny Wren* in the summer of 1968 from a base below Hampstead Road Lock.[10]

On 13 May 1959 British Waterways instituted a waterbus service from Paddington along a 2-mile section of the canal to London Zoo in Regent's Park.[11] It used *Water Buck*, a converted narrow boat that could carry 50 passengers,[12] which proved highly successful. A second boat, *Water Wagtail*, was commissioned for 1960 with a third, *Water Nymph*, soon after. In 1964 89,908 passengers were carried.

Another development was the conversion of the former Midland Railway coal dock at St Pancras into a new yacht basin. The 250ft-long dock had been disused for 20 years and 6,000 tons of silt and sand were dredged out to create moorings for 60 pleasure craft. The basin was formally opened on 6 October 1958 and provided a workshop, store, slipway and toilets,[13] and later became the base for the St Pancras Cruising Club. Other basins were less fortunate; in April 1967 Haggerston was filled in and Northiam followed in July 1976 with the towpath bridge being demolished. Meanwhile under plans first mooted in 1967 some of the privately owned Wenlock Basin was filled in making it narrower, the surviving part being used for moorings.

In June 1963 work started on piling the banks and dredging the surviving short stump of the Cumberland Market Branch for moorings and the site was opened by Turner Marinas Ltd in the autumn and included a floating restaurant.[14] In June 1967 the same company developed moorings opposite the former Great Central Railway's goods yard at Marylebone and in October of the same year further moorings between Warwick Avenue and the western end of Maida Hill Tunnel.[15]

One restriction on the growth of pleasure traffic was the opening hours for the locks, all of which were manned. Normally open from 8am to 5pm from Mondays to Fridays and for four hours on Saturday mornings, it soon became apparent that those using St Pancras Basin and other mooring sites needed longer opening hours at weekends. The problem was that the locks had relatively small weirs and bypass channels and there was a real risk that valuable canal side properties might be flooded. In October 1973 British Waterways produced plans to convert the duplicate chamber at each lock into a weir and this work was carried out in the following year enabling the locks then to be user-operated at all times.

Another development was opening up the towpath to the public, which followed from the government's recognition of the amenity value of the canal. Following an initiative by the Greater London Council, a London Canals Consultative Committee was set up. It first met in July 1966 and included representatives from all the boroughs bordering the canal and from amenity groups. In 1968 Westminster City Council opened up the first stretch of the

Looking down on Hampstead Road Locks, Camden, situated at the end of a 20-mile level stretch of canal. The lock keeper's cottage on the right now serves as Camden's Information Centre and a café and the busy Camden Market now surrounds this area.
Author – 19 May 1984

The Pirate Castle is the headquarters of an active youth club, first established in 1966, that makes full use of the canal for educational purposes. The building also serves as a pumping station to circulate water to keep the electricity cables, that are laid under the towpath, cool. The castellated bridge carries Oval Road across the canal. Author – 19 May 1984

Modern buildings have replaced wharves that used to surround Battlebridge Basin whilst the water space now serves to accommodate a variety of canal craft. Author – 5 June 2003

towpath from Lisson Grove to Regent's Park.[16] Camden Borough Council extended it from the Cumberland Market Branch to Hampstead Road Lock in June 1972 and later on to Islington Tunnel. The through route to Limehouse was completed in May 1982 as the Canalway Project.

One result of the opening up of the towpath has been the establishment of regular organised canal walks, which were inaugurated in March 1977 by Dr Michael Essex-Lopresti and have introduced many thousands of people to different parts of the canal.[17] The walks were interrupted for a time when the Central Electricity Generating Board laid six 400,000-volt cables under the towpath from Lisson Grove to Victoria Park but the board then paved the path to protect its cables and this has produced an all-weather surface for walkers and cyclists. The cables are kept cool by the canal water.

Other amenity developments have been the establishment of the Camley Street Natural Park on derelict land beside the canal at St Pancras in 1982, the opening on 9 March 1992 by the Princess Royal of the London Canal Museum in a former warehouse fronting onto Battlebridge Basin, the opening of the Pirate Castle on 15 October 1977 at Camden as a base for a canal-based youth club,[18] and the redevelopment of much of the canal side land for modern commercial or residential use and to create amenity areas.

Meanwhile at the dock the need for dredging continued and a large-scale exercise was conducted in the summer of 1955 and another in 1960 when 48,340 cubic yards were removed. The handling equipment was also kept up-to-date such as in the autumn of 1958 when Thomas Smith & Sons (Rodley) Ltd contracted to supply three electric portal cranes of between 3 and 6 ton capacity to replace hydraulically-operated cranes installed in the 1920s. Repairs were also carried out to several of the quays such as the north quay, part of which was rebuilt in concrete. Two new steel-framed brick warehouses were also built on this quay behind the railway arches.

In 1961 the swing bridge carrying Narrow Street across the ship lock was replaced by a welded steel structure built by Head Wrightson Teesdale Ltd of Thornaby-on-Tees. Designed in the form of a floating pontoon it was towed down to the Thames in March, lifted into position and formally opened in August. The bridge was fitted with continental-style lifting barriers and flashing traffic lights.

With the dock and the Limehouse Cut now under common ownership and with the two in such close proximity the idea of linking them again, and cutting delays in barges using Limehouse Lock, was revived.[19] On 1 April 1968 the first barges passed through the new link; it was only 200ft long, 50ft wide with a

Regent's Canal Dock, now known as Limehouse Basin, in 2002. Since being closed to shipping the dock has been transformed. The former dock buildings have been demolished, with the exception of the Dock Master's office on the pier head, which became the Barley Mow public house, and the preserved hydraulic pumping station building in Mill Place. There has been extensive residential development such as the six blocks mainly on the site of Bergen Wharf and the striking Marina Heights comprising four blocks on the north side. The dock itself has been reduced in size with parts being filled in to permit the construction of the Limehouse Link road underneath. As part of this a much smaller entrance lock has been built (1989) and a marina now occupies much of the remaining water space (1994). Edward Paget-Tomlinson

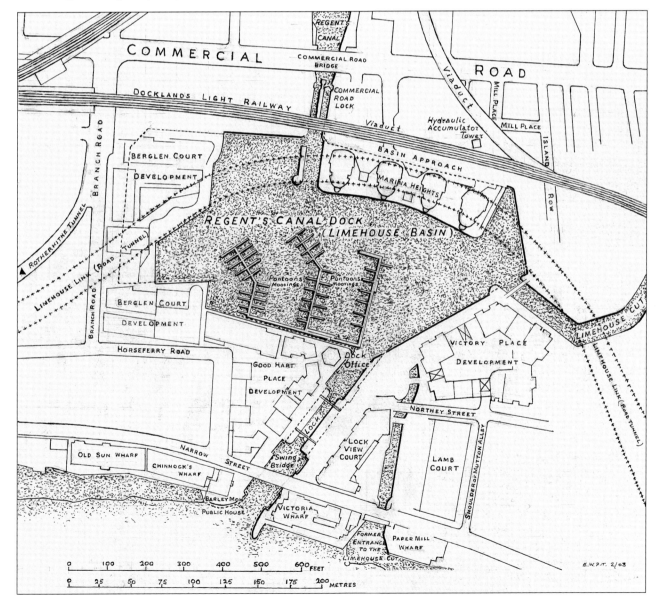

Although no longer in general use for shipping in May 1984, the ship lock at Limehouse was still operating and rather dwarfs this small cruiser. Author

depth of 7ft, its sides formed with steel piles between 40 and 50ft in length.[20] The contract was undertaken by John Shelbourne & Co Ltd and cost some £120,000. The Limehouse Cut immediately south of the new link was then stanked off and the lock was closed and filled in.

On 9 February 1969 British Waterways announced that Regent's Canal Dock was to close to general shipping in May. While 407 ships had used the dock in 1962 involving 210,000 tons of traffic and there had still been 388 ships in 1967 with 160,000 tons and earning a £14,000 profit, there had been a dramatic fall in 1968 to just two per week.[21] Approaches had been made to shipping companies but the trade was now passing to ports such as Harwich and Felixstowe. The dock was not alone in this problem that faced others in London and it closed on 27 May, although ships serving a scrap-metal dealer on the northwest quay continued for another ten years. Despite the closure the through routes to the canal and to the Limehouse Cut remained open.

Thereafter, the future of the dock involved plans for road improvements, the first being for a road passing over the river entrance on a viaduct that would have prevented ships from using the lock. This was dropped but then the Limehouse Link relief road was projected to pass under the north of the dock. As a prelude to this Rees Hough (Civil Engineering) Ltd contracted to rebuild the entrance lock with much smaller dimensions and started work in July 1988. The new lock, which was opened on 20 May 1989 by David

Ingman, Chairman of British Waterways, can accommodate craft 99ft long, 27ft wide with 10ft depth on the cills.[22] It was built inside the old ship lock, used one tenth of the water of its predecessor, and was fitted with modern sector gates manufactured and fitted by Biwater Hydro Power Ltd.

The London Docklands Development Corporation contributed to the cost of the new lock and once it was finished work on the link road could begin. This was constructed by the cut-and-cover method and involved filling in large areas of the dock on the north and west sides. At the same time Limehouse Developments Ltd, a joint venture company between British Waterways and Hunting Gate City Ltd began a major project that involved demolishing the warehouses round the dock with the land being used for housing.

This demolition has included many historic features such as the 1898 pumping station in the old ship lock comprising two engine houses, the large boiler house with an accumulator tower and chimney. The hydraulic plant had closed on 21 April 1920 when the London Hydraulic Power Co took over the supply to the dock and the need for pumping water had diminished with the formation of the Grand Union Canal as water could be supplied from Paddington. Latterly the buildings had been used for storage.

The original hydraulic engine house alongside the Commercial Road Locks suffered a similar fate despite it being the oldest surviving such building in the world. It had a variety of uses after being superseded by the Mill Place plant in 1869 but was

The impressive Marina Heights development, accessed off the Basin Approach Road, now occupies much of the site of the former North quay at Limehouse.
Author – 5 June 2001

demolished in March 1994. The octagonal accumulator tower and chimney of the Mill Place engine, however, has survived and was renovated by the London Docklands Development Corporation in 1995 and is now opened to the public on special days.

Meanwhile, the railway across the north of the dock had closed to passenger traffic on 4 May 1926 but goods survived until 1966. Subsequently the viaduct has been used for the route of the Docklands Light Railway that opened to passengers on 31 August 1987.

In April 1994 British Waterways opened a new marina in the dock, using part of the remaining water space and initially providing 80 berths. The future of the dock, or Limehouse Basin Marina as it is now known, is firmly tied to the leisure market.

In its new role as Limehouse Marina, the former dock now provides moorings for a variety of craft.
Author – 19 April 1999

Left: *The motor vessel* **Kemphaan** *in Regent's Canal Dock alongside the Bergen Wharf discharging to a pair of narrow boats from the Grand Union fleet. The boatman on butty* **Roade** *is clearly concerned by the threat posed to his home by the swim-headed lighter* **Lee**. Waterways Archive, British Waterways Archive, Gloucester

Below: *The motor vessel* **Kemphaan** *discharging to canal craft at the Regent's Canal Dock's Bergen Wharf in 1938.* Waterways Archive, British Waterways Archive, Gloucester

Above: Milborne *discharging to two pairs of British Waterways narrowboats in Regent's Canal Dock in the early 1950s.* Waterways Archive, British Waterways Archive, Gloucester

Right: *Four pairs of Fellows, Morton & Clayton's narrowboats being loaded from a steamer in Regent's Canal Dock. A river lighter looms over the narrowboats.*

Waterways Archive, British Waterways Archive, Gloucester

CHAPTER TEN

TRADE AND TRADERS

In the early days the most important trader on the canal was Pickfords who had moved from Paddington to new purpose-built premises at City Road Basin in December 1820 with the Regent's Canal Company paying them £15,000 for their rented property at Paddington, as compensation for the move and as a contribution towards the cost of their new premises. The land was held from the company on a 99 year lease from 25 December 1819 at an annual rent of £286.

Pickfords were already important carriers by road between Manchester and London when they began using the canals in December 1786.[1] As the canal network spread, so did Pickfords services and they started to use the Grand Junction Canal as soon as the northern section from Braunston to Blisworth in Northamptonshire was opened in September 1796. Even before the canal was opened throughout in March 1805 the firm became a major trader on the route,[2] in 1820 there were over 80 narrowboats in active service and two years later a large building programme was begun to replace older boats and enlarge the fleet still further. A second building programme in the 1830s increased the fleet up to its maximum size of 116 craft by 1838.[3]

On moving from Paddington, Pickfords established their London headquarters south of where City Road crossed the basin and a wharf, warehouses, private side dock and administrative offices were provided. The link with the canal company was strengthened when Joseph Baxendale, the leading partner in the firm, became a Regent's shareholder in June 1824. Other members of the family also became shareholders and in June 1836 Joseph was elected a director of the Regent's Canal Company.

Pickfords' services covered much of the country and handled a wide variety of general cargoes, a high proportion of which involved switching from one route to another at busy transhipment centres like Braunston. This called for a very efficient clerical back-up service to handle the paper work and this was centred on City Road. Transhipment also took place here with imported goods lightered up to the basin for warehousing or loading into the narrowboats while manufactured goods were taken down to the river or the docks. After the fire at the depot in 1824 part of the public wharf in the basin had to be appropriated for Pickfords' use until their premises could be rebuilt.

While Pickfords gave up long-distance canal carrying from the end of 1847 in favour of becoming an agent for the railways, they retained their City Road premises and although canal usage was greatly reduced they still continued to handle some lightered goods between the docks, City Road and the Camden depot.

Another important narrowboat carrier was Crowley Hicklin & Company of Wolverhampton, which had been founded in 1811 based on the former Wolverhampton Boat Company. An early link with the Regent's Canal Company was in 1820 when they transported the steam engines and castings from Boulton & Watt's foundry at Soho in Birmingham to the site of the new Chelsea pumping station. Their London base was then at Paddington but in November 1821 they agreed terms to move to City Road with the canal company providing £3,500 towards the cost of the new buildings with a further £500 being allowed as a rebate on tolls. Thomas Sowter erected the buildings on what was known as 30 & 31 Wharf and the firm, now known as Crowley Hicklin Batty & Company, moved in July 1822; their lease was from 24 June 1821 for 62 years at an annual £90.10s.0d (£90.50).

Like Pickfords, Crowleys had a large fleet of narrowboats and much of their trade comprised import and export goods that were transhipped between barges and narrowboats in the basin. In 1828 the firm extended their buildings on the wharf with the canal company giving further financial help. Crowley's, too, were forced to become railway agents and on 1 January 1849 their long-distance trade and those boats operating between London and the midlands were taken over by the Grand Junction Canal's Carrying Establishment.

This concern had been set up at the end of November 1847 to retain as much as possible of

Pickfords canal business. It acquired many of Pickfords boats, secured much of their remaining canal traffic and went on to purchase other long-distance carrying businesses to consolidate its position.[4] Initially it was based at Paddington but in April 1849 it moved to Crowleys' former premises at City Road, which it held under a sub-lease until the main lease expired when the Regent's formally assigned it to the Grand Junction.

In February 1850 the Grand Junction took a 14-year lease of premises in the Wenlock Basin and moved its boat building and repair operations from Paddington. A year later it was negotiating to establish a depot at Limehouse to develop trade between the canal and the Thames that had previously been confined mainly to Brentford. The Regent's offered to erect a goods shed and wharf in the barge basin north of the railway, and plans were approved in March. A month later the Grand Junction decided it wanted the whole area covered in, agreed to take a 21 year lease and pay a rental equivalent to 7% on the cost. On 2 July 1851 James Little & Son contracted to carry out the work for £1,698 but in the following January the carrier decided it would need more space and this involved relocating the Regent's Canal Company's stabling. Little agreed to this extra work on 7 April for £648. The Grand Junction took up occupation later that year, the rent being agreed at £250.

Early in 1855 the Grand Junction erected additional stabling for 22 horses at City Road but soon afterwards it began to consider steam-powered haulage. At the end of 1859 successful trials were conducted with the steamboat *Pioneer* resulting in the introduction of a series of steam-powered narrowboats operated from City Road on long-distance services and steam tugs operating between Camden and Cowley.[5]

This development had unfortunate consequences when on the morning of 2 October 1874 the steam tug *Ready* was towing a train of boats bound for Nottingham through Regent's Park. The train included *Tilbury*, which had a mixed cargo including several barrels of petroleum and 5 tons of gunpowder. As the boat was passing under the Macclesfield Bridge it exploded killing her crew of three outright. The *Dee* immediately in front in the train was badly damaged

Crowds gathered to inspect the wreckage of the Macclesfield Bridge filling the canal after the massive explosion on 2 October 1874 when a cargo of gunpowder on a boat was ignited. There was widespread damage despite the fact that the canal is in a cutting here.

The Waterways Archive, British Waterways Archive, Gloucester

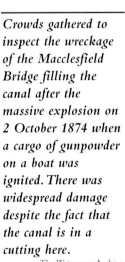

A wide-beam trip boat about to pass under Macclesfield Bridge in Regent's Park, the scene of the horrendous gunpowder explosion in 1874. Author – on 19 May 1984

and her steerer injured, the *Limehouse* immediately behind was sunk, while Macclesfield Bridge was destroyed and nearby properties damaged.[6]

Investigations indicated that the cabin fire had ignited petroleum vapour, which in turn had ignited the gunpowder.[7] The disaster contributed to the passing of the Explosives Act in 1875 tightening up the regulations for the carriage of hazardous substances. Meanwhile the Regent's drafted in its work force to drain the canal to remove the debris of the boats and bridge with the Grand Junction's workmen assisting. With 100 men working day and night the canal was reopened on the fifth day.

By the time of the explosion the Grand Junction's carrying venture had been reduced in size due to losses incurred and much of the long-distance traffic to Manchester, the Potteries and the Midlands had been passed to other carriers. The depot at Limehouse had been given up in May 1872 but the losses had continued, on top of which nearly £80,000 had to be paid in compensation for the damage caused by the explosion, this sum including the cost of re-building Macclesfield Bridge. As a result the Grand Junction gave up its carrying operations at the end of June 1876.[8]

To take over the substantial traffics that remained several new businesses were established. Prominent among these was the London & Staffordshire Carrying Company, which purchased several of the Grand Junction's steamers and other boats and rented a wharf in City Road Basin for its trade, which was mainly to Birmingham and the West Midlands. Meanwhile, Crowleys former premises at 30 Wharf passed to the London & Midland Counties Carrying Company, which had taken over the Grand Junction's trade to Leicester, Nottingham and Derby.

Both these concerns were soon absorbed into the Midlands-based business of Fellows Morton & Company. In 1889 it became Fellows, Morton & Clayton Ltd and occupied 30 & 31 Wharf where it spent considerable sums to improve the storage and handling facilities. It built up an extensive fleet of narrowboats, continued the development of steam-powered craft and later introduced motor-driven craft.[9] City Road was its main London base and it continued to carry a wide variety of goods to and from these premises for the next 60 years, purchasing the freehold of both 30 & 31 Wharf from the canal company in July 1946 for £30,000.

While narrowboats carried a substantial volume of traffic on the canal, the main users were barges. Typical were the craft of the Thames Steam Tug & Lighterage Co Ltd, which had been incorporated on 23 October 1856. By 1859 it was noted as carrying ale on the canal and in 1861, by when it had become one of the main contractors serving several of the railway depots, the minimum quantity that could be carried on its barges without toll penalty was lowered

from 30 to 20 tons as a special concession. The carrier developed particularly strong links with the London & North Western and Great Western railways but served many other customers, handling a wide variety of goods.

The Thames Steam Tug concern eventually became one of the largest barge users on the canal and in 1962 it merged with General Lighterage Ltd to become Thames & General Lighterage Ltd with a fleet of 600 craft and tugs. General Lighterage had

been formed in 1922 and had close links with the Regent's Canal. In May 1927 the canal company provided it with a £3,600 loan towards the purchase of six barges costing £4,800 to help develop a new traffic on the canal. In January 1929 a similar facility was agreed for a further six new barges from Holland costing £725 each, with the company again providing three-quarters of the cost on loan.

Other lighterage concerns were also absorbed into the Thames & General including Vokins & Co Ltd who had operated on the canal for many years and were agents to the Great Central, Great Eastern and Great Northern railways. With the continuing decline in lighterage traffic, however, Thames & General ceased trading at the end of December 1980 when its 17 tugs, several hundred barges and its residual traffics passed to the Cory and Maritime Lighterage companies, both part of the Ocean Group. Thereafter, such barge traffic as remained tended to be confined to the lower end of the river Lee and to Brentford until it all ended in November 1984.[10] One of the last traffics on the Regent's Canal was milk powder coming into the dock and destined for Glaxo Laboratories at Greenford; this trade lasted at least until 1973. The last narrowboat traffic involving exports through the dock ended in April 1968.

Coal was always a major traffic on the canal and eventually most of the barge businesses connected with the trade came together as Charringtons. One of the earliest constituents was John Gardner,[11] a farmer at Mile End, who leased wharf land from the canal company in June 1821. Initially Gardner's craft were mostly sailing barges bringing bricks up from the Medway but as many needed to tranship in the dock he went on to develop a sizeable lighterage business. In 1824 Gardner was given permission to make a lay-by for his barges at Mile End but two years later had still not started, and as complaints were being received about his barges blocking the canal, the company insisted that he carry out the work. Apart from trading on the canal John Gardner also operated on the rivers Lee and Stort.

By 1857 the business was known as Gardner Brothers and was run by grandsons Thomas and Henry Gardner. By 1880 Henry had died, and his son, Henry John, passed over his interest in the business to Thomas's son, another Thomas, who went on to become a major trader on the canal. In 1888 the canal company agreed that he could build a new lay-by at the Mile End wharf, the terms being exactly the same as those for his great-grandfather 60 years before. At about the same time a barge-building and repairing yard was established on the site.[12]

In 1898 Thomas Gardner's business was amalgamated with that of Tomlin & Winn, the two being incorporated to become Gardner Tomlin & Co Ltd with Thomas Gardner as Chairman and principal shareholder and over 200 barges in service.[13]

The coal merchants Charringtons were important traders on the canal and the company maintained its own barge dock just above Mile End Lock. Here work is being carried out on one of the company's fleet of wooden barges. The last wooden barge to be built here was in 1912; thereafter there was a steady changeover to steel vessels.

The Story of Charringtons, book in the author's collection

Charringtons maintained several tugs to tow their barges on parts of the canal. Here the appropriately named tug Regent is in charge of a train of at least four laden barges.   The Story of Charringtons, book in the author's collection

William Tomlin had been a trader on the Regent's Canal probably from the day it opened, and initially was based at Limehouse from where he operated a fleet of barges.[14] By 1843 he had established a wharf at Twig Folly, Bethnal Green,[15] nearly opposite the junction with the Hertford Union Canal, two pieces of land there being leased to William Tomlin & Son in 1847. Later the business became known as Tomlin & Nephew and by 1864 it was called Tomlin & Winn,[16] a barge yard being established at Twig Folly at about the same time. Latterly the firm held the lighterage contracts for the Chartered Gas Light & Coke Company's works at Shoreditch, Haggerston and St Pancras.[17]

In 1903 Gardner Tomlin & Co Ltd amalgamated with Hinton & Horne, one of whose bases was on the canal at St Pancras, and with Locket & Judkins to

become Gardner Locket & Hinton Ltd.[18] Locket & Judkins could also trace their roots back to the earliest days on the canal when the coal trader Edward Wood was allowed to make a lay-by at Kentish Town. By 1838 George Locket was noted as a clerk in the business, which had become Locket & Judkins by 1865. It remained at Kentish Town being allowed to draw water from the canal there for its 14 horses in 1869.

Back in April 1843 William Consett Wright had offered to take land at Limehouse,[19] and a year later he moved all his business to the dock. The business developed with new partners being admitted – in 1851 it was known as Wright Lloyd & Company, in 1857 as Wright Sells Dale & Surtees and in 1859, after a merger with John Charrington's business, it became Charrington Sells Dale & Company with

Wright remaining a partner. Later the name was shortened to Charrington Dale & Company. In April 1861 Charringtons offered to land a minimum of 30,000 tons of coal at the dock provided that a discount was continued. The business concentrated almost entirely on the supply of coal and handled many of the contracts to gas works and later to the electricity generating stations, William Wright was one of the first to use the hydraulic unloading machinery in the dock.

In April 1922 Charrington Dale & Company amalgamated with Gardner Locket & Hinton Ltd to form Charrington Gardner Locket & Co Ltd with Gardner Locket & Hinton contributing 56% of the assets.[20] It was this new company that partnered the Chartered Gas Light & Coke Company in the Regent's Discharging Co Ltd to construct and operate the new mechanised unloading jetty in the northeast corner of the dock in 1926.

Apart from Limehouse Dock the main commercial centre on the canal was City Road Basin where most of the long-distance canal carriers were based. Latterly some of the businesses leasing land from the company made only limited use of the canal and some made no use of it at all. Typical of the latter was Carter Patterson & Company, a great rival of Pickfords. Carter Patterson leased premises on the west side of the basin in November 1895 and developed a granary and stables for horses engaged on collection and delivery services in the capital. After years of rivalry Carter Patterson amalgamated with Pickfords in the autumn of 1912.[21]

In 1900 Pickfords had started to rebuild part of its premises and a small part of the basin immediately

The steam collier Sir David operated by the Gas Light & Coke Company being discharged at the Regent's Discharging Company's jetty in Regent's Canal Dock in 1938. Waterways Archive, British Waterways Archive, Gloucester

southeast of the City Road was filled in and covered by the new buildings. That part of the basin was already very little used and in May 1920 the canal company approved plans by Carter Patterson to fill in the rest of this section. This prompted objections from A. Bridgman & Co Ltd, wooden box and packing case manufacturers with premises on the corner of City Road and Macclesfield Street, who claimed it would be unable to turn its barges there. While the company disputed Bridgmans' rights, the infilling was deferred.

In March 1927 Carter Patterson acquired Bridgmans' lease, closed its depot in the following February and the infilling took place soon after. Carter Patterson went on to purchase the freehold of its premises at the basin for £130,000 in October 1934. Prior to this, the premises had yielded an annual rent of £5,050 for the canal company with a further £850 charge in lieu of tolls as Carter Patterson had made no use of canal transport for many years.

Another important tenant was British Drug Houses Ltd, which eventually had premises on both sides of the basin, linked by an aerial ropeway and later by a footbridge. The drug company had first taken premises on the west side of the basin in 1908 when the previous tenants, wallpaper manufacturers Carlisle & Clegg, had moved to Derby. Ultimately it occupied much of the basin's west side north of the City Road and in November 1915 it also took over four units on the east side of the basin from Lipton Ltd. In March 1937 a new 99 year lease was agreed with the drug company paying an annual rent of £4,150 with a tolls guarantee of £445 but it seems it made little use of the canal.

After the Second World War the remaining use of the basin declined rapidly. Narrowboat operations largely ceased when Fellows, Morton & Clayton's extensive fleet was acquired in 1949 by the nationalised Docks & Inland Waterways Executive, which centred its operations at Brentford. So great was the decline that the London Electricity Board, which occupied a large site northwest of the City Road, applied to redevelop a third of the remaining length of the basin. The plan generated considerable opposition and a Public Enquiry in 1977 resulted in only a short stretch being filled-in.

Today the main users of the water space are young canoeists from the Islington Boat Club that was formed in 1970 and has a club house on the west side of the basin. Most of the waterside warehouses have now been demolished and their sites redeveloped for housing, such as the Grand Junction Wharf and Pickfords Wharf developments on the east side and Crystal Wharf in the northwest corner.

In terms of tonnage Regent's Canal Dock was always the most important location for the company with coal being the major traffic, although only part of what was handled went up the canal, much being transhipped to barges for delivery to wharves on the Thames. In the early days coal merchants dominated the businesses that were established around the dock, typical being Sharp & Rickett who had a wharf in the northwest corner. In March 1853 the partners asked the canal company to equip their wharf with a hydraulic coal hoist, coal stores and an office but they demurred when asked to guarantee that a minimum of 20,000 tons would be handled each year. After lengthy discussions an agreement between the canal company and what had become Rickett & Smith was reached in November 1855 and in the following January Thomas Piper & Son contracted to erect the coal hoist and buildings for £3,369 and nine months later to erect a second hoist for £1,967. W. G. Armstrong & Company provided the machinery for both hoists.

Under the lease agreement Rickett & Smith had to unload 40,000 tons annually but in the year to the end of September 1867 they landed only 22,000 tons. Five years later the firm gave up their facilities on the northwest quay, but they retained a wharf on the west quay although they were still in trouble in 1894 when they only landed 19,940 tons against the specified 60,000. Although the canal company agreed a major concession in their terms, Rickett & Smith left the dock in October 1895, sub-letting their premises to the coal merchants Ray & Son.

Meanwhile, the coal hoists on the northwest quay had a series of short-term tenants, which included Longstaff & Son who had a temporary lease in February 1873. This firm had been founded in 1842 and became a substantial coal trader, a special rebate was agreed in April 1870 if their tonnage exceeded 30,000 tons. In March 1882 a new lease for a wharf in the southwest corner of the dock was agreed for what had become Sargeant Longstaff & Company and this specified a minimum of 45,000 tons. The firm remained an important dock trader until leaving in March 1918.

A somewhat different traffic handled at the dock was ice from Scandinavia. United Carlo Gatti Stevenson & Slater Ltd was the largest company dealing in this trade and it had been established on the northeast quay for many years. In May 1893 the canal company agreed a discount if it brought in 25,000 tons of ice a year. In 1912 the North Pole Ice Company was allowed to bring in between 12 and 15 ships in the season and an extra berth was provided for it by demolishing an old coal jetty on the north side of the dock, but the growth of refrigeration gradually put an end to this traffic.

An important traffic at the dock was constructional materials for John Mowlem & Company, which was well established at least by November 1863 with premises in Narrow Street. In August 1881 Mowlem became the canal company's first tenant of the small new Thames wharf. In March 1886 the wharf was assigned to Alfred Chinnock, a china clay manufacturer, who gave his name to the wharf. Four years later Chinnock assigned the wharf to his Alum China Clay & Vitriol Co Ltd.

The large Victoria Wharf on the Thames had several short-term tenants until John Schwartz, a sugar refiner, leased it from June 1884 at £1,500. His sons, John and William, took over three years later, the business becoming Schwartz Brothers, and later a warehouse was provided for them on the north side of Narrow Street. By 1908 business was declining due to the imposition of a duty on imported sugar and the company converted a warehouse into a bonded store to try to help them out of their difficulties. Despite this, the firm gave up Victoria Wharf and the warehouse at the end of 1910 and both were then let to Little & Johnston, agents for regular shipping services to France, Belgium, Germany and Switzerland.

Little & Johnston remained until the summer of 1916 when Mercantile Lighterage established a new company and took on the lease of the wharf but Little & Johnston gained control of this new company in 1920. Two years later the Bennett Steamship Co Ltd took over the wharf and a year later it secured Chinnocks Wharf as well. Both wharves were transferred in December 1932 to the General Steam North France Lines Ltd, which purchased the freehold of Victoria Wharf for £16,500 in March 1935 with the Regent's being allowed to retain the 'Regent's Canal Dock' name painted on the wall of the premises for a nominal annual rent. Chinnocks Wharf reverted to the canal company in March 1938.

A significant event took place in July 1873 when George Cohen & Son, dealers in old iron at Cable

Street, agreed to rent a wharf on the northwest quay. The firm had been established in 1834 and went on to become the longest standing tenant in the dock. Some problems arose in April 1881 when the canal company allowed W. C. Murrell & Son's corn steamers to use the northwest quay, as Cohens complained of congestion, but they were mollified by being allowed to keep two barges in the dock without payment. Murrell was declared bankrupt in October 1889, bringing his usage of the quay to an end.

Cohens use of the dock steadily built up and they took on additional premises as they became available, such as in September 1910 when two disused coal stores on the northwest quay were demolished. The start made in September 1918 to fill in the barge basin was a prelude to building a new quay wall from their wharf to the Commercial Road Locks. Once the quay had been completed Cohens took a lease of the new area, controlling the entire northwest quay for their scrap metal business.

For many years the largest single user of the dock was John Rupert Spurling, a general trader who was already established at Victoria Park Wharf, Old Ford, on the Hertford Union Canal when he applied for premises at the dock in October 1901. Initially he was refused but a year later the company had a change of heart and leased the southern part of the new Edward Warehouse to him at £500. In September 1903 he leased the middle section and a year later took the whole building at £1,100 and by the middle of 1905 he had erected a mezzanine floor in the building nearly doubling the storage area. Then in March 1906 and after failing to interest the Great Central Railway in the building, the canal company also leased the new Alexandra warehouse to Spurling for £400.

Spurling renewed both leases in 1913 at £1,610 with a guarantee of 20,000 tons of traffic and again in 1919 at a much increased rent of £4,000 although this included an extension to the Alexandra Warehouse; Spurling had acquired a second-hand galvanised-iron building, which he had erected at the northern end nearly doubling the length of the warehouse and extending it almost to the railway viaduct.

Such was the growth of Spurling's business that in December 1908 he agreed to lease the Liverpool Warehouse on the south quay at £655 guaranteeing to handle two ships each week and later he took the adjacent New Shed as well. There was a serious fire in the Liverpool shed in April 1909, which destroyed half of the wooden building, the cause being

George Cohen & Son's scrap yard on the north quay of Regent's Canal Dock in 1911. Cohen first took space on the quay in 1873 and expanded over the years to become the sole occupant of this part of the dock. The company remained in occupation until the early 1980s and was the last to use the dock for general shipping.

Regent's Canal & Dock Co booklet in the author's collection

attributed to a lightning strike. Spurling seems to have been unfortunate in this respect as there had been an equally serious fire at his Victoria Park Wharf in September 1906 that caused serious damage to the premises and blocked the canal when two barges were sunk by falling debris.

In 1915 Spurling agreed to take the newly-constructed west shed on the south quay guaranteeing to handle one ship each week and subsequently several additions were made to the buildings on this quay, some by the canal company and some by Spurling whose business was now J. Spurling Ltd. In June 1928 Spurling got together with the Norddeutscher-Lloyd shipping company of Bremen and they formed Roland-Argo Wharves Ltd, which took over the wharves on the south, southeast and east quays. From the beginning of October 1931 Roland-Argo took over the Medland Wharf as well, increasing its guarantee from 104 to 270 ships each year at the four locations.

In the early 1930s there was a general depression in the country and trading remained difficult and Roland-Argo gradually built up a substantial debt to the company despite a 30% reduction in dock dues being agreed in 1934. By now Norddeutscher-Lloyd had effectively withdrawn and been replaced by Argo-Reederie AG, which stood as guarantor for the rent. The concessions for 1936 totalled £8,408 but by 1 July 1936 Roland-Argo still owed £7,122 for current charges and a further £5,084 for historic debt. The Grand Union Canal Company was becoming increasingly disenchanted with the position, particularly as little of Roland-Argo's traffic used the canal. In May 1937 it decided to review the concessions and this prompted Roland-Argo to agree to give up all its leases on 27 September 1937. The parent concern – Argo-Reederei Richard Adler & Co Ltd of Germany – agreed to maintain the existing service of ships from Hamburg and Bremen to the dock and to clear the outstanding debt by the end of November. Grand Union (Stevedoring & Wharfage) Ltd took over the vacated wharves on 29 September and 1,000 of its shares were issued to Herr Richard Adler for the cranes and other equipment taken over.

In June 1915 H. H. Poole & Co Ltd, ship brokers of Leadenhall Street, had taken premises on the north quay comprising one of the railway arches and an open yard to the north. This business expanded until it controlled most of that quay under nine separate leases, which included eight railway arches and most of the land to the north of them. In May 1922 a new agreement with Pooles consolidated all the agreements into one lease with a £1,050 rental.

Three years later Pooles decided to move to the West India Dock, leaving in the autumn, and a new company was formed to operate from the north quay. It was short-lived and merged with the London & Cologne Shipping Company to form Regent's North Quay Wharf Ltd early in 1928. This concern was an early casualty of the Second World War, which disrupted its German shipping services and it gave up its tenancy at the end of 1939, Grand Union (Stevedoring & Wharfage) Ltd taking over. By now there were only two independent traders in the dock

– Regents Discharging Co Ltd and George Cohen Sons & Co Ltd. The discharging company's traffic was fairly consistent – a typical month was October 1942 when 25,675 tons of coal was transhipped.[22]

In 1943 a new lease was agreed with Cohens, replacing that of 1924. Effective from 25 December 1945, it involved an annual rent of £2,500 with another £1,500 in lieu of dock dues and certain other charges such as for landing and transhipping cargoes. On 3 October 1945, however, there was a major structural failure on the northwest quay that led to a lengthy dispute with Cohens revolving around the wording in the two leases about the responsibility for repairs. In November 1946 W. & C. French Ltd was awarded a £38,925 contract by the canal company to repair the quay and legal proceedings were started against Cohens to recover this cost. The hearing lasted 23 days and was completed in July 1949 with a verdict against the Docks & Inland Waterways Executive, as successors to the Grand Union, on the grounds that the new lease was incorrect in not reflecting the verbal renewal agreement. The Executive appealed but in June 1950 the verdict as upheld.

Cohens continued to use the dock beyond the official closure in May 1969; in 1980 it was still sending out some 15,000 tons of scrap involving an average of one shipment per month, but the traffic came to an end soon afterwards.

Initially the only motive power on the canal was

Whilst tugs were used on the longer lock-free stretches of the canal, they were not so useful where there were several locks. As early as April 1930 Charrington Gardner & Lockett & Co Ltd had introduced a small tractor to tow coal barges to Kensal Green Gasworks and the practice spread, particularly after the Second World War. Here a tractor is towing a loaded timber barge above St Pancras Locks on 30 July 1953.

The Waterways Archive, British Waterways Archive, Gloucester

*The tug **Brent** undergoing trials near the Macclesfield Bridge in Regent's Park in 1928. The tug had been built at the Bushell Brothers boatyard at Tring in Hertfordshire and both Charles and Joseph Bushell were on board for the trial. By now tugs were in regular use on the longer lock free stretches of the canal.*

The Waterways Archive,
British Waterways Archive, Gloucester

provided by horses and the canal company maintained stables at key locations such as Hampstead Road, City Road and Limehouse. The introduction of the tug at Islington prompted a string of inventors to offer the company other forms of traction such as when David Gordon's steamboat was tried out between Paddington and Regent's Park Basin in November 1828. While the paddle wheels were enclosed to prevent the wash damaging the canal banks the boat was not found to be suitable and tests on a series of other craft yielded similar results.

Matters remained the same until March 1852 when the company's traffic manager suggested introducing a steam tug on the upper level between Hampstead and Paddington to speed up traffic. John Inshaw of Birmingham provided a tug on trial and it performed satisfactorily, prompting the company to offer a prize for the best design of tug capable of handling three barges, of 80 tons each, at a minimum speed of 2mph. The competition took place in August 1855 and Inshaw's entry, a screw tug named *Birmingham*, was judged the winner. The company awarded him the £100 prize and purchased his tug for £450. It entered service on 1 November and performed satisfactorily, but seems to have ceased operating by 1865 possibly because of damage caused to the banks.

Ten years later the company was again looking to using steam tugs instead of horses between Hampstead Road and Paddington and elsewhere on the canal but no suitable boat could be found.

Instead, and following a review of expenditure, the company contracted out horse towing between Islington Tunnel and Paddington to John Walker from 1 February 1899 for three years. Under this arrangement the horses and equipment remained the company's property and the contractor provided labour, fodder and veterinary care. This was a prelude to Thomas Tilling Ltd taking over the entire towing contract on the canal for an initial three-year term from 1 January 1923. The contractor undertook to have 28 horses and drivers available and to provide two horse keepers and all the necessary equipment. As part of the deal Tillings purchased 24 horses from the company for £732, paying another £80 for 26 sets of harness and other equipment.

There was a different development in January 1863 when the company commissioned Joshua Horton to build three wrought-iron barges for £350 each to be hired out to traders to help them build up traffic on the canal. *Iron Albert* was delivered in November and *Iron Alfred* and *Iron Arthur* soon afterwards. All three were soon let out to traders at a rental of around £5 per month and in June 1869 a further five barges of 100-ton capacity were ordered from Bayliss Jones & Bayliss for £374 each – all five had been delivered by April 1870; they were *Beatrice*, *Confidence*, *Director*, *Leopold* and *Peabody*.

The company continued to provide a towing service through Islington Tunnel, although there were interruptions at times such as in March 1837 when the boat sprang a leak and was taken to a shipyard on the Thames for repairs. At such times barges and boats had to be legged through. Normally, barges were not allowed to pass through the tunnel after 8pm when the tug ceased operating but from early in 1837 the company began offering extended hours for barges, in return for an additional fee. Narrowboats, which could pass one another inside, were allowed to pass through the tunnel outside the normal hours without charge.

Increasing barge traffic necessitated more powerful engines and in 1840 Ovid Topham, provided an 8hp engine for £736 while John Fuller built a new wooden hull for it for £258. This tug served until 1900 by which time it was nearly worn out and the

machinery kept breaking down and was increasingly costly to repair. A new tug was then provided by the Blenheim Engineering Company for £1,250 and it served until March 1921 when a self-propelled steam tug, converted from a naval pinnace and named *Ruislip*, was purchased from O. J. Cavell for £1,075 to do away with the cable haulage system. Initially it proved satisfactory and two similar tugs were purchased from Cavell, the first in May for £1,123 for towing between Hampstead Road and Paddington, and the second in September for £1,125; they were named *Brent* and *Northolt* after the principal feeders to the canal.

After a few months problems began to be experienced with the new system at the Islington

A cluster of craft on the first stretch of the Regent's Canal west of Maida Hill Tunnel in about 1952. The tug **Ruislip** *has been towing the Thames Steam Tug & Lighterage Company's barge* **Retort** *loaded with timber whilst the motor narrow boat* **Vanguard**, *then employed on maintenance duties, has charge of another barge.*

Tunnel and on 28 September the tug driver was overcome by fumes. Less than a month later, four men employed on the tug collapsed and to counteract this a covered enclosure was provided to protect the steerer. This eased the position but on 10 July 1923 both the steerer and the engineer were overcome during a passage through the tunnel. The steerer fell overboard and drowned. At the ensuing inquest the coroner recommended steps to prevent a similar accident and this led to the cable-tug system, which had operated for nearly 80 years without major incident, being brought back into use on 24 July. In December 1927 *Ruislip* was fitted with a 50hp Bolinder semi-diesel engine costing £613 and supplied by James Pollock Sons & Co Ltd of Faversham who specifically guaranteed that it would not be injurious to health. The cable haulage system was then finally dispensed with.

By this time *Brent*, which operated on the Long Level, was in poor condition. It was replaced in the middle of 1928 by a new wooden tug built by Bushell Brothers of Tring for £1,130 and fitted with a 44hp Kromhout diesel engine costing £544. In August 1929 it was decided to replace the equally aged *Ruislip* and Bushells provided a new wooden hull costing £650 with the engine and fittings bringing the total cost to £3,200. Similarly in October 1928 a new steel ice-breaking tug was ordered from the Steel Barrel Co Ltd of Uxbridge for £2,044 – called *Aldenham* this starting a new practice of naming the tugs after the company's reservoirs.

In August 1936 Pollocks agreed to supply a new steel tug for the Islington Tunnel service to replace the more vulnerable wooden vessel and *Tring* was delivered early in 1937 costing £2,376. *Tring* remained in service until 1952 when three all-steel welded tugs were built at Lowestoft by Brooke Marine to handle barges in the London area and particularly through the tunnel. These tugs were equipped with 62hp Lister diesel engines and could tow seven barges laden with 600 tons at 1½mph.[23] They were named *Naseby, Olton* and *Sulby* and continued to handle the barges until commercial traffic on the Regent's Canal finally came to an end.

The tunnel tug **Tring** *emerges from the eastern end of Islington Tunnel with a hopper barge in tow, whilst a Charringtons coal barge waits to make the passage.*

The Waterways Archive, British Waterways Archive, Gloucester

NOTES

CHAPTER ONE

1. A Design for bringing a Navigable River from Rickmansworth to St. Giles-in-the-Fields, 1641 with an Answer. Institute of Civil Engineers Library (Reprinted 1720).
2. Spencer, Herbert, *London's Canal*, 1961. (A plan is in Marylebone Central Library).
3. *Ibid*. A variation of this scheme appeared in September 1802 as the North London Canal from Waltham Abbey to the Thames with branches to Spa Fields and Shoreditch.
4. Grand Junction Canal Act – 33 Geo III c80 – 30 April 1793.
5. Paddington Branch Canal Act – 35 Geo III c43 – 28 April 1795.
6. Faulkner, Alan, *The Grand Junction Canal*, 1993.
7. *Northampton Mercury*, 18 July 1801.
8. *Rees's Encyclopaedia*, Vol VI, 1819.
9. John Rennie (1761–1821) was engineer to the Kennet & Avon, Lancaster and Rochdale canals among many other involvements.
10. Grand Junction Canal gauging register, Vol 1, 1802.
11. Nash went on to make a major contribution to building the canal and was actively involved in many of the negotiations (see Chapter 4).
12. Morgan was born in Wales in about 1773. An architect and engineer, he was a close associate of John Nash for many years.
13. Saunders, Ann, *Regent's Park,* 1969.
14. Sir Thomas Bernard (1750–1818) was also a notable philanthropist (see Chapter 4).
15. The records of the venture prior to incorporation are held in the Waterways Archive at Gloucester and are thought to have been compiled by Colonel John Drinkwater.
16. Preliminary minutes – 4 February 1812.
17. Regent's Canal Act – 52 Geo III c195 – 13 July 1812.

CHAPTER TWO

1. Regent's Park Branch Canal Act – 53 Geo III c32 – 15 April 1813.
2. Between 1804 and 1806 Jones had been involved in the construction of the Grand Surrey Docks. His brothers, Charles and George, were involved with the tunnels at Braunston, Blisworth and Langleybury on the Grand Junction Canal.
3. McIntosh was born in Scotland in 1768 and by 1812 had become one of the country's leading civil engineering contractors. He died at Wakefield in August 1840. 'Hugh McIntosh, National Contractor', M. M. Chrimes, *Transactions of the Newcomen Society*, Vol 66, 1994/5.
4. This date is specified in *The Principal Events connected with the Formation of the Regent's or London Canal* – a chronology compiled by Colonel John Drinkwater in 1830. Some accounts give the 14 October as the supposed commencement date.
5. Josias Jessop (1781–1826), engineer, was the second son of canal engineer William Jessop.
6. The award was made to the engineer Henry Provis, who had worked on the Grand Junction Canal, but it seems he copied a design by William Jessop.
7. Regent's Canal Company's General Assembly minutes, 9 August 1816. (Public Record Office Rail 860/1)
8. Conyers Morrell, Reverend R. *The Story of Agar Town*, 1935.
9. Plans of the proposed deviations dated 30 September 1815 are in the London Metropolitan Archives – ref. MR/UP/6L & 6M.
10. Regent's Canal Third Act – 56 Geo III c85 – 2 July 1816.

CHAPTER THREE

1. Regent's Canal Third Act – 56 Geo III c85 – 2 July 1816.
2. A tontine was an annuity shared by subscribers whose share increased as participants died until the last

survivor got the lot. Sometimes there was a specified date when those who survived shared the proceeds.

3. Poor Employment Act – 57 Geo III c34 – 16 June 1817, which provided for the appointment of The Exchequer Bill Loan Commissioners.
4. Thomas Telford (1757-1834) was one of the leading canal and civil engineers of the day. He was the principal consulting engineer to the Exchequer Bill Loan Commissioners.
5. Limehouse and City Road Basin Act – 59 Geo III c66 – 14 June 1819.

CHAPTER FOUR

1. *The County Chronicle*, 6 June 1820.
2. Regent's Canal Company minutes, 12 May 1820 (PRO RAIL 860/18).
3. For example Eyre's Tunnel, Hawley's Lock, Thornhill's Bridge, Sturt's Lock, Acton's Lock, and Johnson's Lock.
4. The opening was widely reported as, for example, in *The Morning Chronicle*, 2 August 1820.
5. Grand Junction Canal General Committee Minutes 12 April 1802.
6. *Ibid*, 20 January 1804 and 10 February 1807.
7. Grand Junction Canal Gauging Register, Vol 1, 1802.
8. *The London Encyclopaedia*, 1983.
9. *Ibid*.
10. Summerson, Sir John, *John Nash*, 1949.
11. *The London Encyclopaedia*, 1983.

CHAPTER FIVE

1. Grand Junction Canal Water Act – 38 Geo III c33 – 26 May 1798.
2. Grand Junction Canal Water Works Act – 51 Geo III c169 – 15 June 1811.
3. A heading was an underground tunnel or passage – in this case a pipeline.
4. The standard lock measure was 56,000 gallons – enough to fill an average 14ft wide lock.
5. William Congreve (1772–1828) succeeded his father as a baronet in April 1814. He was a Fellow of the Royal Society and wrote many scientific papers. He also served as an MP until his death at Toulouse.
6. Patent No 3670 – Congreve's Improved Modes of Constructing Locks and Sluices of Canals etc – 23 March 1813.
7. These details were contained in the auctioneers' sale particulars.
8. William Chadwell Mylne was the engineer to the New River Company.
9. John Rennie junior (1794–1874) later became Sir John Rennie. His father, John Rennie (1761-1821), was also a famous engineer.
10. Bryan Donkin (1768–1855) was a versatile and respected mechanical engineer at the time.
11. Water Supply Agreement Act – 59 Geo III c111 – 21 June 1819.
12. Contained within the Limehouse and City Road Basin Act – 59 Geo III c66 – 14 June 1819.
13. Pritchard was involved in civil engineering where he gained a reputation for canal tunnelling work, being in partnership with his son-in-law William Hoof. He was actively involved in both Maida Hill and Islington tunnels where his work was highly regarded by James Morgan.
14. Anderson was the GJWWC's first Resident Engineer, serving under John Rennie, its Consulting Engineer
15. Revised Water Agreement Act – 7 Geo IV c140 – 31 May 1826.
16. Regent's Canal Report to its shareholders, December 1834.
17. In the early years the canal company's records often refer to this as Cool Duck Lane, but its present name has been used here.
18. Hoof had gone into partnership with Daniel Pritchard (his father-in-law) in the 1820s forming Pritchard & Hoof, canal tunnelling contractors. Hoof died in 1855 aged 67.

CHAPTER SIX

1. Twenty-eight wharves had been established round the basin by 31 March 1828 producing £1,969 annual

rent to the company. The 1830 edition of *Robson's London Commercial Directory* records 40 traders at the basin and the 1843 edition 51.

2. *Aris's Birmingham Gazette*, 1 March 1824.

3. The Act authorising the market was 12 Geo IV c14 assented on 3 May 1830.

4. Everard, Stirling *The History of the Gas Light & Coke Company, 1812 – 1949*, 1949.

5. Regent's Canal Committee minutes, 23 August 1820 (PRO RAIL 860/18).

6. Select Committee on the Port of London, 1836.

7. Thereafter Nash was much less involved in the company's affairs but he remained on the committee until his death on the Isle of Wight in May 1835.

8. Finance Act – 1 & 2 Geo IV c43 – 19 April 1821 (authorised the Exchequer Bill Loan Commissioners to lend more money).

9. Exchequer Bill Loan Commissioners Act – 1 & 2 Geo IV c111 – 10 July 1821.

10. Exchequer Bill Loan Commissioners Act – 3 Geo IV c86 – 26 July 1822.

11. Exchequer Bill Loan Commissioners Act – 5 Geo IV c77 – 17 June 1824.

12. It seems certain that Colonel John Drinkwater compiled these figures for his chronology.

13. The Act was 5 Geo IV c47 assented on 17 May 1824.

14. An article by Grahame Boyes on 'The Exchequer Bill Loan Commissioners as a source of canal railway finance' in the *Journal of the Railway & Canal Historical Society* – Vol 24, No. 3 – November 1978 gives more details about the Commissioners.

CHAPTER SEVEN

1. The original London & Birmingham Railway Act was assented on 6 May 1833 and the Euston extension was authorised on 3 July 1835. Other incorporation and authorisation dates in this chapter were Eastern Counties Railway 4 July 1836, Commercial Railway 28 July 1836, Great Northern Railway 26 June 1846, North London Railway 26 August 1846, North London Railway (Broad Street Extension) 22 July 1861, Midland Railway (London Extension) 22 June 1863, Great Eastern Railway (Bethnal Green to Hackney) 27 July 1864, Metropolitan & St Johns Wood Railway 29 July 1864, Manchester, Sheffield & Lincolnshire Railway (London Extension) 28 March 1893.

2. Borley, H.V., *Chronology of London Railways*, 1982. Most of the railway opening dates in this chapter are from the same source.

3. Wrottesley, John, *The Great Northern Railway, Volume 1*, 1979. Volumes 2 & 3 record that a second tunnel under the canal was opened in 1878 and a third in 1892.

4. *The Observer*, 27 October 1851.

5. *Illustrated London News*, 28 May 1853.

6. Plimsoll is better known for establishing the Plimsoll line to limit the amount of cargo ships could carry.

7. Midland Railway (South Construction Committee) minutes, 3 May 1865.

8. Agar's estate had been acquired by the Ecclesiastical Commissioners in about 1852.

9. *The Regent's Canal & Dock Co* (booklet), July 1911.

10. Radford was born in 1816, worked for Hugh McIntosh and then for the Grand Junction Water Works, which brought him to the notice of the canal company. He died in May 1854, aged 38, not long after leaving the company's service

11. James Meadows Rendel was born in 1799 and worked under Thomas Telford from about 1817. He moved to London in about 1836 where he concentrated on river and harbour works. He was President of the Institution of Civil Engineers in 1852/3 and died in November 1856.

12. Regent's Canal & Dock Company Act – 38 & 39 Vic c206 – 11 August 1875.

13. Regent's Canal & Dock Company Dissolution Act – 40 & 41 Vic c205 – 6 August 1877.

14. Regent's Canal City & Docks Railway Company Act – 45 & 46 Vic c262 – 18 August 1882.

15. The actual agreement was dated 25 September 1847 with John and James Knight. Plans of the new lock are in the Waterways Archive at Gloucester (BW 1533/84 and 1534/84).

16. Regent's Canal Company minutes, 6 June 1849 (PRO RAIL 860/42).

17. *The Regent's Canal Dock and the Hydraulic Accumulator Tower* (Greater London Industrial Archaeology Society, 1996) records that James Rendel was an early proponent of hydraulic power and a friend of William Armstrong.
18. William George Armstrong (1810–1900) invented the world's first efficient hydraulic crane for the docks at Newcastle and went on to found W. G. Armstrong & Company at Elswick on the Tyne in 1847. He was knighted in 1859 for services to the armaments industry.
19. The link was first mentioned in the 18 July 1848 minutes of the Lee Trustees.
20. Lee Trustees minutes, 17 December 1853.
21. The plan signed by Edwin Thomas and John Fowler and dated 30 November 1863 is held in the London Metropolitan Archives, (MR/UP/727).
22. The plan signed by Edwin Thomas and John Fowler and dated November 1864 in the London Metropolitan Archives (Ref. MR/UP/772) shows the full extent of the proposed works.
23. Limehouse Basin Act – 28 & 29 Vic c365 – 5 July 1865.
24. Regent's Canal Company minutes, 4 August 1869 (PRO RAIL 860/56).
25. The lock at the entrance to the Limehouse Cut was reconstructed and re-opened on 24 January 1866 (Lee Trustees minutes 18 May 1865 and 24 January 1866).
26. Hertford Union Canal Purchase Act – 18 & 19 Vic c95 – 26 June 1855.
27. The park was opened in 1845, being laid out between 1842 and 1845 by James Pennethorne who was Mary Nash's adopted son. Pennethorne took over John Nash's practice in 1834.
28. This bridge on the Acton estate was a belated requirement of the 1812 Act which, with the passage of time, the company had tried to avoid. The landowners contributed £255 to the cost as the bridge was built wider than required under the Act.
29. Details and a plan of this bridge are held in the Royal Engineer's Specialist Collection at Chatham.
30. Brent Reservoir Act – 14 & 15 Vic c32 – 5 June 1851.
31. Details of Warner and the inn are contained in the Wembley History Society's booklet *The Welsh Harp Reservoir, 1835 to 1985*.
32. Makin, George, 'The Great Flood' (*Waterways World*, September 1986).
33. Regent's Canal Company's minutes, 16 July 1883 (PRO RAIL 860/62). This opening date differs from 4 December 1882, which is quoted in the Grand Junction Canal Company's minutes, but water may have been let into parts of the new branch to facilitate its construction.
34. Morgan died at Hammersmith in February 1856 and was buried in London's Brompton Cemetery.

CHAPTER EIGHT

1. Establishment of separate canal undertaking – 46 & 47 Vic c164 – 2 August 1883.
2. Establishment of City Lines undertaking – 46 & 47 Vic c212 – 20 August 1883.
3. Power to establish further separate undertakings – 48 & 49 Vic c138 – 31 July 1885.
4. Extension of time – 50 & 51 Vic c51 – 23 May 1887.
5. Further extension of time – 53 & 54 Vic c200 – 20 August 1890.
6. Abandonment of City Lines and renaming of company – 55 & 56 Vic c188 – 27 June 1892.
7. Regent's Canal and Dock Company Act – 63 & 64 Vic c118 – 30 July 1900.
8. Borley, H.V., *Chronology of London Railways*, 1982. The other railway opening dates in this chapter are from the same source.
9. Canal Improvements Act – 59 & 60 Vic c184 – 7 August 1896.
10. Figures taken from a report prepared by John Glass.
11. Sir W. G. Armstrong Mitchell & Co merged with Sir Joseph Whitworth & Co of Manchester in 1897 to form Sir W.G. Armstrong Whitworth & Co Ltd.
12. Everard, Stirling, *The Gas Light & Coke Company, 1812–1949*, 1949.
13. *Ibid.*
14. Information from Tom Ridge of the Ragged School Museum.
15. The high duty pumps were so called as they had to overcome a 27ft rise over almost a mile of pipeline

between the dock at Limehouse and Mile End Lock. The low duty pumps has only to force water up from the tidal Thames into the dock.

16. Canal Control Committee papers (PRO MT 52/4).
17. *Ibid*.
18. Grand Junction Canal board minutes, 10 March 1926 (PRO RAIL 830/46).
19. *Ibid*, 12 October 1927 (PRO RAIL 830/47).
20. Grand Junction Canal Purchase Act – 18 & 19 Geo V c98 – 3 August 1928 and the Warwick Canals Purchase Act – 18 & 19 Geo V. c99 – 3 August 1928.
21. Faulkner, Alan, *The Warwick Canals*, 1985.
22. Grand Union Canal board minutes, 9 January 1929 (PRO RAIL 860/86).

CHAPTER NINE

1. *The Times*, 31 March 1932.
2. Faulkner, Alan, *The George & The Mary*, 1973.
3. Faulkner, Alan, *The Warwick Canals*, 1985.
4. Evidence of John Miller in support of the 1943 Bill.
5. Amended powers Act – 6 & 7 Geo VI c5 – 6 July 1943.
6. The closure was reported in *The Star*, 24 July 1940.
7. Details of the fleet kindly supplied by Roy Fenton of the World Ship Society.
8. *Waterways* (British Waterways magazine), No 14, November/December 1957.
9. *The Bulletin*, (Journal of the Inland Waterways Association), No 27, May 1951.
10. *Windlass* (Journal of the London & Home Counties Branch of the Inland Waterways Association), No 66, June 1968.
11. The Zoological Gardens were opened on 27 April 1828 initially on a five-acre site south of the canal but they extended steadily and now cover 36 acres and straddle the canal.
12. *Waterways*, No 33, July/August 1959.
13. *Waterways,* No 25, November 1958.
14. *Windlass*, No 36, June 1963.
15. *Windlass*, No 63, December 1967.
16. *Windlass*, No 71, October 1968.
17. *Windlass*, No 136, January 1977. Dr. Essex-Lopresti went on to produce *Exploring the Regent's Canal*, a comprehensive guidebook to the canal published in 1987.
18. *Windlass*, No 140, November 1977 (The ceremony was performed by the Lord Mayor of London).
19. The works were authorised by the Act – 13 & 14 Eliz 2 c23 assented in 1965.
20. *Windlass*, No 66, April 1968.
21. *Windlass*, No 76, April 1969.
22. *New Ways* (British Waterways Staff Newspaper), July/August 1989.

CHAPTER TEN

1. Turnbull, Gerard, *Traffic and Transport* (An Economic History of Pickfords), 1979.
2. The Grand Junction gauging tables show Pickfords had nine boats on the section of the canal south of Blisworth in 1802. In the first month after the tunnel was opened a further eight boats were gauged and a year later the cumulative total had doubled to 33.
3. Turnbull – op. cit. (At least twenty-four new boats were gauged by the Grand Junction in 1823).
4. Faulkner, Alan, *The Grand Junction Canal*, 1993.
5. Faulkner – *op. cit.*
6. The disaster was widely reported including in *The Illustrated London News*, 10 October 1874.
7. *Fire Protection Association Journal*, No 37, April 1957.
8. Faulkner – *op. cit.*
9. Faulkner, Alan, *FMC* (A short history of Fellows, Morton & Clayton Limited), 1975.

10. A short-lived service between February 1982 and November 1984 was provided by Lee & Brentford Lighterage trading to the British Waterways Board's Brentford depot and, via Regent's Canal Dock, with its Enfield depot.

11. John Gardner (1779–1850). His son, John Irvine Gardner, was also involved in the business.

12. The yard was reputed to build one wooden barge each year, the last being *Japan* in 1912. It remained in business repairing wooden barges until the 1950s, by which time most craft were of steel construction.

13. Fraser-Stephen, Elspeth, *Two Centuries in the London Coal Trade* (The Story of Charringtons), 1952.

14. The Grand Junction gauging register (PRO RAIL 830/57) shows a 70 ton barge being gauged for Tomlin on 19 February 1822.

15. *Robson's London Commercial Directory*, 1843.

16. A William Winn, who resigned as a clerk from the Regent's Canal Dock office in March 1850 may have been connected with the business.

17. In March 1876 the Chartered Gas Light & Coke Company took over both the Imperial Gas Light & Coke Company, with its works at St Pancras and Shoreditch, and the Independent Gas Company, with its works at Haggerston. It had already acquired the Western Gas Light Company at Kensal Green in November 1872.

18. Fraser-Stephen, Elspeth – *op. cit.*

19. Joseph Wright established the business in 1731.

20. Fraser-Stephen, Elspeth – *op. cit.*

21. Turnbull, Gerard – *op. cit.*

22. The Chartered Gas Light & Coke Company had a fleet of steam colliers that delivered to the dock. Under an agreement dated 5 September 1894 it qualified for a significant toll rebate if its annual traffic reached 220,000 tons and this rebate was earned in many subsequent years.

23. *Lock & Quay*, (Journal of the Docks & Inland Waterways Executive), September 1952.

APPENDIX ONE

1 The Acts of Parliament

1	52 Geo III	c195	13 Jul 1812	Incorporation. Main canal from Paddington to Limehouse & Aske Terrace Branch; capital £400,000.
2	53 Geo III	c32	15 Apr 1813	Regent's Park Branch.
3	56 Geo III	c85	2 Jul 1816	Defining line on Agar's estate; extra capital £200,000; supplying Thames water to Grand Junction Canal.
4	59 Geo III	c66	14 Jun 1819	City Road Branch; deepening Limehouse Basin; extra capital £200,000.
5	59 Geo III	c111	22 Jun 1819	Water supply agreement with Grand Junction Canal and Grand Junction Water Works companies.
6	1&2 Geo IV	c43	19 Apr 1821	Exchequer Bill Loan Commissioners may advance money; extra £200,000 capital.
7	5 Geo IV	c47	17 May 1824	Incorporation Hertford Union Canal.
8	7 Geo IV	c140	31 May 1826	Amended water supply agreement.
9	14 & 15 Vic	c32	5 Jun 1851	Enlargement Welsh Harp reservoir.
10	18 & 19 Vic	c95	26 Jun 1855	Purchase Hertford Union Canal.
11	28 & 29 Vic	c365	5 Jul 1865	Limehouse Basin improvements; extra £240,000 capital.
12	38 & 39 Vic	c206	11 Aug 1875	Incorporation Regent's Canal & Dock Company.
13	40 & 41 Vic	c205	6 Aug 1877	Dissolution Regent's Canal & Dock Company.
14	45 & 46 Vic	c262	18 Aug 1882	Incorporation Regent's Canal City & Docks Railway Company.
15	46 & 47 Vic	c164	2 Aug 1883	Establishment of separate canal undertaking with £1,500,000 capital
16	46 & 47 Vic	c212	20 Aug 1883	Establishment separate City Lines undertaking.
17	48 & 49 Vic	c138	31 Jul 1885	Power to establish separate railway undertakings; payment of interest on capital.
18	50 & 51 Vic	c51	23 May 1887	Extension of time.
19	53 & 54 Vic	c200	14 Aug 1890	Further extension of time.
20	55 & 56 Vic	c188	27 Jun 1892	Abandonment of City Lines; further extension of time for the rest; renamed North Metropolitan Railway & Canal Company.
21	57 & 58 Vic	c199	17 Aug 1894	Canal Tolls & Charges Confirmation.
22	59 & 60 Vic	c184	7 Aug 1896	Canal improvements and other works.
23	63 & 64 Vic	c118	30 Jul 1900	Consolidation of loan debt; renamed Regent's Canal & Dock Company.
24	4 Edward 7	c132	22 Jul 1904	Canal Tolls & Charges Confirmation.
25	18&19 Geo V	c98	3 Aug 1927	Purchase of Grand Junction Canal; renamed Grand Union Canal Company.
26	18 & 19 Geo V	c99	3 Aug 1927	Purchase of the Warwick canals.

2 Authorised Share Capital

(A) Regent's Canal Company

1812 Act	By shares	£300,000
	By shares or by mortgage	£100,000
1816 Act	By shares, half shares or mortgage	£200,000
1819 Act	By shares or by mortgage	£200,000
1821 Act	By shares or by mortgage	£200,000
	Total	**£1,000,000**

The 1865 Act extinguished the company's money-raising powers under former Acts except for the existing capital of £816,625 (nominal £2,701,800) and the existing mortgage debt of £109,550.

1865 Act		
	Existing share capital	£816,625
	By new ordinary or preference shares	£180,000
	Existing mortgages	£109,550
	By mortgages re existing capital (max. £250,000)	£140,450
	By mortgages re additional capital	£60,000
	Total	**£1,306,625**
	of which shares	*£996,625*
	borrowing	*£310,000*

(B) Regent's Canal City & Docks Railway Company

1882 Act		
	By shares (canal and railway capital)	£8,100,000
	By mortgages (£239,000 for each £810,000 raised)	£2,390,000
	Borrowings already authorised by the 1865 Act	£310,000
	Total	**£10,800,000**

1883 Act		
	Separate canal capital established	£1,500,000
	Separate canal borrowing established	£115,000
	If balance of capital raised, further borrowing	£75,000
	Existing canal borrowing powers	£310,000
Sub Total	*£1,500,000 in shares & £500,000 in borrowings*	**£2,000,000**
1892 Act	By mortgages an additional	£300,000
1896 Act	By ordinary or preference shares	£200,000
	If balance of capital raised, further borrowing	£65,000
	Total	**£2,565,000**
	of which shares	*£1,700,000*
	borrowing	*£865,000*

The company was renamed the North Metropolitan Railway & Canal Company in 1892 and then the Regent's Canal & Dock Company in 1900.

Under the 1883 Canal Capital Act the railway capital was established at £6,600,000 in shares and £2,200,000 in borrowing, making £8,800,000 in all. The 1885 Act increased the shares by £660,000 to £7,260,000 for the payment of interest. Under the 1892 Act abandoning the City lines the share capital was first reduced to £4,291,800 but then increased by £410,000 to £4,701,800 for the payment of interest. Borrowings were reduced to £1,430,600 making a total of £6,132,400 for the undertaking.

The 1928 Grand Union Act extinguished the company's powers under former Acts for borrowing, except for the existing debentures of £842,284.

(C) Grand Union Canal Company

1927 Act		
	Existing powers for raising capital	£1,700,000
	Capital for Grand Junction shareholders	£801,442
	By ordinary or preference shares	£200,000
	Existing borrowings	£842,284
	Debentures for Grand Junction Company	£285,709
	By borrowing re additional Grand Junction capital	£94,559
	By borrowing up to half of additional capital	£200,000
	Total	**£4,123,994**
	of which shares	*£2,701,442*
	borrowing	*£1,422,552*

The 1928 Act actually specified £760,536 for the Grand Junction shares but the higher amount of £801,442 seems to have been issued.

3 Issued Share Capital

1811–15	2,541	at £100	Original subscription	£254,100	£254,100
1817–19	3,730	at £25	Resumption of work	£93,250	£347,350
1819	600	at £25	To keep capital/loan ratio	£15,000	£362,550
1819	1,223	at £25	Limehouse Basin	£30,575	£392,925
1819–20	4,200	at £25	Completion of works	£105,000	£497,925
1827–8	9,124	at £25	To repay government loan	£228,100	£726,025
1850	250	at £16	Limehouse property	£5,000	£731,025
1850	1,600	at £16	Limehouse property	£25,600	£756,625
1851	3,750	at £16	Limehouse/Brent Reservoir	£60,000	£816,625
1865	4,682	at £20	Limehouse extension	£93,640	£910,265
1867	1,589	at £20	Limehouse extension	£31,780	£942,045
1867–68	1,689	at £20	Limehouse extension	£33,780	£975,825
1868	1,040	at £20	Limehouse extension	£20,800	£996,625
Total	36,018 (Nominal value £2,701,800)				**£996,625**

In 1874 36,018 shares at a nominal £25 were converted into £900,450 of stock.

1883	Initial capital of canal undertaking	£1,275,000
1893	Additional capital issued at par	£83,100
1928	Grand Junction Canal purchase	£801,442
	Total	**£2,159,542**

4 Dividend Table

(A) Regent's Canal Company *(For consistency given in decimal format throughout)*

Interim date	Rate (£)	Final date	Rate (£)	Total (£)	Cost
		03.06.29[1]	0.625	0.625	£13,386.25
		02.06.30[1]	0.625	0.625	£13,386.25
		01.06.31[1]	0.675	0.675	£14,457.15
		06.06.32[1]	0.675	0.675	£14,457.15
		05.06.33[1]	0.675	0.675	£14,457.15
		04.06.34[1]	0.700	0.700	£14,992.60
		03.06.35[1]	Nil	Nil	Nil
		01.06.36[1]	0.600	0.600	£12,850.80
		07.06.37[1]	0.600	0.600	£12,850.80
		06 06.38[1]	0.600	0.600	£12,850.80
		05.06.39[1]	0.350	0.350	£7,496.30
		03.06.40[1]	0.350	0.350	£7,496.30
		02.06.41[1]	0.400	0.400	£8,567.20
		01.06.42[1]	0.625	0.625	£13,386.25
07.06.43[1]	0.875	06.12.43	0.450	1.325	£28,378.85
05.06.44	0.500	04.12.44	0.450	0.950	£20,347.10
04.06.45	0.600	03.12.45	0.600	1.200	£25,701.60
03.06.46	0.600	02.12.46	0.600	1.200	£25,701.60
02.06.47	0.625	01.12.47	0.625	1.250	£26,772.50
07.06.48	0.625	06.12.48	0.550	1.175	£25,166.15
06.06.49	0.500	05.12.49	0.500	1.000	£21,418.00
05.06.50	0.500	04.12.50	0.575	1.075	£24,088.10
04.06.51	0.575	03.12.51	0.500	1.075	£25,018.10

Interim date	Rate (£)	Final date	Rate (£)	Total (£)	Cost
02.06.52	0.500	01.12.52	0.425	0.925	£23,116.65
01.06.53	0.400	07.12.53	0.450	0.850	£22,965.30
07.06.54	0.450	06.12.54	0.400	0.850	£22,965.30
06.06.55	0.400	05.12.55	0.425	0.825	£22,289.85
04.06.56	0.425	03.12.56	0.425	0.850	£22,965.30
03.06.57	0.475	02.12.57	0.425	0.900	£24,316.20
02.06.58	0.475	01.12.58	0.425	0.900	£24,316.20
01.06.59	0.400	07.12.59	0.425	0.825	£22,289.65
06.06.60	0.600	05.12.60	0.625	1.225	£33,097.05
05.06.61	0.600	04.12.61	0.625	1.225	£33,097.05
04.06.62	0.675	03.12.62	0.600	1.275	£34,447.95
03.06.63	0.700	02.12.63	0.650	1.350	£36,473.30
01.06.64	0.750	07.12.64	0.650	1.400	£37,825.20
07.07.65	0.700	06.12.65	0.650	1.350	£36,474.30
25.04.66[2]	0.800	31.10.66	0.650	1.450	£39,176.10
24.04.67	0.700	30.10.67	0.650	1.350	£36,474.30
29.04.68	0.625	28.10.68	0.500	1.125	£30,395.25
28.04.69	0.500	27.10.69	0.450	0.950	£33,659.10
27.04.70	0.500	26.10.70	0.400	0.900	£32,416.20
26.04.71	0.425	25.10.71	0.350	0.775	£27,913.95
24.04.72	0.425	30.10.72	0.400	0.825	£29,714.85
30.04.73	0.525	29.10.73	0.475	1.000	£36,018.00
29.04.74[3]	0.650			0.650	£23,411.70

(B) Regent's Canal Company (after share consolidation)

Interim date	Rate (£)	Final date	Rate (£)	Total (£)	Cost
		28.10.74	1.900	1.900	£17,108.50
28.04.75	2.187	27.10.75	2.187	4.375	£39,394.67
26.04.76	2.437	25.10.76	2.375	4.812	£43,334.16
25.04.77	2.500	31.10.77	2.250	4.750	£42,771.37
24.04.78[4]	2.500	30.10.78	2.250	4.750	£42,771.37
30.04.79[4]	2.500	29.10.79	2.250	4.750	£42,771.37
29.04.80[4]	2.500	27.10.80	2.250	4.750	£42,711.37
27.04.81	2.500	26.10.81	2.375	4.875	£43,896.94
26.04.82	2.500	25.10.82	2.500	5.000	£45,022.50
25.04.83[5]	2,500			2.500	£22,511.25

(C) Regent's Canal City & Docks Railway Company

Interim date	Rate (£)	Final date	Rate (£)	Total (£)	Cost
		30.09.83	2.000	2.000	£25,500.00
28.03.84	2.000	29.09.84	2.000	4.000	£51,000.00
27.03.85	2.000	30.09.85	2.000	4.000	£51,000.00
26.03.86	2.000	30.09.86	1.000	3.000	£38,250.00
04.03.87[6]	1.125	30.09.87	1.125	2.250	£28,687.50
27.03.88	1.625	28.09.88	1.125	2.750	£35,062.50
01.03.89	1.500	30.09.89	1.250	2.750	£35,062.50
28.03.90	1.625	30.09.90	1.375	3.000	£38,250.00
20.03.91	1.375	30.09.91	1.250	2.625	£33,486.75
31.03.92	1.750	30.09.92	1.250	3.000	£38,250.00
17.03.93	1.500	29.09.93	0.850	2.350	£30,668.85

Interim date	Rate (£)	Final date	Rate (£)	Total (£)	Cost
16.03.94	1.150	07.09.94	0.875	2.025	£27,501.52
15.03.95	1.000	27.09.95	0.625	1.625	£22,069.13
27.03.96	1.375	29.09.96	1.125	2.500	£33,952.51
30.03.97	1.375	07.09.97	1.000	2.375	£32,254.88
18.02.98[7]	1.250	06.09.88	0.875	2.125	£28,859.63
14.02.99[7]	1.250	19.09.99	0.875	2.125	£28,859.63
20.03.00	1.250	25.09.00	1.000	2.250	£30,557.25
26.03.01	1.125	03.09.01	1.000	2.125	£28,859.63
11.02.02	1.375	01.08.02	1.125	2.500	£33,952.51
17.02.03	1.375	04.08.03	1.125	2.500	£33,952.51
02.02.04	1.375	19.08.04	1.000	2.375	£32,254.88
28.02.05	1.250	04.08.05	1.000	2.250	£30,557.25
16.02.06	1.250	03.08.06	1.000	2.250	£30,557.25
21.02.07	1.250	02.08.07	1.000	2.250	£30,557.25
27.02.08	1.000	06.08.08	1.000	2.000	£27,162.00
21.02.09	1.000	06.08.09	0.875	1.875	£25,464.38
25.02.10	1.000	05.08.10	0.875	1.875	£25,464.38
28.02.11	1.000	01.08.11	0.875	1.875	£25,464.38
27.02.12	1.000	01.08.12	0.500	1.500	£20,371.50
25.02.13	0.875	01.08.13	0.625	1.500	£20,371.50
24.02.14	0.500	07.08.14	0.500	1.000	£13,581.00
23.02.15	0.500	06.08.15	Nil	0.500	£6,790.50
29.02.16	Nil	08.08.16	Nil	Nil	Nil
27.02.17	Nil	25.09.17	Nil	Nil	Nil
26.03.18	0.500	09.08.18	0.500	1.000	£13,581.00
25.02.19	0.500	01.08.19	0.562	1.062	£14,429.81
24.02.20	0.562	10.08.20	0.562	1.124	£15,278.62
22.03.21	0.562	09.08.21	Nil	0.562	£7,639.31
21.03.22	0.750	04.08.22	0.500	1.250	£16,976.25
20.03.23	0.750	10.08.23	0.500	1.250	£16,976.25
18.03.24	0.750	12.08.24	0.875	1.625	£22,070.12
17.03.25	1.125	14.08.25	0.875	2.000	£27,163.00
16.03.26	1.125	13.08.26	0.500	1.625	£22,069.12
15.03.27	1.125	16.08.27	1,125	2,250	£30,557.24
27.02.28	1.250	17.08.28	1.250	2.500	£33,952.50

The company was renamed the North Metropolitan Railway & Canal Company in 1892 and then the Regent's Canal & Dock Company in 1900.

1 From 1829 to 1842 the dividend was payable in July on the year's profits to the end of 31 March. From 1843 the dividends were payable half yearly in July and January on the profits for the preceding six months ended 31 March and 30 September.

2 From 1866 the half yearly meetings were switched from the first Wednesday in June and December to the last Wednesday in April and October. The dividend was paid in May and November but still covered to the end of March and September.

3 On 29 April 1874 the decision was taken to consolidate the 36,018 shares of £25 each to become £900,450 of ordinary stock. These shares had been issued at various prices and had actually brought in £996,625.

4 The figures for 1878, 1879 and part of 1880 have been estimated.

5 On 31 March 1883 the canal was sold to the Regent's Canal City & Docks Railway Company for £1,170,585, ie £1.30 per £1 of ordinary stock. The first accounts of the new company allowed for interest at 4% to be paid on the canal capital stock of £1,275,000.

6 From 30 June 1886 onwards, and as the capital for the railway plans had not been raised, the interest was paid only in so far as the profits of the canal permitted – ie it was effectively a dividend.

7 Under the 1883 company the meetings were initially held in March and September. In 1898 and 1899 this was varied with the first meetings being held in February. From 1902 the meetings were usually held in February and August. In all cases the dividend was paid a few days after the meeting.

APPENDIX TWO

Distance Tables

This table is a mixture of past and present features on the canal. With closures and subsequent rebuilding works the sites of many of the wharves, small basins, gas and electricity works that are shown have been redeveloped. This process seems set to continue.

The bridge numbering shown in square brackets is from the 1827 sequence. Those missing from the main line sequence are: 6 – Collateral Cut Bridge (on Regent's Park Branch); 22 – City Road Bridge (across City Road Basin); 39 – Queen Street Swing Bridge (across the original Limehouse entrance lock).

(L) and (R) refer to the left and right side of the canal in the direction of travel.

Regent's Canal		**Miles**	**Yards**
Broadwater, Paddington: Junction with the Grand Junction Canal			
(now known as Little Venice, or Browning's Pool)	OD 96.85	0	0
Warwick Avenue Bridge (A404) [Paddington No 1]		0	90
Paddington Stop Lock		0	100
Maida Hill Tunnel – south-western end (272 yards)		0	570
Maida Hill Tunnel – north-eastern end		0	840
Borough of Marylebone's Power Station (R)		0	900
Lisson Grove Bridge (B507) [Eyre's Tunnel No 2 – 53 yards]		0	1025
St Johns Wood Power Station – London Power Co (L)		0	1150
Great Central Railway's goods yard (R)		0	1150
Modern footbridge		0	1375
Railway bridge – ex Great Central line into Marylebone		0	1450
Railway bridge – Metropolitan line into Baker Street		0	1485
Park Road Bridge, Finchley Road (A41) [Chapel No 3]		0	1550
Charlbert Street Footbridge & River Tyburn Aqueduct		1	245
Macclesfield Bridge, Avenue Road, North Gate [No 4]		1	505
Primrose Hill footbridge		1	845
Footbridge into London Zoo		1	1050
Zoo water bus landing stage (R)		1	1170
Footbridge into London Zoo		1	1300
Broad Walk Footbridge		1	1390
Junction with Cumberland Market Branch (1,230 yards) (R)		1	1445
Prince Albert Road Bridge (A205) [Water Meeting No 5]		1	1480
Regent's Park Road Bridge [Grafton Bridge No 7]		1	1555
Gloucester Avenue Bridge [Fitzroy Bridge No 8]		2	40
Railway bridge – ex London & North Western line into Euston (1906)		2	85
Railway bridge – ex London & Birmingham line into Euston (1837)		2	100
Railway bridge – ex London & Birmingham Railway siding		2	140
Railway bridge – ex London & Birmingham Railway siding		2	175
Oval Road Bridge [Southampton Bridge No 9]		2	185
Ice Well Wharf & basin (R)		2	280
Camden Railway Basin (ex London & North Western Railway) (L)		2	285
Bewlay Cliff Wharf & basin (R)		2	295
North Western Stone Wharf & basin (R)		2	340
Turnover Bridge (diagonal)		2	345
Hampstead Road Basin (Dingwall's Dock – Purfleet Wharf) (L)		2	350

		Miles	Yards
Hampstead Road Lock No 1 – fall 6ft 8in	OD 90.14	2	380
Bridge Wharf & basin (L)		2	430
Chalk Farm Road Bridge (A502) [Hampstead Road No 10]		2	440
Hawley's Wharf (R)		2	520
Hawley's Lock No 2 – fall 6ft 9in	OD 83.39	2	525
Camden Brewery Wharf (R)		2	550
Kentish Town Lock No 3 – fall 7ft 3in	OD 76.14	2	630
Kentish Town Wharf (R)		2	660
Kentish Town Bridge, Kentish Town Road [No 11]		2	680
Modern footbridge		2	730
Camden Street Bridge (A400) [Camden No 12]		2	830
Fleet Ditch sewer passes under canal		2	875
Camden Road Bridge (A503) [North Road No 13]		2	900
Royal College Street Bridge (A5202) [College Street No 14]		2	1025
Eagle Wharf (R)		2	1075
Bangor Wharf & basin – St. Pancras Borough Council (R)		2	1095
St. Pancras Way Bridge [Grays Inn Lane No 15]		2	1185
Pratt Wharf (R)		2	1200
Star Wharf (R)		2	1275
Railway bridge – ex Midland siding into ale warehouse		2	1520
Midland Railway Ale & Porter Stores (R)		2	1530
Pancras Bridge [No 16]		2	1570
Camley Street Bridge, access to Goods Depot [Oblique No 17]		3	0
Railway bridge – ex Midland line into St. Pancras		3	55
Railway bridge – ex Midland line into goods depot (site of new Channel Tunnel Rail Link crossing)		3	65
St. Pancras Basin (ex Midland Railway) (R)		3	80
St. Pancras Lock No 4 – fall 7ft 3in	OD 68.85	3	205
Great Northern Railway stone & coal basin (L)		3	240
Railway bridge – ex Great Northern siding to coal drops		3	260
Somers Bridge [No 18]		3	500
Stop gates protecting Great Northern Railway tunnels		3	500
Railway bridge – ex Great Northern siding into gasworks		3	510
Great Northern Railway's Granary basin (L)		3	540
Granary Bridge – Goods Way		3	580
Gasworks basin (Imperial Gas Light & Coke Company) (R)		3	620
Great Northern Railway passes underneath canal in tunnels		3	695
Flour Mill Wharf (R)		3	695
York Road Bridge (A5200) [Maiden Lane No 19]		3	760
Stop gates protecting Great Northern Railway tunnels		3	780
Horsfall's Basin (Battlebridge Basin – 150 yards) (R)		3	885
Timber Yard Wharf (R)		3	980
Lime Kilns Wharf (R)		3	1030
Pembroke Wharf (R)		3	1090
Thornhill Wharf (R)		3	1140
Caledonian Road Bridge (A5203) [Thornhill's No 20]		3	1170
Islington Tunnel – western end (960 yards)		3	1315
Islington Tunnel – eastern end		4	515
Danbury Street Bridge [Frog Lane No 21]		4	615

		Miles	Yards
City Road Lock No 5 – fall 7ft 7in	OD 61.27	4	795
Regent's Canal Company's yard (R)		4	830
City Road Basin (originally 550 yards) (R)		4	860
Wharf Road Bridge		4	960
Wenlock Basin (360 yards) (ex John Edwards) (R)		4	1025
City Saw Mills (R)		4	1115
Packington Street Bridge (B144) [Islington Footpath No 23]		4	1205
Britannia Wharf (R)		4	1215
Cowley Wharf (R)		4	1250
Blenheim Wharf (R)		4	1355
Sturt's Lock No 6 – fall 7ft 0in	OD 54.27	4	1420
Iron Works Wharf (R)		4	1465
City Wharf (later Eagle Dock) (R)		4	1515
Times Wharf (R)		4	1570
Canonbury Road Bridge, New North Road (A1200) [Sturt's No 24]		4	1635
Bridge Mills (R)		4	1645
Crown Wharf (R)		4	1685
Southgate Road Bridge (B102) [Rosemary Branch No 25]		5	145
Rosemary Branch Wharf (R)		5	225
Stone Wharf (R)		5	250
Whitmore Road Bridge [Hoxton No 26]		5	510
Red Lion Stone Wharf (R)		5	530
Timber Wharf (R)		5	590
Dowgate Wharf (R)		5	610
Stone Wharf (R)		5	650
Canal Road Basin (R)		5	675
Tuscany Wharf (R)		5	745
Kingsland Basin (240 yards) (ex William Rhodes) (L)		5	765
Medway Wharf (R)		5	775
Bridge Stone Wharf (R)		5	805
Kingsland Road Bridge (A10) [No 27]		5	860
Timber Wharf (R)		5	880
Railway bridge – ex North London line into Broad Street		5	950
Gasworks basin (Independent Gas Light & Coke Company) (R)		5	1120
Haggerston Road Bridge [Agastone No 28]		5	1380
Haggerston Timber Yard (R)		5	1400
Stone Yard (R)		5	1445
Kent Wharf (R)		5	1490
Queens Road Bridge, Great Cambridge Street (B108)		5	1515
Queens Road Wharf (R)		5	1535
Haggerston Basin (230 yards) (Imperial Gas Light & Coke Co, later Shoreditch Borough Electricity Works) (R)		5	1590
Acton's Lock No 7 – fall 7ft 11in	OD 46.35	6	90
Cat & Mutton Bridge, Broadway Market [Hackney Footpath 29]		6	210
Coal Wharf (R)		6	230
Red Star Wharf (J. S. Darwen & Sons) (R)		6	265
Shoreditch Lay-by (Imperial Gas Light & Coke Company) (R)		6	420
Lion Wharf (R)		6	430
Railway bridge – ex Great Eastern line into Liverpool Street		6	580

		Miles	Yards
Cambridge Heath Coal Dock (later timber dock) (R)		6	605
Mare Street Bridge (A107) [Cambridge Heath No 30]		6	635
Lime Wharf (R)		6	655
Northiam Basin (Gerver's Dock) (L)		6	740
Timber Yard (L)		6	785
Chalk Warehouse (later saw mills) (R)		6	805
Saw Mills (R)		6	1065
Bonner Hall Bridge – approach road to Victoria Park [No 31]		6	1310
Old Ford Lock No 8 – fall 7ft 9in	OD 38.60	6	1600
Old Ford Road Bridge (B118) [Oldford No 32]		6	1720
Bridge Basin (R)		6	1740
Junction with Hertford Union Canal (2,110 yards) (L)		7	30
Twig Folly Wharf & Tomlin's barge repairing yard (R)		7	185
Twig Folly Bridge, Roman Road (B119) [Oldford Footpath No 33]		7	205
Cumberland Wharf (R)		7	230
Victoria Wharf (R)		7	270
Palmer's Wharf (R)		7	430
Devonshire Street Goods Depot (ex Great Eastern Railway) (R)		7	600
Young's Wharf (R)		7	605
Railway Bridge – ex Eastern Counties line into Liverpool Street		7	625
Devonshire Street Coal Drops (ex Great Eastern Railway) (R)		7	630
Dust Yard, Stepney Borough Council (R)		7	655
Commercial Wharf (R)		7	855
Charringtons barge repairing yard (R)		7	890
Mile End Lock No 9 – fall 7ft 11in	OD 30.68	7	920
Globe Bridge, Mile End Road (A11) [Mile End No 34]		7	1060
Globe Wharf (R)		7	1160
Gunmaker's Arms Bridge, Solebay Street [Stepney Footpath 35]		7	1230
Devon Wharf (R)		7	1245
Riga Wharf (J. King & Co Ltd) (R)		7	1335
Newcastle Wharf (R)		7	1430
Johnson's Lock No 10 – fall 7ft 0in	OD 23.68	7	1605
Commercial Gas Company's Lay-by (R)		7	1630
Victory Bridge, Ben Johnson Road [Rhodeswell Common No 36]		8	15
Railway Bridge – ex London & Blackwall line into Fenchurch Street		8	300
Stonebridge Wharf (R)		8	475
Salmon Lane Lock No 11 – fall 6ft 10in	OD 16.85	8	485
Parnham Street Footbridge		8	525
Salmon Lane Wharf (R)		8	585
Salmon Lane Bridge [No 37]		8	605
Railway bridge – ex London & Blackwall spur (Limehouse Curve)		8	635
Brunton's Wharf (R)		8	675
Commercial Road Bridge (A13) [No 38]		8	805
Commercial Road Lock No 12- fall 5ft 7in	OD 11.27	8	835
Railway bridge – ex London & Blackwall line into Fenchurch Street		8	855
Entrance to Regent's Canal Dock (Limehouse Basin)		8	865
Exit from Regent's Canal Dock (Limehouse Basin)		8	1040
Regent's Canal Ship Lock No 13 – fall from 11ft 3in to nil		8	1075
Narrow Street Swing Bridge [No 40]		8	1175
Junction with the River Thames		8	1210

City Road Basin

		Miles	Yards
Junction with Main Line	OD 61.27	0	0
Regent's Canal Company's Weigh Dock (R) (*built 1821*)		0	20
Side dock (L) (*built 1825*)		0	75
Side dock (L) (*built 1824*) (St Lukes Vestry Wharf)		0	140
Side dock (L) (*built 1822*)		0	190
Side dock (L) (*built 1820*) (Fellows Morton & Clayton Ltd)		0	285
End of basin (2005)		0	340
City Road Bridge [No 22]		0	390
Side dock (R) (*built 1824*)		0	405
Side dock (L) (*built 1823, extended 1824*) (Pickfords)		0	495
Original terminus of basin		0	550

The side docks and the southern section of the basin have been filled in.

Cumberland Market Branch (Regent's Park Branch)

		Miles	Yards
Junction with Main Line	OD 96.85	0	0
Gloucester Gate Bridge [No 6]		0	425
Entrance to Cumberland Market Basin		0	990
Terminus of basin		0	1230

Only a short stub of the branch remains, the rest having been filled in during the Second World War.

Hertford Union Canal

		Miles	Yards
Old Ford, Junction with Regent's Canal	OD 38.60	0	0
Regent's Canal Towing Path Bridge		0	5
Old Ford Stop Lock		0	10
Victoria Park Wharves (R)		0	65
Park Wharf (R)		0	175
Grove Road Bridge (A1205)		0	225
Crown Wharf (R)		0	245
Old Ford Road Bridge (B118) (Skew Bridge)		0	540
Saw Mills (R)		0	760
Three Colt Bridge, Gunmakers Lane		0	890
Victoria Park Mills (R)		0	940
Entrance to dry dock (R)		0	1285
Old Ford Upper Lock No 1 – fall 9ft 0in	OD 29.60	0	1305
Parnell Road Bridge		0	1340
Parnell Road Dry Dock (R)		0	1375
Old Ford Middle Lock No 2 – fall 8ft 1in	OD 21.50	0	1535
Wick Lane Bridge		0	1565
Site of railway bridge – ex North London line to West India Docks		0	1635
Blackwall Tunnel Northern Approach Bridge (A102M)		0	1640
Wansbeck Road Bridge		0	1670
Timber Yard (R)		0	1725
Old Ford Lower Lock No 3 – fall 2ft 11in	OD 18.58	1	35
Junction with the river Lee Navigation		1	350

APPENDIX THREE

Construction of The Canal

Phase One: October 1812 to September 1815
Paddington to Hampstead Road (3,900 yards)

Bridge and lock numbers in this list refer to the official plan on the opening of the canal.

Contract	Contractor	Awarded
Excavation – main work	Hugh McIntosh	Sep 1812
Excavation – part of Marylebone Park	Samuel Jones	Sep 1812
Paddington Bridge No 1 (Warwick Avenue)	Direct labour	Dec 1814
Paddington Stop Lock	Direct labour	Aug 1815
Maida Hill Tunnel (272 yards)	Direct labour	Dec 1812
Lisson Grove Bridge No 2 (Eyre's Tunnel – 53 yards)	Direct labour ★	Feb 1814
Chapel Bridge No 3 (Park Road)	Direct labour ★	Apr 1814
River Tyburn Aqueduct	Direct labour ★	Dec 1814
Regent's Park Bridge (foundations only)	Direct labour	Dec 1814
Water Meeting Bridge No 4 (Prince Albert Road)	Direct labour ★	Apr 1814
Southampton Bridge No 6 (Oval Road)	Direct labour ★	Apr 1814
Hampstead Road Lock – masonry work	Direct labour	Jul 1814
Hampstead Road Lock – caissons & machinery	Maudslay & Co	Jul 1814
Hampstead Road Bridge No 7	Direct labour	Jul 1814
Hampstead Road Lock House	Direct labour	Jan 1815

★ In the absence of the Committee of Works' records it has not been possible to verify whether these bridges were constructed by direct labour or if contractors were employed.

Regent's Park Branch (1,230 yards)

Contract	Contractor	Awarded
Excavation	Hugh McIntosh	Sep 1813
Collateral Cut Bridge No 5 (Parkway)	Direct labour	Apr 1814

Islington Tunnel (960 yards)

Contract	Contractor	Awarded
First phase	Direct labour	Sep 1814

Phase Two: August 1817 to August 1820
Paddington to Hampstead Road (3,900 yards)

Contract	Contractor	Awarded
Toll House, Paddington Stop	John Knight	Jul 1820
St Johns Wood Sewer (Eyre's Estate)	Richardson & Want	Aug 1818
Regent's Park Bridge (Macclesfield Bridge)	Francis Read	Oct 1817
Hampstead Road Lock No 1 – rebuilding	Francis Read	Sep 1819
Hampstead Road Bridge No 7 – alterations	Francis Read	Sep 1819

Hampstead Road to Islington Tunnel (2,695 yards)

Contract	Contractor	Awarded
Excavation	Hugh McIntosh	Jul 1818
Hawley's Lock No 2	Francis Read	Jun 1819

Kentish Town Lock No 3	Richardson & Want	Jun 1819
Kentish Town Bridge No 8	Richardson & Want	Jun 1819
Camden Bridge No 9 (Camden Street)	Richardson & Want	Jun 1819
College Street Bridge 10 (Royal College Street)	Richardson & Want	Jun 1819
Grays Inn Lane Bridge 11 (St. Pancras Way)	Richardson & Want	Jun 1819
Fleet Ditch Sewer	Richardson & Want	May 1819
Pancras Bridge No 12 (no equivalent today)	Richardson & Want	Nov 1818
Oblique Bridge No 13 (Camley Street)	Richardson & Want	Nov 1818
Pancras Lock No 4	Richardson & Want	Jan 1819
Somers Bridge No 14 (Goods Way)	Richardson & Want	Nov 1818
Maiden Lane Bridge No 15	Richardson & Want	Aug 1818
Earthworks, Horsfall's Basin	Hugh McIntosh	Jul 1818
Thornhill's Bridge No 16 (Caledonian Road)	Richardson & Want	Aug 1818
Hawley's & Pancras lock houses	Francis Read	Jun 1820

Islington Tunnel (960 yards)

Contract	Contractor	Awarded
Second phase (resumption of work)	Direct labour	Aug 1817

Islington Tunnel to the Rosemary Branch (1,390 yards)

Contract	Contractor	Awarded
Excavation	Hugh McIntosh	Sep 1819
Frog Lane Bridge No 17 (Danbury Street)	Atherly & Sowter	Oct 1819
City Road Lock No 5	Atherly & Sowter	Oct 1819
City Road Lock & Toll House	Thomas Sowter	Jun 1820
Islington Footpath Bridge 19 (Packington Street)	Atherly & Sowter	Oct 1819
Sturt's Lock No 6	Robert Streather	Nov 1819
Sturt's Lock House	Robert Streather	Jun 1820
Sturt's Bridge No 20 (New North Road)	Richardson & Want	Nov 1819
Rosemary Branch Bridge No 21 (Southgate Road)	Robert Streather	Nov 1819

City Road Basin (550 yards)

Contract	Contractor	Awarded
Excavation	Hugh McIntosh	Sep 1819
City Road Bridge No 18	Richardson & Want	Nov 1819

Rosemary Branch to Cambridge Heath (2,250 yards)

Contract	Contractor	Awarded
Excavation	George & John Roe	Jan 1819
Hoxton Bridge No 22 (Whitmore Road)	Robert Streather	Nov 1819
Kingsland Road Bridge No 23	Robert Streather	Nov 1819
Agastone Bridge No 24 (Queensbridge Road)	Robert Streather	Aug 1819
Hackney Footpath Bridge No 25 (Broadway Market)	Robert Streather	Jun 1819
Acton's Lock No 7	Robert Streather	Jun 1819
Cambridge Heath Bridge No 26 (Mare Street)	Robert Streather	Apr 1819
Acton's Lock House	Robert Streather	Jun 1820

Cambridge Heath to Mile End (2,185 yards)

Contract	Contractor	Awarded
Excavation	George Roe	May 1818

Bonner Hall Bridge No 27	Richardson & Want	Sep 1819
Oldford Lock No 8	Richardson & Want	Nov 1819
Oldford Lock House	Robert Streather	Jun 1820
Oldford Road Bridge No 28	Hugh McIntosh	May 1818
Oldford Footpath Bridge 29 (Roman Road)	Hugh McIntosh	May 1818
Mile End Lock No 9	Richardson & Want	Nov 1819
Mile End Lock House	John Knight	Jun 1820
Mile End Bridge No 30	Richardson & Want	Aug 1818

Mile End to Commercial Road Bridge (1,505 yards)

Contract	Contractor	Awarded
Excavation	George Roe	Jan 1818
Stepney Footpath Bridge No 31 (Solebay Street)	Richardson & Want	May 1818
Johnson's Lock No 10	Richardson & Want	Nov 1818
Rhodeswell Common Bridge No 32 (Ben Johnson Road)	Francis Read	May 1818
Rhodeswell Sewer	Francis Read	May 1818
Salmon Lane Lock No 11	Richardson & Want	Nov 1818
Salmon Lane Toll House	John Knight	Jul 1820
Johnson's & Salmon Lane lock houses	John Knight	Jun 1820
Salmon Lane Bridge No 33	Hugh McIntosh	May 1818
Commercial Road Bridge No 34	Hugh McIntosh	May 1818

Commercial Road to the River Thames (405 yards)

Contract	Contractor	Awarded
Commercial Road Lock No 12	Hugh McIntosh	Oct 1819
Commercial Road Lock House	John Knight	Jun 1820
Excavation – Limehouse Basin	Hugh McIntosh	Mar 1818
Excavation – ship entrance channel	Hugh McIntosh	Mar 1818
Limehouse Ship Lock No 13	Hugh McIntosh	Mar 1818
Queen Street Bridge No 35 (swing bridge)	Salisbury & Co	Jun 1819
Narrow Street Bridge No 36 (swing bridge)	Salisbury & Co	Jun 1819
Cast-iron ship lock gates	Salisbury & Co.	Jun 1819
Dock Master's house, Limehouse	John Knight	Jul 1820

Chelsea Engine House

Contract	Contractor	Awarded
Supplying cast-iron pipes	Salisbury & Co	Aug 1818
Laying down pipeline to Paddington	Daniel Pritchard	Jun 1819
Bricks for the engine and boiler house	Thomas Theobald	Aug 1819
Erecting engine and boiler house	Daniel Pritchard	Sep 1819
Cast-iron roof for engine and boiler house	Hunter & English	Sep 1819
Cocks, branch pipes, sluices etc	Hunter & English	Sep 1819
Two steam engines	Boulton & Watt	Oct 1819
Laying down suction pipes etc into river	Daniel Pritchard	Jun 1820

Some Important Contracts up to 1928

Contract	Contractor	Date	Price
Camden Bridge	Sowter & Dale	Apr 1825	£1,776
Grafton Bridge	Sowter & Dale	May 1826	£965

Fitzroy Bridge (skew arch)	Sowter & Dale	Jul 1826	£1.075
Brent Reservoir	William Hoof	Oct 1834	£2,747
Brent Reservoir extension	William Hoof	Jul 1837	£3,435
Great Cambridge Street Bridge	Grissell & Peto	Mar 1839	£1,315
Extension to Regent's Canal Dock	John Hart	Oct 1840	£4,320
Limehouse Barge Lock	Knight & Son	Aug 1847	£15,584
Extension to Regent's Canal Dock	Jonas Gregson	Oct 1850	£2,950
Hydraulic dock cranes & machinery	W. G. Armstrong	May 1851	£8,700
Hydraulic engine houses & pipes	John Jay	Apr 1852	£10,930
Brent Reservoir Extension	John Jay	Apr 1852	£9,937
Lee Junction works	George Myers	Feb 1853	£8,624
Dock extension & new ship lock	Mansfield Price & Co (cancelled)	Mar 1867	£91,300
Swing bridge, lock gates & hydraulics	W. G. Armstrong & Co	Jul 1867	£22,415
Steam engine for new hydraulic plant	W. G. Armstrong & Co	Dec 1868	£4,474
Liverpool Warehouse, South Quay	Direct labour	Jan 1870	£1,280
New gasworks transhipping jetty	John Mowlem & Co	Jul 1891	£3,200
Hydraulic cranes for transhipping jetty	Sir W. G. Armstrong & Co	ul 1891	£2,480
New warehouse, South Quay	Whitford & Co	Jul 1894	£1,750
Pumping machinery & pipeline	Tangyes Ltd.	Nov 1896	£18,330
Dock improvements	Henry Lovatt & Co	Mar 1897	£70,412
New pumping station building	Henry Lovatt & Co	Mar 1897	£8,392
New hydraulic-pumping engines	Sir W. G. Armstrong & Co	Jun 1897	£11,750
Three upper level engine houses	Henry Lovatt & Co	Sep 1897	£3,003
Pumping plant (Old Ford, Sturt's)	Tangyes Ltd.	Jan 1899	£7,840
Pumping station buildings & pipeline	Henry Lovatt & Co	Feb 1899	£14,060
Edward Warehouse, Southeast Quay	Watts Johnson & Co	Feb 1902	£6,157
Alexandra Warehouse, Northeast Quay	Sheffield Brothers	Dec 1903	£2,595
West Warehouse, South Quay	Rees & Kirby	Nov 1914	£2,552
Medland Wharf & Warehouse, East Quay	Armstrong Whitworth & Co Ltd.	Jul 1920	£13,992
Bergen Wharf & Warehouse	Armstrong Whitworth & Co Ltd.	Jul 1920	£27,815
Closing off barge lock	Armstrong Whitworth & Co Ltd.	Apr 924	£3,656
Extension of Northwest Quay	Armstrong Whitworth & Co Ltd.	Dec 1924	£13,518
10-ton gantry crane on North Quay	Stothert & Pitt Ltd.	Jan 1928	£4,730

APPENDIX FOUR

Books by Alan Faulkner

Barlows (Samuel Barlow Coal Co. Ltd.) (1987)

Claytons of Oldbury (1978)

FMC (Fellows, Morton & Clayton Ltd) (1975)

Fenland Barge Traffic (1972)

The George & The Mary (Grand Union Canal Carrying Co) (1973)

The Grand Junction Canal (1972, revised 1993)

The Grand Union Canal in Hertfordshire (1987, revised 1993)

The Regent's Canal: London's Hidden Waterway (2005)

Tankers Knottingley (John Harker Ltd) (1976)

Severn & Canal and Cadburys (1981)

The Warwick Canals (1986)

Willow Wren (1986)

INDEX